Practical Beginning Theory
A Fundamentals Worktext

EIGHTH EDITION

Bruce Benward

University of Wisconsin, Madison (Emeritus)

Barbara Garvey Jackson

University of Arkansas, Fayetteville (Emerita)

Bruce R. Jackson

Lincoln University, Jefferson City, MO

Boston   Burr Ridge, IL   Dubuque, IA   Madison, WI   New York   San Francisco   St. Louis
Bangkok   Bogatá   Caracas   Lisbon   London   Madrid
Mexico City   Milan   New Delhi   Seoul   Singapore   Sydney   Taipei   Toronto

McGraw-Hill College

A Division of The **McGraw·Hill** *Companies*

PRACTICAL BEGINNING THEORY: A FUNDAMENTALS WORKTEXT

13 14 QVS/QVS 5 4 3

ISBN 978-0-07-234797-5
MHID 0-07-234797-X

Vice president/Editor-in-chief: *Thalia Dorwick*
Editorial director: *Phillip A. Butcher*
Sponsoring editor: *Christopher Freitag*
Developmental editor: *Nadia Bidwell*
Marketing manager: *David Patterson*
Project manager: *Margaret Rathke*
Production associate: *Debra R. Benson*
Designer: *Kiera Cunningham*
Supplement coordinator: *Carol Loreth*
Compositor: *A-R Editions*
Typeface: *10/12 New Aster*
Printer: *Quad/Graphics/Dubuque*

www.mhhe.com

Contents

Preface   v
Introduction   vii

PART I

The Musician's Raw Materials   1

1   The Properties of Individual Sounds   1
2   The Notation of Musical Sounds: Pitch   5
3   Pitch and the Keyboard   15
4   The Notation of Musical Sounds: Rhythm   25
5   Other Notational Signs   39

PART II

Combinations of Materials to Create Tonality, Scales, Key Signatures, Intervals, and Triads   45

6   Introduction to the Tonal Center   45
7   The Major Scale: Major and Minor Seconds   49
8   Intervals: Unison, Octave, and Major and Minor Thirds   59
9   The Major Triad and the Interval of the Perfect Fifth   69
10   The Circle of Fifths and the Key Signatures of the Major Scales   83
11   The Minor Scales   95
12   Intervals: Fourths, Fifths, and the Tritone   105
13   The Minor Triad   115
14   More Intervals: Major and Minor Sixths and Sevenths, and More Augmented and Diminished Intervals   121
15   Harmonic and Melodic Minor Scales   131
16   Augmented and Diminished Triads, The Whole-Tone Scale   139
17   Inversion of Intervals, Compound Intervals   149

PART III, IV, and V

Rhythm and Meter, Melody, and Harmony   157

PART III

Rhythm and Meter   159

18   Simple Duple, Triple, and Quadruple Meters   159
19   Syncopation   173
20   Triplets   183
21   Compound Meters   191

PART IV

Melody   199

22   Movement and Rest in Melody   199
23   Conjunct and Disjunct Motion, Melodic Direction   211
24   Rhythmic and Melodic Motives, Melodic Repetition and Sequence   221

PART V

Harmony   229

25   Triad Arrangements   229
26   Triads in Succession   237
27   Nonharmonic Tones   249
28   Harmonizing a Melody   259
29   Further Harmonizations Using I, ii, ii⁷, IV, V, and V⁷   273
30   Chord Symbols and Their Application in Jazz, Blues, and Popular Music   279

Appendix 1   Introduction to Musical Forms   289
Appendix 2   Keyboard Harmony Supplement   295
Appendix 3   Fingerboard Harmony for Guitar   297

Glossary   301
Index to Musical Examples   315
General Index   318

 # *Preface*

To the Teacher

Although the revision process allows authors an excellent opportunity to update and improve their texts, it is essential that the authors maintain the characteristics that were most useful in the previous editions. For that reason, teachers and students will continue to find this text straightforward and thorough. It is demanding—yet rewarding. Further, the significant background material, always a feature in past editions, has not been compromised, nor has the authors' strict attention to detail.

This eighth edition of *Practical Beginning Theory* is an appropriate text for use in music fundamentals courses at the community college and college levels. It is also well suited to pre-college students who are preparing for entrance to college or professional school as music majors and to high school music theory courses.

The text assumes no prior musical training, poses no threat to beginning students, and sets a flexible pace suitable to the average student as well as to the gifted. The drills are designed to be valuable and interesting to both categories of students. Headings are accentuated, key terms are boldfaced and can be found quickly in the glossary, and the chronologies inside the back (**The Old World**) and front (**The New World**) cover pages are to help develop a time perspective for music in the course.

The music from which examples in the text are drawn can be used as an excellent basis for a listening list for students who wish to begin or enhance their own collections. Thus, the listening experience involves listening for academic achievement and to develop particular skills and listening for pleasure as well.

The harmony section emphasizes practicality, utility, and above all clarity. The last chapter, new to this edition, deals with the harmonic basis of jazz, popular music, and blues and the chord symbol notation used in that music. Some students will already have tried to use some of this material on their own, and here all will have a guide to the essentials of these styles.

Considerable prominence is given to the integration of music theory with keyboard instruments, guitar, and voice. Such coordination between theory and actual practice has been emphasized throughout the text. The exercises on the CD included with the book use various instrumental sounds for melodic examples and computer-generated organ, piano, and harpsichord sounds for harmonic examples.

Practical Beginning Theory is designed to be flexible, supporting whatever musical preferences the teacher might cherish—classical music, pieces in the European tradition, folk literature, popular music, jazz, and blues.

Because of the variety and diverse types of assignments, this text can be used even when outside-of-class learning facilities are minimal. A valuable learning environment can be sustained even where there is no access to a keyboard laboratory, listening room for ear training, computer lab, or adequate music library. The CD enables the student to practice ear training wherever he or she has access to a CD player.

The text has perforated pages, which are especially helpful in tearing out assignments for grading.

The appendices offer supplemental material on musical forms, keyboard harmony, and fingerboard harmony for guitar.

Teacher's Manual

The *Teacher's Manual* serves two purposes. It contains the music for the ear training segment of the course, and it offers a number of suggested strategies and applications for teachers who might find them valuable.

It provides tactics through the ear training assignments to help students develop a step-by-step rationale to narrow the gap between musical theories and their applications. Experienced teachers might already employ many of the strategies described here or have found others equally effective, whereas those who might be teaching the course for the first time will find the strategies a stimulating aid in incubating ideas of their own.

Ancillary Materials

The ear training exercises are available on the CD included with this text. Additional practice materials, using the same techniques, instructions, and strategies and using the same letter outline as in the text, can be found on the Internet. Please visit our Web site at **http://www.mhhe.com/socscience/music/texts.htm.**

Introduction

What Is Music?

Music is the art of sound moving through time to form a structure that evokes a response from the feelings and senses of the hearer. The sound elements selected to create this structure vary in different cultures and historical periods. Within any given culture there is a common practice that determines which combinations of sound will be accepted by the listener as logical and a body of principles that codify their use.

How Is Music Used?

Ancient cultures considered music to have healing powers, and the Greeks and others believed that it had an effect on the development of good or bad qualities of human character and that its regulated use was important for education. Music has been used in worship in every culture. It has urged troops on to battle and heroism (drums and bugles provided means of sending messages in the field before telephone and radio), it has provided entertainment for all social classes, and it has a symbolic role in governments (national feelings aroused by national songs) and revolutions (the "Marseillaise" in the French Revolution). The practice of going to a concert hall to hear music is relatively modern, but public concerts now make music of all kinds available to a very wide public. Recordings also make it possible for a listener almost anywhere in the world to hear almost any kind of music simply by playing a CD or cassette!

What Is Music Theory?

Whatever the purpose for which music was originally produced, musicians use certain common principles to manipulate sound material. These principles are included in the study of **music theory.** Although theory involves some study of the physical laws of sound, full study of these physical laws is reserved for the study of physics or **acoustics** (the science of sound).

In this course you will learn about the sound materials used in the Western world in modern times. Music of ancient times and of other cultures of the modern world, such as Oriental and African civilizations, is often organized along quite different lines, and from these different principles, coherent and intelligible art forms also result.

The study of music theory is divided into three parts: *rhythm, melody,* and *harmony.* The study of **rhythm** covers time relationships between beats, patterns of note values, meter, and so on. **Melody,** because it is movement from one pitch to another in a time relationship, involves both rhythm and pitch. Melodic patterns often use broken chords or imply harmonic relationships, so the study of melody also involves harmony. **Harmony** is the study of the arrangements of pitches that sound together (*chords*) and the movement from one chord to another. Because movement is involved, rhythmic relationships exist in the study of harmony; as one chord moves to another, the separate members of the chord may create melodic patterns as they move to the following notes, so there is also melody in harmony!

Where Did the Examples in the Text Come From?

Knowledge of style differences and of the purposes for which different kinds of music were written also helps make music speak more intensely to you. We have provided some guides that will allow you to view the examples in the book in a wider setting. There is more treatment of this aspect of music in courses in *music appreciation, music literature,* or *music history.* On the Internet you will find a listening list of complete works that can be heard in addition to the examples drawn from them in the text. A chronology of musical people and events correlated with other historical people and events can be found inside the back (**The Old World**) and front (**The New World**) covers.

Class Discussion Assignment

As you begin this course, try to think of as many situations as possible in your lives in which music is necessary or desirable. You might find it interesting to think of this question again at the end of the course and see whether you have discovered new ways in which you use music or whether you have noticed it around you.

PART 1 · The Musician's Raw Materials

All music must manipulate certain basic elements—the pitch, duration, intensity, and timbre of each tone and the rhythmic and melodic relationships that result from combining tones in succession. In this first part, you will study the properties of sound and the notation of individual sounds that show their relation to each other in pitch and rhythm.

Chapter 1 · The Properties of Individual Sounds

Pitch, Duration, Intensity, Timbre

Every isolated musical sound has four properties that give it its particular character: *pitch, duration, intensity,* and *timbre.*

Pitch is the property that the ear perceives as the *high* or *low* character of the sound. The sensation of *highness* or *lowness* is the ear's response to the frequency of the vibrations of the sounding body; the more rapidly the object vibrates, the higher the sound will be heard to be. Pitch is perceived only when the sounding body vibrates with a regular number of vibrations per second. If the vibrations are irregular, the sound is without pitch and is called *noise.*

Duration is the length of time the tone sounds.

Intensity is what the ear perceives as the *loudness* or *softness* of the sounds.

Timbre is the property that distinguishes the sound of a violin from that of the human voice or that of the oboe from the clarinet. It is often referred to as *tone color* or *tone quality.* It is caused by the complex components of each sound called *overtones.* Overtones are a series of higher pitches that are mixed in the sound of every musical tone and that maintain invariable pitch relations to the *fundamental tone.* The tones of different instruments contain these overtones in varying degrees of intensity. The ear does not usually perceive them as separate pitches but as a total sound property called *timbre.* The notes that make up the first part of the overtone series for the note A follow. The series goes on to infinity, theoretically, although the extreme upper limits of the series would then be beyond the range of human hearing. Your teacher can play this series for you to hear. When you have learned to read the notation, you should return to this example and play it yourself.

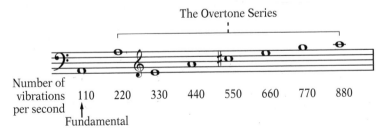

The Overtone Series

Number of vibrations per second   110   220   330   440   550   660   770   880

Fundamental

The most important aspect of these properties to the musician is the aural effect perceived. In the exercises that follow, you will be asked to hear changes in the various properties of sound from one tone to another.

The Instruments That Produce the Different Timbres

Musical instruments are classified into families on the basis of the methods by which the sound is produced. *String instruments* are those that sound when a bow is drawn across the string causing the string to vibrate. Instruments of this family can also be sounded by plucking their strings. *Wind instruments* sound by means of a vibrating column of air in a tube or pipe. There are two groups of wind instruments: the *brass* family, in whose instruments lengths of tubing produce the notes of the overtone series, and the *woodwind* family, in which finger holes are used in a pipe to produce different pitches by changing the length of the column of air. Instruments in which the sound is produced by striking the sounding body are called *percussion* instruments.

Members of the *string* family played with a bow include the violin, viola, violoncello, double bass, and earlier instruments from the Renaissance and Baroque eras, such as the viola da gamba. All these instruments are sometimes played by plucking the strings. Some string instruments are always played by plucking the strings. Members of the *plucked string* family also have *frets,* that is, division points on the fingerboard behind which the finger is placed to produce the desired pitch. Members of this family (often called the family of *fretted* instruments) include the guitar, lute, banjo, ukelele, and balalaika. The harp is another type of instrument with strings whose sound is produced by plucking.

Members of the *brass* family include the bugle (which has only one possible length of tubing and can thus only play the notes of *one* overtone series), the trumpet (which like most instruments of this family can change the length of the tubing by means of valves, and which thus, unlike the bugle, has a complete scale), the cornet, the tuba, the trombone (which changes the length of its tubing by means of a slide), the French horn, and the euphonium.

Members of the *woodwind* family include the flute, clarinet, oboe, bassoon, English horn, and the various saxophones. All these instruments except the flute use a vibrating reed to produce the sound.

Members of the *percussion* family include tympani, snare drums, castanets, chimes, cymbals, triangle, and a variety of other drums and special instruments. One large and important category of percussion instruments includes those with bars arranged like keyboards and struck with mallets; these include the xylophone, marimba, and vibraphone.

A very important group of instruments uses a *keyboard* to activate the sound-producing agent. Among the *keyboard instruments,* the piano produces its sound by means of hammers striking the strings, the organ uses air columns in pipes to produce its sound, and the harpsichord sound results from *plectra* that pluck the strings.

In the twentieth century some instruments have been adapted or invented to use electric means of producing or enhancing the sounds they make. *Electronic sounds* may be amplifications of natural sounds, they may be electrically produced sounds similar to the sounds of natural instruments, or they may be completely new qualities of sound. Many popular music groups of the present day use electronic means of producing sounds. There are various electronic plucked and keyboard instruments. An instrument that can use electronic techniques to put together synthetic sounds of various sorts is the *synthesizer* which has been useful to both serious composers and composers in the popular music field.

Music made up entirely or in part by electronic sound may be preserved on tape. Some music is composed especially for tape, using sounds and adaptations of sounds that are possible only by this means. The effects and combinations of sound of such *electronic music* cannot be represented adequately by standard musical notation.

Class Demonstration Assignment

Members of the class who play various musical instruments should demonstrate their instruments to the class, showing how the sound is produced and how the various pitches are obtained. Students who play brass instruments can demonstrate the way their instruments use the overtone series, and string instrument players can show string division and its effect on pitch.

Sight singing assignment

You must be able to use your own voice to express yourself musically. An important first step is the ability to match pitches, whatever the timbre producing the pitch to be matched. A series of tones will be played by your teacher. Each tone will be played twice. After the second sound is played, sing it back, using the neutral syllable "la." The pitch will then be sounded again to give you a chance to check yourself.

$\mathscr{E}$AR TRAINING ASSIGNMENT

A. You will hear two tones, one followed closely by the other. One pitch is higher than the other. Place an X in the blank of the higher pitch. Each example will be played only once. The first example is worked correctly for you.

EXAMPLE:

You hear:

1. __X__   _____

2. _____   _____

3. _____   _____

4. _____   _____

5. _____   _____

6. _____   _____

7. _____   _____

8. _____   _____

9. _____   _____

10. _____   _____

B. In each of the following exercises you hear two tones, one followed closely by the other. In each exercise *one* of the four properties of musical sound has been altered. The four properties of musical sound are:

    1. Pitch   2. Duration   3. Intensity   4. Timbre

Three of the properties will remain the same in each exercise; only *one* property will be changed. Place a line under the one that has been altered. The first example is worked correctly for you.

EXAMPLE: (Two different timbres)

Answer:				
	1. Pitch	Duration	Intensity	<u>Timbre</u>
	2. Pitch	Duration	Intensity	Timbre
	3. Pitch	Duration	Intensity	Timbre
	4. Pitch	Duration	Intensity	Timbre
	5. Pitch	Duration	Intensity	Timbre
	6. Pitch	Duration	Intensity	Timbre
	7. Pitch	Duration	Intensity	Timbre
	8. Pitch	Duration	Intensity	Timbre
	9. Pitch	Duration	Intensity	Timbre
	10. Pitch	Duration	Intensity	Timbre

C. In each of these exercises you will hear two tones, one followed closely by the other. *Two* of the four properties of musical sound have been altered. Remember that *two* of the properties will remain the same in each exercise; *two* will change. Underline the two that have been altered.

1. Pitch   Duration   Intensity   Timbre
2. Pitch   Duration   Intensity   Timbre
3. Pitch   Duration   Intensity   Timbre
4. Pitch   Duration   Intensity   Timbre
5. Pitch   Duration   Intensity   Timbre
6. Pitch   Duration   Intensity   Timbre
7. Pitch   Duration   Intensity   Timbre
8. Pitch   Duration   Intensity   Timbre
9. Pitch   Duration   Intensity   Timbre
10. Pitch   Duration   Intensity   Timbre

Chapter 2 · The Notation of Musical Sounds: Pitch

Notes on the Staff

The most common type of musical notation shows pitch by placing symbols called **notes** on a graph of *five lines and four spaces* known as the **staff.** The location of the note on the staff represents the highness or lowness of the pitch. The principle of the staff was adopted in Europe in the eleventh century. Although the shape of the notes was different then, the graph principle has remained the same.

Medieval staff   Modern staff

Lower   Higher   Lower   Higher

Clefs

The actual pitch of the note has always been determined by referring to a sign placed at the left end of the staff called the **clef.** It designates the exact pitch of the line on which it stands, and all the other lines and spaces are related to that line. Because the range of notes on any one staff is limited, various clefs are used to notate music at different pitch levels. The clef commonly used for pitches in the range of voices of women and children and the upper half of the piano keyboard is called the **treble clef.** It is placed on the second line of the staff, making that line represent G just above the middle of the piano keyboard. The form of the modern sign is derived from an ancient ornate letter G, with the lower circular portion enclosing the second line of the staff—the note G.

The clef used for notes in the male voice range and the lower half of the piano keyboard is called the **bass clef.** It marks the position of the F below the middle of the piano keyboard and takes its shape from an old form of the letter F.

Other clefs in common use are the **C clefs,** which mark the position of middle C. The most common positions for the C clef are:

Alto clef   Tenor clef

Today C clefs are most often used for instrumental music. The viola reads alto clef, and the cello, bassoon, and trombone use tenor clef for their upper ranges. In this book all the exercises will be in treble or bass clef.

The Names of the Notes

When the clef sign is in place, every other line and space acquires an exact pitch in relation to it. Each pitch is given a letter name, going up in alphabetical order.

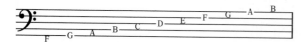 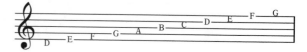

The letters used for note names are the first seven letters of the alphabet—A B C D E F G. After G, the series begins again. By comparing the repeated letter series with the corresponding notes on the piano keyboard, you will see that the pattern of white and black keys repeats with the alphabetical series. If you play each of the notes of the same letter name on the keyboard, you will hear that there is a strong similarity, almost a feeling of identity, between the notes. The similarity of sound is evidence of a close mathematical relationship between the tones, for as you go from left to right on the keyboard (that is, *up* in relation to the pitches), each repeated letter has exactly twice as many vibrations as the one preceding it.

Each line and space corresponds to a white key of the piano keyboard, as shown on the following diagram. Play each note on the piano, using the diagram as a guide.

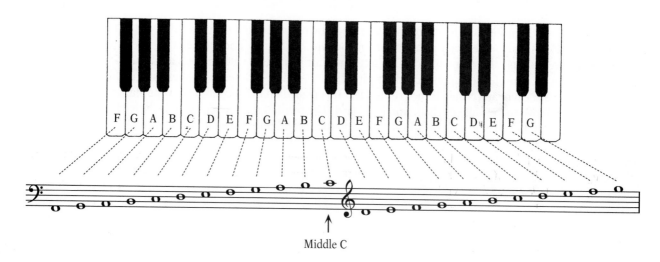

Middle C

For notes beyond the range of the five-line staff, small line segments called **ledger lines** are used above or below the staff so that higher or lower notes may be written. The C in the middle of the preceding example is written with a ledger line.

The Interval of the Octave

The distance between any two musical tones is called an **interval.** If two notes of an interval are sounded together, the interval is a **harmonic interval.** When they are sounded successively, the interval is a **melodic interval.** The interval from a tone to the next note with the same letter name is called an **octave.**

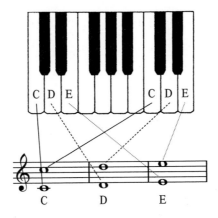

In music for the piano and other keyboard instruments, two staves are used, forming the **grand staff.** The lower staff is usually notated in bass clef and the upper in treble clef. The note that is on the first ledger line below the treble clef is known as **middle C.** That same pitch is the first ledger line above the bass clef.

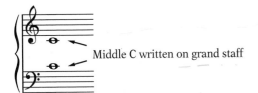

Middle C written on grand staff

The System for Naming Specific Pitches

There is a convenient system for referring to specific notes in their proper octave without using staff notation. The octave beginning with *middle C* (one-line octave) uses the symbols *c'*, *d'*, *e'*, and so on; the next octave uses *c''*, *d''*, *e''*, and so on; the octave above that is *c'''*, *d'''*, *e'''*, and so on. The octave below *c'* is notated *c, d, e,* and so on; the next octave down is *C, D, E,* and so on; and the octave below that would be *C'*. The whole system is shown in the following. (The system using *c¹, c², c³, c⁴* is also used by many writers.)

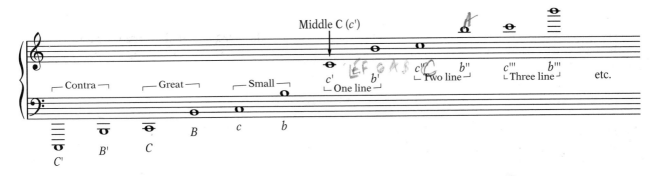

This system will be used (in *italic print*) when referring to a specific pitch throughout the text. If a general pitch name (not referring to a specific note in a particular octave) is used, a capital roman letter will be used, as in the sentence: A piece in the key of C major usually ends on a C. This system is the one now preferred for writing about music.

Octave is sometimes abbreviated 8ᵛᵃ. The range of the staff can be extended by using an *octave sign* (*8va---*) to show that notes included in the bracket are played an octave higher when the sign is above the notes and an octave lower when it is below them.

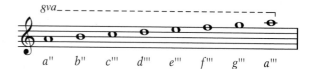

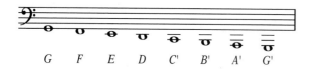
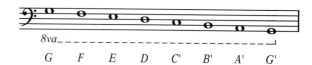

𝒩otation for Guitar

Music for fretted instruments, such as the guitar and bass guitar, is notated in three ways: staff notation, chord symbols, and tablature. In many pieces of jazz and popular music, all three methods of notation may be employed.

1. The guitar may use a staff notation just as other instruments and the voice do. Music for the guitar is written on a single staff using the treble clef. For the guitar, the notes on the staff sound one octave lower on the instrument than the notated pitch. The placement of notes on a staff different from the actual sound is called *transposition* and is used by many instruments, including the bass guitar, which *transposes* the pitch down one octave just like the guitar.

2. The guitar may use chord symbols, which serve as a simple form of harmonic shorthand that contains three pieces of information. First, a chord symbol is always a capitalized letter and indicates the *root* of the chord. Second, it indicates the quality of the **triad** (see page 143) (major uses capital letter only, minor adds *m* or *mi*, augmented adds ⁺, or diminished adds °). Finally, the chord symbol indicates all additional **color tones** (such as the seventh), which are tones added to the basic triad. Although chord symbols indicate what notes can be included in the chord, they do not indicate the order of notes (called **chord voicing**), what notes can be doubled, and strumming patterns or rhythms to be used. Chord symbols and their sevenths are covered in Chapter 28.

3. The guitar may use a system of notation called **tablature,** in which each individual note is dictated by placing a dot onto a diagram of the fingerboard. This pictorial approach to music notation is a very old system of notation and was in use long before staff notation was invented. Guitar tablature is explained in Appendix 3.

𝒮IGHT SINGING ASSIGNMENT

A pitch will be given to you on the piano. Sing that pitch, then sing the note an octave higher, and then sing the first pitch again. These exercises may be worked out in two different ways.

1. *For the classroom:* The teacher plays the whole notes, and the student immediately sings the black notes.
2. *For individual drill:* The student plays the whole notes on an instrument (outside class) and immediately sings the black notes. It is advisable also for the student to play the black notes on a pitch pipe, on the piano, or on another instrument *after* singing them. This acts as a final check on the accuracy of singing.

To be sung by students with treble voices:

To be sung by students with lower voices:

$\mathcal{W}$RITTEN ASSIGNMENT

A clear and legible musical handwriting is essential to the musician. The purpose of these exercises is not simply to acquaint you with the shape of the notes, with which you may already be familiar, but to give you practice in perfecting the legible musical manuscript, which is so important in communicating musical ideas to the performer who reads your manuscript. You should continue to practice and perfect a clear and legible manuscript in all subsequent written drills, even when it is not specifically mentioned in the instructions.

A. 1. The steps in writing a treble clef are:

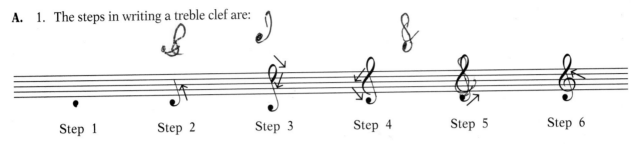

Step 1   Step 2   Step 3   Step 4   Step 5   Step 6

Following this method, write ten treble clefs on the following staff. Be sure that the relation of the parts of the clef to the staff lines is kept exact in all the clefs you write.

2. The steps in writing a bass clef are:

Step 1   Step 2   Step 3   Step 4   Step 5

Following this method, write ten bass clefs on the following staff. Be careful to see that the two dots to the right of the clef sign are on either side of the fourth line of the staff.

B. Whole notes are written as:

Stroke 1 + Stroke 2 = Whole note   Stroke 1 + Stroke 2 = Whole note

Using this method, write one whole note on each line and each space of the staff provided. Then write the proper letter symbol for each note in its proper octave.

C. Ledger lines are spaced with the same distance between them as that between the lines of the staff. They are just long enough to extend slightly beyond the note on each side.

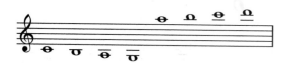

Place the note on the last ledger line or in the space beyond the last ledger line. *Never* use a ledger line beyond the note.

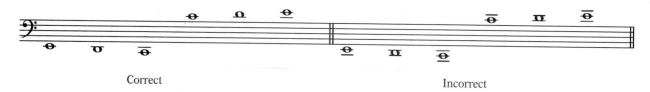

Correct   Incorrect

Write the notes called for in the following exercises. Be sure to use the correct notation for notes with ledger lines. Then write the proper letter symbol for each note in its proper octave.

EXAMPLE:

Given   Answer

1. Write the note an octave above the note given. Use a treble clef.

a'   a''

2. Write the note an octave below the note given. Use a bass clef.

3. Write the note an octave above the note given. Use a bass clef.

4. Write the note an octave above the note given. Use a treble clef.

5. Write the note an octave below the note given. Use a bass clef.

6. Write the note an octave below the note given. Use a treble clef.

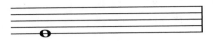

D. Here you see a series of notes. Label each with its letter name showing the correct octave. The first example is worked correctly for you.

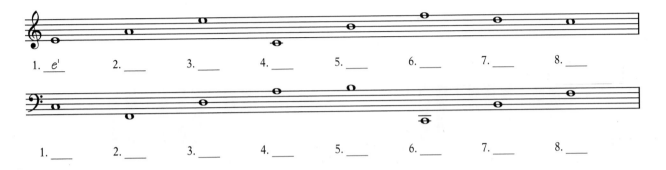

1. _e¹_ 2. ___ 3. ___ 4. ___ 5. ___ 6. ___ 7. ___ 8. ___

1. ___ 2. ___ 3. ___ 4. ___ 5. ___ 6. ___ 7. ___ 8. ___

Under the staff is a series of note names. Write each note in its proper place on the staff.

EXAMPLE:

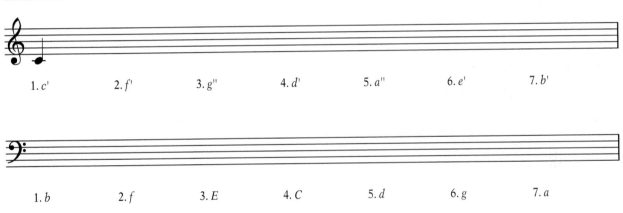

1. c¹   2. f¹   3. g"   4. d¹   5. a"   6. e¹   7. b¹

1. b   2. f   3. E   4. C   5. d   6. g   7. a

E. A diagram of a keyboard accompanies each of the following groups of notes. Draw a line from each note to the appropriate key on the diagram. After finding each group of notes on the diagram, play them on the piano. The example is worked correctly for you.

EXAMPLE:

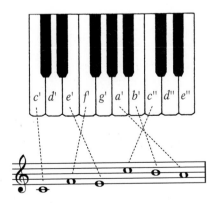

2.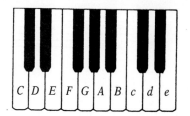

5.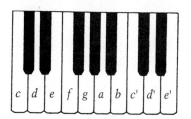

3.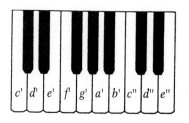

6.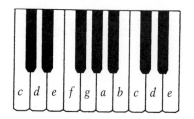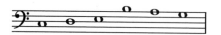

4.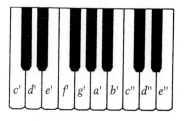

ℰAR TRAINING ASSIGNMENT

A. Generally speaking, tones sounding *higher than middle c'* are written in the *treble clef.* In each exercise you will hear middle C (the C in the middle of the piano keyboard) *first,* followed by a group of three other tones. Indicate which of the three tones should be written in the treble clef and which should be written in the bass clef by circling the proper clef in each instance. The example is illustrated and worked correctly for you.

EXAMPLE:
The teacher plays this:

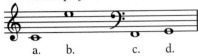

    a.   b.   c.   d.

Answer:

1. a. Middle C   2. a. Middle C   3. a. Middle C   4. a. Middle C   5. a. Middle C

6. a. Middle C   7. a. Middle C   8. a. Middle C   9. a Middle C   10. a. Middle C

B. In each of the following exercises you will hear four harmonic intervals. *Three* will be octaves, and *one* will be some other interval. Circle the letters here that represent the octaves. Each exercise will be played twice. The example is illustrated and is worked correctly.

EXAMPLE: You will hear:

1. (a.)   (b.)   c.   (d.)
2. a.   b.   c.   d.
3. a.   b.   c.   d.
4. a.   b.   c.   d.
5. a.   b.   c.   d.
6. a.   b.   c.   d.
7. a.   b.   c.   d.
8. a.   b.   c.   d.
9. a.   b.   c.   d.
10. a.   b.   c.   d.

C. In each of the following exercises you will hear a group of three melodic intervals. *Two* will be octaves, and *one* will be some other interval. Circle the following letters that represent the interval of an octave. The example is illustrated and is worked correctly. Each exercise will be played twice.

EXAMPLE: You will hear:

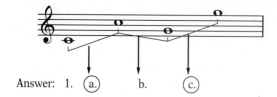

Answer: 1. (a.)   b.   (c.)

2. a. Between the 1st and 2nd note
    b. Between the 2nd and 3rd note
    c. Between the 3rd and 4th note

3. a. Between the 1st and 2nd note
    b. Between the 2nd and 3rd note
    c. Between the 3rd and 4th note

4. a. Between the 1st and 2nd note
    b. Between the 2nd and 3rd note
    c. Between the 3rd and 4th note

5. a. Between the 1st and 2nd note
    b. Between the 2nd and 3rd note
    c. Between the 3rd and 4th note

6. a. Between the 1st and 2nd note
    b. Between the 2nd and 3rd note
    c. Between the 3rd and 4th note

7. a. Between the 1st and 2nd note
    b. Between the 2nd and 3rd note
    c. Between the 3rd and 4th note

8. a. Between the 1st and 2nd note
    b. Between the 2nd and 3rd note
    c. Between the 3rd and 4th note

9. a. Between the 1st and 2nd note
    b. Between the 2nd and 3rd note
    c. Between the 3rd and 4th note

10. a. Between the 1st and 2nd note
    b. Between the 2nd and 3rd note
    c. Between the 3rd and 4th note

The Octave, the Half Step, and the Whole Step

Within each octave of the piano keyboard there is a fixed relationship between the black and white keys. The octave whose lowest note is *middle C* (the note on the first ledger line below the treble clef staff) is the middle octave of the keyboard (*c'–c''*).

The interval between notes of the same letter name is the *octave*. This relationship gives order to the larger divisions of the pitch range. The *smallest* division in use in most of the music of Western civilization is the distance between *two adjacent keys on the piano*. This distance is called a **half step** or a *semitone*.

Half steps

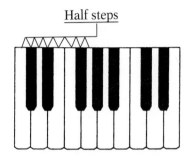

Intervals smaller than the half step and slides, or **glissandi,** through a continuous pitch stream are used in music in other parts of the world and in some twentieth-century European and American music.

There are two places within any octave from C to C in which the adjacent keys on the piano are both white keys: E and F, and B and C. These are the only white keys with *only one half step* between them. All other white keys are separated by a black key, so the distance between them is *two* half steps, or a **whole step** (also called a *whole tone*).

Half steps

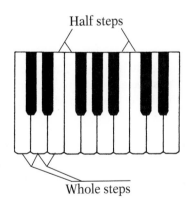

Whole steps

Movement from one note to the next adjacent note (half step or whole step) is called **stepwise motion.**

Sharps, Flats, and Naturals

To notate all the possible pitches on the keyboard, additional signs are needed to raise or lower the pitch of the seven letter names (A B C D E F G).

The pitch is raised a half step when a **sharp** (♯) is placed in front of the note and lowered a half step when a **flat** (♭) is placed before the note.

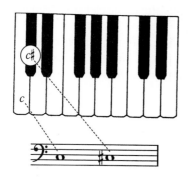
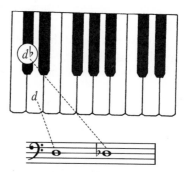

A **natural** (♮) cancels the preceding sharp or flat.

A double sign is used to raise or lower the pitch further. Thus, a **double flat** (♭♭) lowers the note by two half steps, and a **double sharp (𝄪)** raises it by the same amount. To cancel part of a double flat or double sharp so that one half step of alteration remains, a combination of the sharp or flat sign and the natural sign is used.

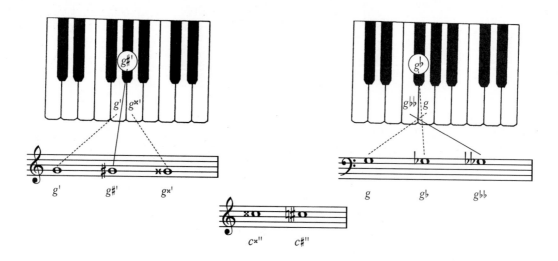

Enharmonic Spellings

As you see, the same key of the keyboard may be given different names, depending on the way it is notated. Notes that sound alike but are notated differently are said to be **enharmonic.**

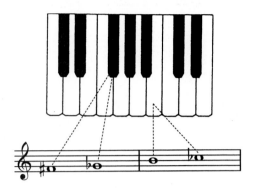

Enharmonic spellings

The Scale

A **scale** is an orderly sequence of the notes within an octave. It summarizes the notes available for use in a particular context. You will learn many specific patterns later.

The Chromatic Scale

When all twelve different notes within the octave are arranged in order, the result is a **chromatic scale.** Sharps are used to notate the ascending scale; flats, the descending scale.

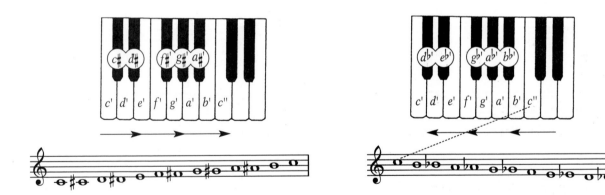

When you write a chromatic scale, be sure that the white-key half-step pairs (E–F and B–C) are notated as natural notes.

Sıght singing assignment

A. A pitch will be given to you from the piano or pitch pipe. Sing that pitch, then sing the half step up or down from that pitch as shown by the notation, then sing the first pitch again.

B. The next exercise is for singing half steps and whole steps. When you hear the note played, sing that pitch; then sing the *half step above* it, return to the first pitch, sing the *whole step above* it, and return to the starting pitch. For exercises 7 through 12, practice the same pattern *descending* from the given note.

*W*RITTEN ASSIGNMENT

Developing a good musical handwriting helps everything you need to do in preparing a musical score.

1. Sharps are notated as follows:

Be sure that the sharp is to the *left* of the note and that the lines enclose the line or space on which the note is placed. Using the above method, write a sharp before each of the following notes.

2. Flats are notated as follows:

Be sure that the flat is to the *left* of the note and that the line or space on which the note stands is enclosed by the curved section of the sign. Using the above method, write a flat before each of the following notes.

3. Naturals are notated as follows:

The square section of the sign should enclose the line or space on which the note stands. Using the preceding method, write a natural before each of the following notes.

A. After each of the following notes, write the sharped note a half step above the given note. Locate each note of the pair on the keyboard diagram.

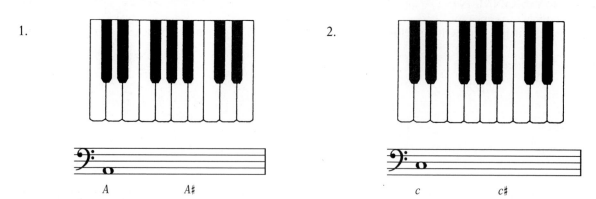

1.

2.

A   A♯   c   c♯

B. After each of the following notes, write the flatted note a half step below the given note. Locate each note of the pair on the keyboard diagram.

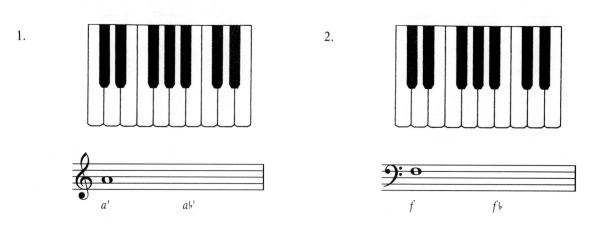

1.

2.

a'   a♭'   f   f♭

C. Write one-octave chromatic scales, both ascending and descending. Use the correct spelling in sharps for the ascending scale and flats for the descending scale on each of the given tones. After writing the examples, play each scale on the piano. Under each note write the specific name of the note as it is found in the chart on page 7. Use the chart to check your results.

1.

2.

D. Following are several pairs of notes. Some are enharmonic spellings of the same sound, and others are not. Locate the correct enharmonic pairs and circle them. Change the second note of the other pairs to make them enharmonic also. Locate the key on the keyboard diagram that would be used to play both notes of all the enharmonic pairs of notes.

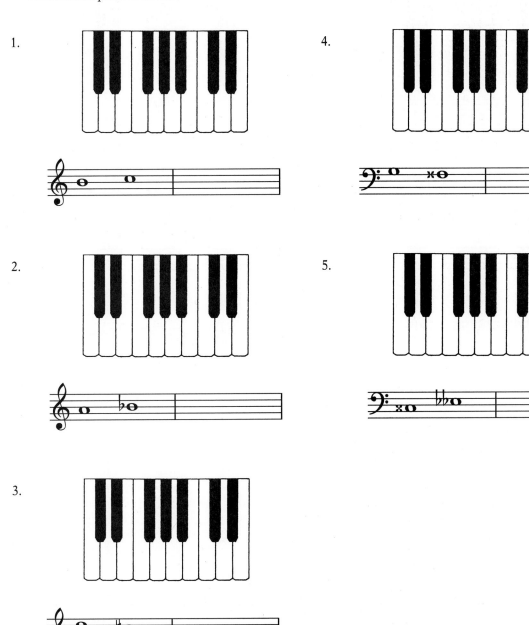

E. Each of the following examples includes one pair of enharmonic notes. Circle the two enharmonic tones on each staff. Then play each example on the piano.

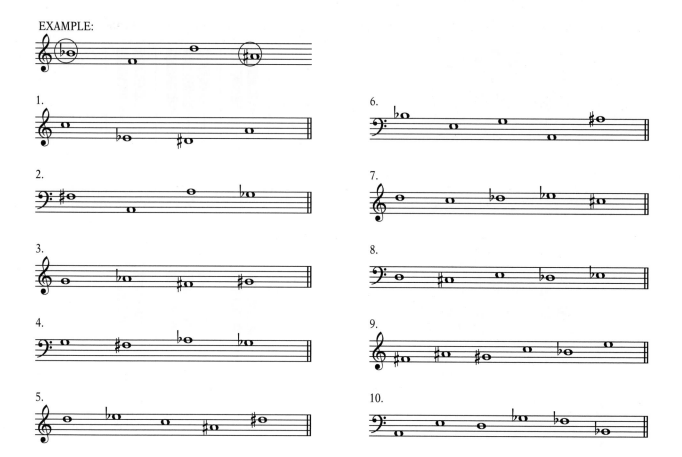

$\mathcal{E}$AR TRAINING ASSIGNMENT

A. You will hear three isolated melodic intervals. In each exercise *one* of these will be a half step, and the other *two* intervals will be larger than a half step. Circle the letter designating the half step.

EXAMPLE: You will hear:

Answer: 1. a.   b.   (c.)

2. a.   b.   c.

3. a.   b.   c.

4. a.   b.   c.

5. a.   b.   c.

6. a.   b.   c.

7. a.   b.   c.

8. a.   b.   c.

9. a.   b.   c.

10. a.   b.   c.

B. You will hear three isolated melodic intervals. *Two* will be whole steps, and *one* will be a half step. Circle the letter designating the half step.

1. a.   b.   c.

2. a.   b.   c.

3. a.   b.   c.

4. a.   b.   c.

5. a.   b.   c.

6. a.   b.   c.

7. a.   b.   c.

8. a.   b.   c.

9. a.   b.   c.

10. a.   b.   c.

Chapter 4 ▪ The Notation of Musical Sounds: Rhythm

What Is Rhythm?

Music is the art of sound organized in time. **Rhythm** is the force that generates, controls, and organizes movement and time relationships. Rhythmic organization is not limited to music; we perceive it as a life-giving force in our own bodies in the regularity of our heartbeat, breathing, walking, sleeping, and waking. We feel day and night, the turn of the seasons, and even birth and death to be rhythmic organizations of experience. The arts of poetry, drama, and dance also depend for their effect on the organization of materials in time. The drive for rhythmic organization is so strong that the concept is even extended to arts such as painting and sculpture, in which the relation of the parts to each other and to the whole object is seen as a kind of movement.

The Beat

Rhythm in music involves all time relationships. It includes everything from the progression from one large division of a musical form to another down to the underlying pulse, which, like the heartbeat, is present continuously in most music. The study of rhythm begins with the underlying pulse, or *beat.*

The **beat** is a regularly recurring pulse that measures the duration of musical events. It also has the property of forming groups with an **accent** or stress, for the principal beat of the group. The stressed beat is called **1,** and the remaining beats in the group are counted from the accented beat.

① 2 <u>1</u> 2 <u>1</u> 2 <u>1</u> 2 or ① 2 3 <u>1</u> 2 3 <u>1</u> 2 3 <u>1</u> 2 3

This grouping of beats can be felt even in a series of pulses of absolutely equal intensity. It probably results from an inner human need to organize experience into patterns. It is this urge to organize that causes optical illusions. If you look at a series of equidistant dots, you may see them group themselves in twos or threes at will.

. . . .

If some of the dots are slightly darkened, or *accented,* one grouping will be seen.

• . • . • . • . • . •

By changing the accent, another grouping appears.

• . . • . . • . . • .

In musical notation, these groups would be expressed as in the examples below. The > (*accent mark*) shows the stressed notes.

Grouping I (duple meter)

Grouping II (triple meter)

It is important to remember that these natural stresses are generally very subtle. It would be unmusical to overemphasize them in playing!

$\mathcal{M}$eter

The simplest groups of beats contain two or three beats. Larger groups are the result of combining the smaller groups. When groups of beats with regularly recurring accents occur in music, we call it **meter.** If the groups fall in groups of *two* pulses, the meter is **duple;** when in groups of three, the meter is **triple.** Each group of beats with a regularly recurring accent is called a **measure,** or **bar.** In music notation, the end of each measure is indicated by a vertical line drawn through the staff known as the **bar line** (see the previous examples).

Not all music is **metric.** Some of the old music of the Catholic Church (Gregorian chant) is not measured in this way, and electronic and other twentieth-century types of music use **nonmetric** means of organizing musical time. In the ear training exercises you will hear some examples.

$\mathcal{N}$otes and Their Values

In modern musical notation, the relative duration of each individual note is shown by its shape and coloring.

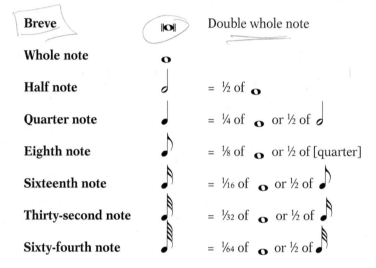

Breve	
	ǁoǁ Double whole note
Whole note	o
Half note	♩ = ½ of o
Quarter note	♩ = ¼ of o or ½ of ♩
Eighth note	♪ = ⅛ of o or ½ of [quarter]
Sixteenth note	♬ = ¹⁄₁₆ of o or ½ of ♪
Thirty-second note	= ¹⁄₃₂ of o or ½ of ♬
Sixty-fourth note	= ¹⁄₆₄ of o or ½ of

A note consists of one to three parts that can be assembled to represent the desired value. These are the **note-head,** the **stem,** and the **flag.**

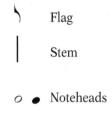

$\backslash$ Flag

| Stem

o ● Noteheads

The noteheads of whole and half notes are not filled in, but all note values smaller than the half note have black noteheads. All notes except the whole note have a stem. Flags are added to the eighth notes and all smaller note values. Each flag added to the stem decreases the value by one-half.

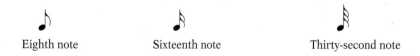

Eighth note   Sixteenth note   Thirty-second note

A group of notes with flags may instead be connected by a **beam,** a heavy line (or lines) connecting the ends of the stems. When a beam is used, flags are not used. See examples on page 30.

Adding Length to a Note with a Dot or a Tie

So far, all the note values have been related to each other in a *one-to-two relationship;* that is, each note value was equal to two of the next smaller value unit. A new symbol is necessary to express a value equal to *three* of the next unit. This symbol is the **dot** added to the right of the notehead to increase the value of the note by one-half.

When a note is placed on a space, the dot is written on the space. For clarity, if the note is on a line, the dot is placed on the space above.

A **tie,** a curved line connecting the noteheads of two notes of the same pitch, is used to indicate that the note values are to be added together. By means of the tie, a note of any duration can be written.

The Rest

Silence is also a means of musical expression. The **rest** shows the duration of the silence. The values of rests correspond exactly to the notes with the same name.

Whole rest	▬	=	Whole note
Half rest	▬	=	Half note
Quarter rest	𝄽	=	Quarter note
Eighth rest	𝄾	=	Eighth note
Sixteenth rest	𝄿	=	Sixteenth note
Thirty-second rest	𝅀	=	Thirty-second note

Dotted rests have the same value as dotted notes. Rests are never tied because a succession of rests produces an uninterrupted silence without the use of an additional sign.

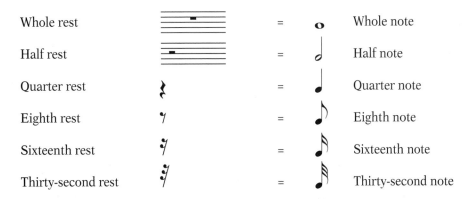

Beat Units and the Time Signature

Any note value may serve as the *unit* that receives the beat, and all other values are related to it in accordance with the preceding tables of values. The most common **beat units** are the quarter note and the eighth note. The beat unit is shown at the beginning of the piece by the lower one of two numbers found at the right of the clef sign. The top figure shows the number of beats in each measure. This pair of numbers is the **time signature.**

Neidhart von Reuenthal (ca. 1190–c. 1236), "Sinc an, Guldin Huon!" (Sing on, Golden Cockerel!)*

Three quarter notes per measure   Three eighth notes per measure
———————————————— Triple time signatures ————————————————

The basic plan of the note unit and the number of beats in each measure is called the *meter*. The numbers of the time signature are always written so that the middle line of the staff comes between them. The time signature is placed at the beginning of a piece of music, just to the right of the clef sign. Unlike the clef sign, *it is not repeated on any of the following lines unless there is a change in the meter.*

Franz Schubert (1797–1828), "Heiden-Röslein" (Hedge-Rose) (1815)

Two quarter notes per measure (a duple time signature)

Simple Meter

When the regular division of the unit is into two subdivisions, as in all the preceding examples, the meter is called **simple meter.**

Clara Schumann (1819–1896), *Trio in G Minor*, Op. 17, Allegretto (1847)

Violin

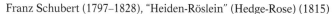

Simple duple meter

The abbreviation *op.* stands for **opus,** an Italian word meaning *work.* It is often found after the title of a composition to refer to a musical work or group of works that were published together, and it indicates the order of publication; that is, this is the *seventeenth* work published by this composer. If another number is found after the opus number, it will indicate the number of the piece within a group of works published together.

The Upbeat

If beats or parts of beats occur before the first bar line, it is called an **upbeat, anacrusis,** or **pickup.** The preceding example has an eighth-note anacrusis.

---

* The examples are labeled with the composer's name, the dates of birth and death, the title of the complete work, the part of the work from which the excerpt is drawn, and, where possible, the date or approximate date of composition. A + sign at the end of a caption indicates that the composer is an American.

Compound Meter

In certain meters, the beat unit has *three* subdivisions. The beat unit in this kind of meter is always a dotted note, and the lower number of the time signature refers to the *subdivision unit* rather than to the *beat unit*. This type of meter is called **compound meter.**

 Six eighth notes per measure as shown by the time signature.
Two beat units of one dotted quarter note each.

In all compound meters, the upper number of the time signature is a number divisible by three, that is, 6, 9, or 12. The number of beat units in compound meter is the upper number divided by *three*.

Joseph Haydn (1732–1809), *The Creation,* "With Verdure Clad" (1796–98)

With ver - dure clad the fields ap - pear, _ De - light - ful to ___ the ra - vish'd sense. _

Compound duple meter

Richard Wagner (1813–1883), *Die Walküre,* "The Ride of the Valkyries" (1852–56)

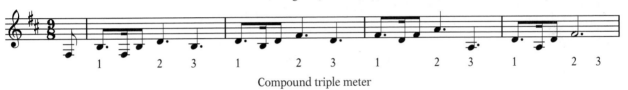

Compound triple meter

Triplets

To divide a note that normally has two subdivisions into three parts, three notes are written as a group with the numeral 3 above them. The same principle is used for more unusual groups, such as five or seven subdivisions. The group of three, which is by far the most common, is called a **triplet.**

Triplets

The number 3 is centered above the triplet at the stem end. If the notes of the triplet are not beamed, gapped brackets, one on either side of the numeral, are used to enclose the triplet group.

Eduard Lalo (1823–1892), *Symphonie Espagnole,* Op. 21, Allegro non troppo (1875)

Quarter-note triplets

Johannes Brahms (1833–1897), *Sonata in E Minor for Cello and Piano,* Op. 38, Third Movement (1862–65)

Eighth-note triplets

Grouping Notes with Beams

When several notes with flags are grouped together, they may be connected by a heavy line called a **beam** in place of the individual flags. If the notes have more than one flag, they are replaced by an equal number of beams. In instrumental music, beams are used to show the grouping of notes in relation to the beat, as in the following example. In vocal music, the choice of beams or flags depends on the syllable division of the text, although modern engravers often choose instrumental beaming rather than vocal flagging.

The beam can be used with notes of different values, as long as they all have values smaller than a quarter note.

The grouping of notes within the meter is shown by beams.

More about Meter

As you remember, rhythmic pulses tend to be grouped in twos or threes. Meters are classified by the number of beats per measure. The most common meters are **duple** (two beats per measure), **triple** (three beats per measure), and **quadruple** (four beats per measure, a multiple of duple meter). Such unusual meters as quintuple or septuple meter (with five or seven beats in a measure) are actually combinations of groups of two and three beats within one measure.

Piotr Ilyitch Tschaikovsky (1840–1893), *Symphony No. 6 in B Minor ("Pathétique"),* Second Movement (1893)

Quintuple meter

Some folk music and some twentieth-century music use meters that change frequently (**changing meter**) and can have fascinating results.

Béla Bartók (1881–1945), *Concerto for Orchestra,* "Intermezzo Interotto" (Interrupted Intermezzo) (1944)

Tempo

The pace at which the beat moves may be fast or slow. The speed, or **tempo,** of the beat is usually indicated by Italian words. For example, **andante** means a slow, walking tempo; **moderato** means a moderate speed; **allegro** means rapidly; and so on. Some French and German composers use terms in their native languages rather than Italian. In the twentieth century, a few English-speaking composers have used English tempo markings. The Italian words, however, are in such universal use that they can be understood easily by all composers and performers throughout the world, no matter what language they speak.

Tempo may be indicated precisely by referring to the **metronome,** a machine invented in 1816 by Beethoven's friend Maelzel. It can be adjusted to beat any desired number of regular pulses per minute.

If the notation "M.M. ♩ = 60" appears at the beginning of a composition, the tempo of the music is sixty quarter-note beats per minute. The initials stand for "Maelzel's Metronome." Metronome markings are not always given by the composer and are not found in any music before Beethoven because he was the first composer to use the machine. Any marking of this kind that you see in earlier music has been added by a more recent editor and was not originally provided by the composer.

SIGHT SINGING ASSIGNMENT

A. The following exercises are for rhythm. Sing or say the regular meter beat indicated and, at the same time, clap the note values as shown. These exercises may also be practiced by tapping the rhythm with one hand while beating time with the other hand or with your foot. If desired, the metronome can be used to set the beat. Professional musicians practice with this device, and you will also find it helpful.

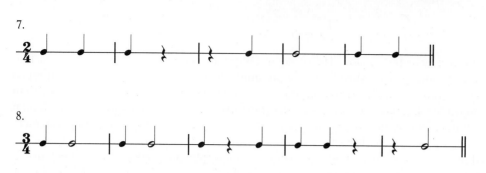

This skill can be practiced with real music. You can use tunes from a hymnal, lead sheet, or other songbook to practice singing or saying just the rhythm of a tune.

B. Each of the following exercises contains a four- or five-note melody that can be played on a piano or other instrument. First sing the notes along with the instrument using the note names. Then sing the notes without instrumental aid, again using the note names. Remember, although men and women sing in different octaves (men commonly in the range of the bass clef and women in the range of the treble clef), you should sing in the range that is comfortable for you. It is important to develop quick note reading skill in *both* clefs. Women may have to sing the bass clef examples one octave higher (as if they were written in treble clef) and men the treble clef examples one octave lower (as if they were written in bass clef).

EXAMPLE:

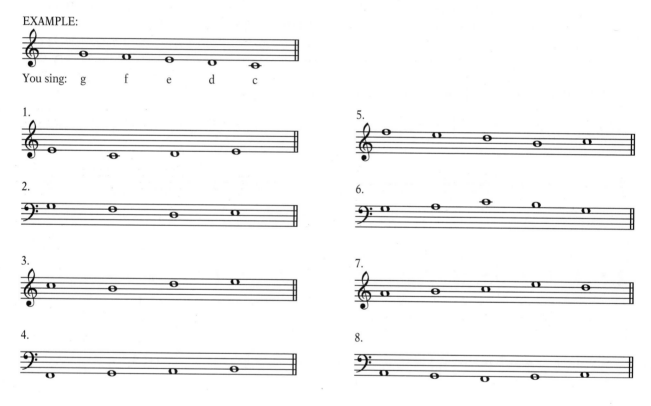

You can do this same exercise with any piece of music: a hymn tune from a hymnal, a piece of instrumental music, or a *lead sheet** from a popular music *fake book*. To develop fluidity in music reading, you need to develop speed and accuracy through repetition and practice. Apply this exercise to other pieces of music. When accidentals are indicated, simply say the note name with the accidental. The development of accurate pitch note reading skill, not rhythm, is important here.

---

* A lead sheet is a tune marked with chord changes and other information for use by jazz and popular musicians. A fake book is a collection of lead sheets. See Chapter 30 for a full explanation.

$\mathcal{W}$RITTEN ASSIGNMENT

A. There are two methods of notating quarter notes in music manuscript.
Method 1: For use with ordinary pen or pencil and for rapid writing in dictation or written assignments. In this method the notes are constructed of straight line segments ("stick method"). Use the following procedure:

Step 1   Step 2   Step 1   Step 2   Step 1   Step 2   Step 1   Step 2

Notes below the center line have the stem going up on the right.   Notes on or above the center line have the stem going down on the left.

Use the staff provided to make a quarter note on each line and space. Middle C (*c′*) is written as an example.

Method 2: For use with a special music manuscript or drawing pen. With a manuscript pen, it is possible to make oval filled-in noteheads with two strokes of the pen, using the same method used for writing whole notes or half notes but turning the pen so that the ink covers the whole notehead. Oval noteheads may also be written with a pencil by drawing an empty notehead and coloring in the space with a pencil.

Use the staff provided to make quarter notes with oval noteheads on each line and space. Middle C (*c′*) is written as an example.

B. Eighth notes are formed by adding a flag to a quarter note as in the following examples:

Quarter + flag   =   eighth note   Quarter + flag   =   eighth note

The flag is placed on the right size of the stem, no matter which way the stem is pointed. The arrows show the direction the pen or pencil follows to add the flag.

Use the staff provided to write an eighth note on each line and space. *c′* is given as an example.

C. Smaller note values add flags or beams as necessary. Make each of the eighth notes on the staff provided into a sixteenth note. The examples are worked correctly for you.

EXAMPLES:

Flag added   Beam added

Write a single sixteenth note on each line and each space of the staff below. *c'* is given as an example.

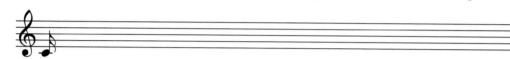

Using the following noteheads, make eighth-note groups with a beam connecting each group of four notes. The example is worked correctly for you. The direction of stems is shown by the first note of each group.

Example   Solution

Using the following noteheads, make sixteenth-note groups with a beam connecting each group of four notes. The example is worked correctly for you. The direction of stems is shown by the first note of each group.

Example   Solution

In the last group above, note that the stem of the first note goes up, so that the notes in the whole group will be going in the correct direction.

D. The *whole rest* is written as a heavy rectangle, half a space in width, suspended from the fourth line of the staff. It is in the same place on the staff for all clefs, as are all other rests. The whole rest should be placed in the center of the measure. Sometimes a **C** time signature is used for quadruple meter instead of $\frac{4}{4}$. It means the same thing.

Whole rest

Write a whole rest in each measure on the staff provided.

The *half rest* is written as a heavy rectangle, half a space in width, resting above the middle line of the staff. It is not centered in the measure.

Half rest

Write two half rests in each measure on the staff provided.

The *quarter rest* is written in music manuscript as shown here. In printed music, it has a somewhat different form, as shown.

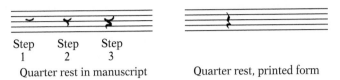

Step 1   Step 2   Step 3

Quarter rest in manuscript   Quarter rest, printed form

Write four quarter rests, using the manuscript method just illustrated, in each measure of the staff provided.

The method for writing an *eighth rest* is shown here.

Step 1   Step 2   Step 3

Eighth rest

Write four eighth rests in each measure provided.

To make smaller note values, extend the long line farther down and add additional flags below the top one.

Sixteenth rest   Thirty-second rest

Write four sixteenth rests in each measure provided.

E. Place the correct meter signature in the correct location for each example.

EXAMPLE:

*E*AR TRAINING ASSIGNMENT

A. You will hear ten short melodies. Each melody is either $\frac{2}{4}$ or $\frac{3}{4}$ time (duple meter or triple meter). In each exercise, indicate the meter by circling the correct time signature. Each exercise should be played twice.

1. $\frac{2}{4}$ $\frac{3}{4}$ 6. $\frac{2}{4}$ $\frac{3}{4}$

2. $\frac{2}{4}$ $\frac{3}{4}$ 7. $\frac{2}{4}$ $\frac{3}{4}$

3. $\frac{2}{4}$ $\frac{3}{4}$ 8. $\frac{2}{4}$ $\frac{3}{4}$

4. $\frac{2}{4}$ $\frac{3}{4}$ 9. $\frac{2}{4}$ $\frac{3}{4}$

5. $\frac{2}{4}$ $\frac{3}{4}$ 10. $\frac{2}{4}$ $\frac{3}{4}$

B. *Recognition of Tempi.* In each of the following exercises you will hear a short excerpt of music in one of the tempi described in the text. Underline the correct tempo. The tempo markings used are:

Adagio = Very slow
Andante = Slow (walking tempo)
Moderato = Moderate
Allegro = Fast
Presto = Very fast

1. a. Andante   b. Moderato   c. Presto

2. a. Andante   b. Allegro   c. Presto

3. a. Andante   b. Allegro   c. Presto

4. a. Adagio   b. Andante   c. Presto

5. a. Adagio   b. Moderato   c. Allegro

6. a. Adagio   b. Moderato   c. Presto

C. *Recognition of Meter.* In each exercise you will hear a short excerpt of music in one of the meters described in the text. Underline the correct meter.

1. a. Duple   b. Triple   c. Quintuple

2. a. Compound duple   b. Compound triple   c. Neither

3. a. Duple   b. Triple   c. Changing meter

4. a. Triple   b. Quintuple   c. Duple

5. a. Triple   b. Quadruple   c. Neither

Dynamic Signs

The level of intensity of the sound and variations in the amount of sound are expressed by **dynamic signs.** Those in most common use are given in the following list. Italian is the conventional language for describing the dynamics of a composition.

SYMBOL	TERM	EFFECT
p	**piano**	Soft
pp	**pianissimo**	Very soft
f	**forte**	Loud
ff	**fortissimo**	Very loud
mp	**mezzo piano**	Moderately soft
mf	**mezzo forte**	Moderately loud
——— or *cresc.*	**crescendo**	Gradually get louder
——— or *decresc.* or *dim.*	**decrescendo** or **diminuendo**	Gradually get softer
fp	**forte piano**	Loud, then suddenly soft
sf or *sfz*	**sforzando**	A sudden strong accent on the note marked
>	**accent**	A strong stress on the note marked

The Double Bar

The **double bar** is used to mark the end of important sections or the end of a piece. It consists of a pair of bar lines placed close together. When it is used for the end of a piece, the second line is heavier than the first, as shown here. When it appears at the end of the section within the piece, the two lines are the same.

Frédéric Chopin (1810–1849), *Prelude No. 7* (for piano), Op. 28 (1839)

In piano music a *phrase marking* (curved line above or below the notes of the group) is often used to show each musical sentence, or *phrase.* The performance style of the phrases in the Chopin *Prelude* above is *legato* (smooth).

Repeat Signs

If a section is to be repeated, two dots are placed in front of a double bar, and a double bar with two dots facing the opposite direction is placed at the beginning of the section being repeated. This is called a **repeat sign.**

Violin

Tempo di Menuetto

Clara Schumann (1819–1896), *Trio in G Minor*, Op. 17, Scherzo (1847)

Lengthening a Note with a Fermata

There are also signs that show changes of rhythm or tempo. If a single note or rest is to be held longer than its notated value, a sign called a **fermata** is placed over it. The length of the note with a fermata depends on the context of the composition. Often it lengthens the note to about twice its value.

"The Boar's Head," anonymous English carol

fermata

Gradual Change of Tempo

If the tempo is to be increased gradually, the score is marked **accelerando** (*accel.*); if decreased, **ritardando** or *ritenuto* (*rit.*).

Staccato and Legato

Some signs indicate the style of performance—for example, whether notes are to be played smoothly (**legato**) or in a detached manner (**staccato**). A curved line called a **slur** shows legato groups of notes. In string music this also means that the notes are played on one bow stroke and in wind music with no articulation between the notes. **Dots** (or wedges) placed above or below the noteheads indicate staccato notes. These markings are also called **articulation signs.**

Ludwig van Beethoven (1770–1827), *Symphony No. 5 in C Minor*, Op. 67, Fourth Movement (1807–08)

Flute

Allegro

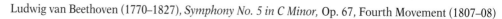

A Few Ornament Signs

The example above has **grace notes** in measures 3 and 4. These are notes in smaller type with a slash through the stem. They are played quickly just before the beat. The notes to which they are attached are the *principal notes* and are played on the beat. They are common ornaments in the nineteenth and twentieth centuries. Other ornaments that can be indicated by special signs are the **trill** *tr* and the **turn** ∽.

Similar looking ornamental notes were used in the seventeenth and eighteenth centuries. These are played on the beat and take half the value of the principal note. One of these is the **appoggiatura,** shown in the example below. It is helpful to know the time period of a piece you are playing in order to know what rules apply to the reading of ornament signs. In some periods trills begin on the principal note, and in other periods they begin above the principal note.

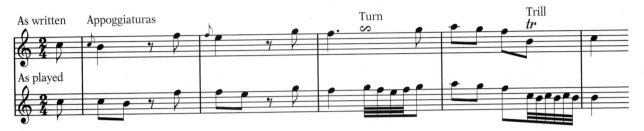

The number of notes in a trill is variable and the rhythm is approximate.
In Baroque and Classical music the trill will start on the higher note.

Find some ornaments in music that you are learning to share with the class. There are many more types of ornaments, so you can probably find several that are not in your textbook.

SIGHT SINGING ASSIGNMENT

A. *Continued Practice of Rhythm.* Sustain the following notes for the durations called for by the notation. Tap the beat as you sing. Sing the syllable *la* or *ta* for the pitch indicated. Sing exercises on a single pitch. They may also be practiced by tapping the rhythm with one hand while beating time with your other hand or with your foot.

*E*AR TRAINING ASSIGNMENT

Recognition of Performance Techniques. Each of the following exercises consists of a short phrase of music. Each composition will be performed in *one* of the two following manners:

1. *Staccato*—shortening the duration of the note, producing a detached, separated effect with a short silence between notes.

2. *Legato*—no interruption of sound between notes. One note is followed immediately by the next with no silence between. One note blends into the next.

   In each exercise underline the answer that best describes the manner of performance.

   1. Staccato   Legato

   2. Staccato   Legato

   3. Staccato   Legato

   4. Staccato   Legato

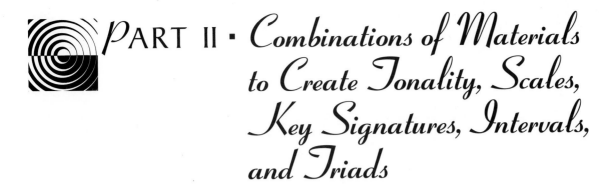

PART II · Combinations of Materials to Create Tonality, Scales, Key Signatures, Intervals, and Triads

The second part of this text treats the way the basic materials you learned in Part I can be combined to create the feeling of a **tonal center** (**tonality**), organized in **scales,** with **key signatures** that show immediately what tonal materials can be expected in a piece of music and placed together simultaneously to produce intervals (two pitches sounded together) or **chords** (more than two pitches at once). The most important of all chords are those three-note chords whose members are three notes apart (the **triad**). Most of the music with which you are familiar is harmonized with triads. Part of what creates the feeling that one particular note, the **tonic,** is the center, or resting place, of a tonality is the way in which those chords are arranged in relation to each other.

When you have learned these basic combinations, you can see how the broad categories of *rhythm, melody,* and *harmony* function, using the raw materials you learned in Part I of the text and the combinations you are about to explore in Part II.

Chapter 6 · Introduction to the Tonal Center

What Is Tonality?

Just as time relations in music are given shape by the beat and meter, pitch relations are given a sense of direction by a tonal center to which the composition returns at the end to give a feeling of completion. The *tonic,* or note that serves as a *tonal center,* exercises a strong pull on the other tones used with it, so that moving away from the tonic produces a somewhat restless feeling, whereas arrival at the tonal center gives a sense of relaxation and stability. The organization of music around a tonal center is called *tonality.*

To illustrate the strong pull of the tonal center, sing the whole tune for "My Country 'Tis of Thee" and stop on the next-to-last note. You will feel that the impetus to move on and resolve the tension by singing the last note is extremely strong.

The notes that are used with any given tone to create the feeling that it is the tonal center must be chosen with care. When these tones are arranged in alphabetical order within the octave of the tonal center, the result is a *scale.* The tonal center, or tonic, is always the first and last note of the scale in the well-known modern scales, **major** and **minor.**

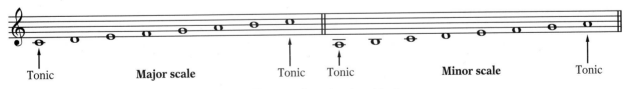

Tonic   **Major scale**   Tonic   Tonic   **Minor scale**   Tonic

Two different scales using the white keys

There are other scale systems, as in these two melodies. Play them over on the piano or another instrument and note how the tonal atmosphere differs as the scale on which the melody is based is changed.

Modest Musorgsky (1839–1881), *Pictures at an Exhibition,* Promenade Theme (1874)

Pentatonic (five-note) scale   Melody based on pentatonic scale shown

The Gregorian chant of old church music, some folk music, and some popular music uses scales called **modes.** One of these scales is the Dorian mode, shown below. Note that the example does not have a time signature.

Requiem, "Dies Irae" (Day of Wrath), Gregorian chant (13th century)

Dorian mode

Can Tonality Be Avoided?

Some music of the twentieth century avoids creating the feeling of a tonal center by using all the twelve chromatic tones in a prearranged order that does not lay particular emphasis on any one pitch in the composition as a whole. This method of composing is based on a **twelve-tone row** rather than on a scale. Following is a melody based on a twelve-tone row with numbers showing the pitch order used in this piece.

Arnold Schoenberg (1874–1951), *String Quartet No. 4* (no key), First Movement (1933)

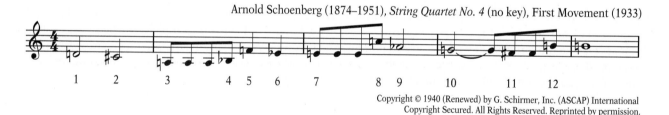

1   2   3   4   5   6   7   8 9   10   11   12

Music that avoids the feeling of a tonal center by this means or by any other means is said to be **atonal,** that is, without a tonal center. Much electronic music does not use a tonal center.

SIGHT SINGING ASSIGNMENT

A. Below are six melodies. Sing each melody using note names. All examples end on the tonic.

EAR TRAINING ASSIGNMENT

In each of the following exercises you will hear a short melody. Some of these melodies will end on the tonal center and some will end elsewhere. *All will begin on the tonal center.* Underline the proper answer in each exercise. For example, you will hear:

EXAMPLE:

Answer: 1. <u>Ends on the tonic.</u>   Ends elsewhere.

2. Ends on the tonic.   Ends elsewhere.

3. Ends on the tonic.   Ends elsewhere.

4. Ends on the tonic.   Ends elsewhere.

5. Ends on the tonic.   Ends elsewhere.

6. Ends on the tonic.   Ends elsewhere.

7. Ends on the tonic.   Ends elsewhere.

8. Ends on the tonic.   Ends elsewhere.

9. Ends on the tonic.   Ends elsewhere.

10. Ends on the tonic.   Ends elsewhere.

Chapter 7 ▪ The Major Scale: Major and Minor Seconds

The Major Scale

The composers of the past 300 years have used two arrangements of tones around a tonal center (scales) in preference to any others. These two are the **major scale** and the **minor scale.** Each scale has its own pattern of whole and half steps. Composers of the present day use many other scale patterns in addition to the major and minor scales.

Scales are described by the arrangement of whole and half steps between the scale tones. A typical major scale is produced by playing all the white keys from C to the next C on the piano. Half steps occur between the third and fourth notes (E and F) and between the seventh and eighth notes (B and C) of the scale. Remember that the tonal center (C) is also called the *tonic.*

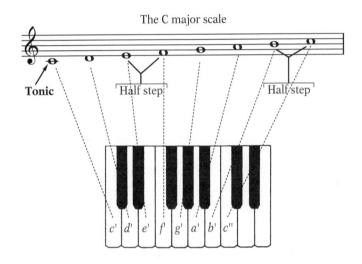

The C major scale

When a piece uses the C major scale, we say it is "in the key of C major." Every note of the C major scale is used in this melody in the key of C major. Notice that it begins and ends on the tonic.

Philipp Nicolai (1556–1608), "Wachet auf!" (Sleepers, Awake!) (1599)
(a hymn tune used by Johann Sebastian Bach and many other composers)

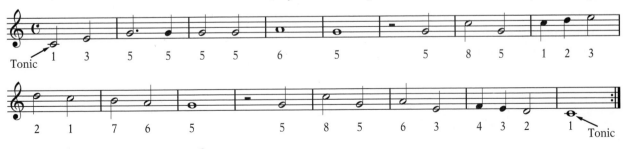

The major scale may have any note as its tonic, as long as sharps or flats are used so that the scale has *half steps between the third and fourth and the seventh and eighth degrees and whole steps between all the other scale degrees.*

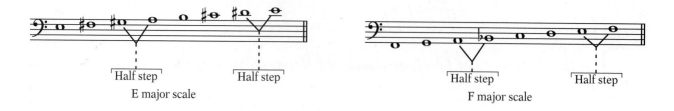

E major scale · F major scale

Each **scale** degree (note of the scale) is named by number, counting up from the tonic. The eighth note of a scale is the tonic note again, and could be sung as 1.

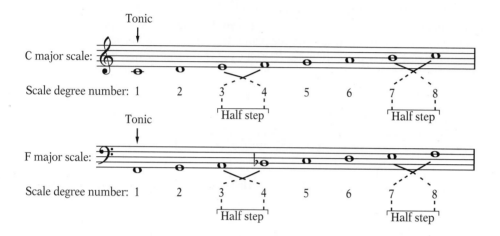

Scale names always include the letter name of the tonic note and the term describing their structure (whether major, minor, or some other mode or pattern). Thus, it is *wrong* to speak simply of the "C scale"; one *must* distinguish between the "C major scale" and "C minor scale." Both parts of the name *must* be used because many other scales could be written with the same beginning note (tonic).

C major scale · C minor scale

In writing major and minor scales, be careful to keep the letter names of the notes in *alphabetical order* even though other ways of spelling some sounds might seem more practical at the moment.

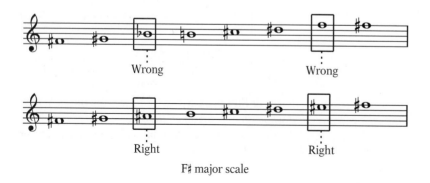

Major and Minor Seconds

The difference in pitch between two notes is an **interval.** The distance from one letter name to the next letter name is called a **second.** If this distance is a half step, the interval is a *minor* (small) *second;* if it is a whole step, it is a *major* (large) *second.*

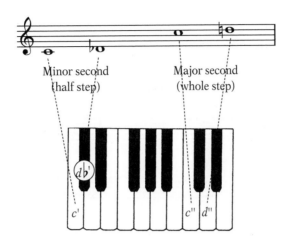

Minor second (half step)

Major second (whole step)

Major second is abbreviated *M2;* minor second, *m2*. In the major scale, major and minor seconds are found in the following order.

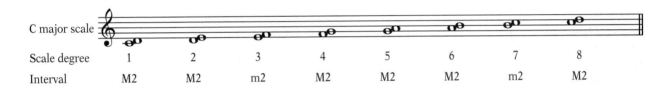

C major scale								
Scale degree	1	2	3	4	5	6	7	8
Interval	M2	M2	m2	M2	M2	M2	m2	M2

Half step is a more general term than *minor second;* the distance between any two adjacent keys on the keyboard is a half step, whereas minor seconds are half steps in which each note has a different letter name. The same is true for whole steps and major seconds. To be called a second, the interval must consist of tones with adjacent letter names.

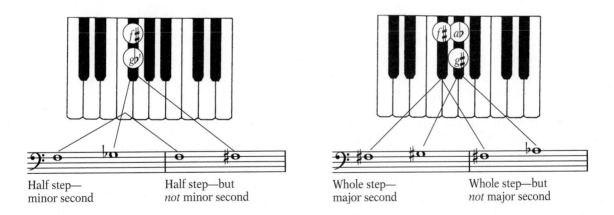

Half step— minor second

Half step—but *not* minor second

Whole step— major second

Whole step—but *not* major second

Thus, the rule that in major and minor scales the letter names must be in alphabetical order can also be worded to read: *in major and minor scales the adjacent intervals must all be seconds.*

Melodic and Harmonic Intervals

The seconds in scales and melodies are *melodic intervals*. Intervals sounded together are *harmonic intervals*. There is a wonderful movement in the *Concerto for Orchestra* by the twentieth-century Hungarian composer Béla Bartók that presents several melodies, using pairs of like instruments playing the melodies set in parallel lines, with a different harmonic interval between the lines for each new pair of instruments. As we study each interval we will see how that interval sounds in this piece in the passage in which it is used. Listen to a recording of the whole movement to see how the examples fit into the larger whole. Are all the seconds that are used as harmonic intervals in this example the same size? What size are they?

Trumpets in C   Béla Bartók (1881–1945), *Concerto for Orchestra*, "Giuoco delle Coppie" (Game of Pairs) (1944)

© Copyright 1946 by Hawkes & Son (London) Ltd.; Copyright Renewed. Reprinted by permission of Boosey and Hawkes, Inc.

Con sord. (sordino) means "with mute," a device that softens the sound of an instrument and changes its timbre somewhat.

Sight singing assignment

Note: For those students and teachers who prefer to sight sing with a syllable system, two systems in common use are given here for reference. The syllables themselves originated in the Middle Ages as an aid to learning relationships between notes and learning the large repertory of Church chant easily and quickly.

System I (movable *do*) In this syllable system, each syllable belongs to a note of the scale, with the tonic note (1) as *do* in major and *la* in minor: In the scale below and in many examples, the top octave above the starting tonic is numbered 8.

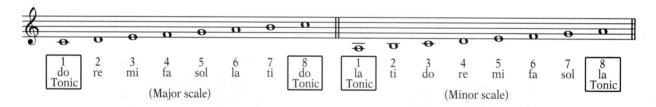

In all keys these syllables may be substituted for the corresponding numbers to sing any of the exercises given, as long as *tonic* is *do* in major and *tonic* is *la* in minor.

System II (fixed *do*) In this system, the syllables are used for fixed pitches. Thus, C is always *do*, D is always *re*, and so on. The complete system also has syllables for chromatic notes:

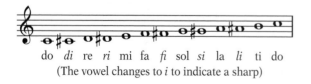

do *di* re *ri* mi fa *fi* sol *si* la *li* ti do
(The vowel changes to *i* to indicate a sharp)

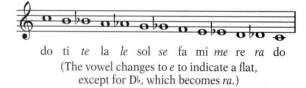

do ti *te* la *le* sol *se* fa mi *me* re *ra* do
(The vowel changes to *e* to indicate a flat,
except for D♭, which becomes *ra*.)

Syllables are not given elsewhere in the text to leave the teacher free to choose whichever system is preferred.

A. Sing the following short melodies using the scale numbers as provided under the notes. You may sing syllables by one of the systems described above instead.

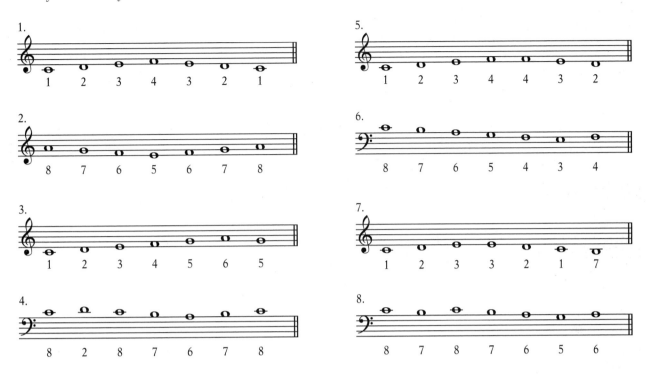

1.

1 2 3 4 3 2 1

5.

1 2 3 4 4 3 2

2.

8 7 6 5 6 7 8

6.

8 7 6 5 4 3 4

3.

1 2 3 4 5 6 5

7.

1 2 3 3 2 1 7

4.

8 2 8 7 6 7 8

8.

8 7 8 7 6 5 6

B. Sing the following short melodies providing the correct scale numbers (or syllables) as you sing.

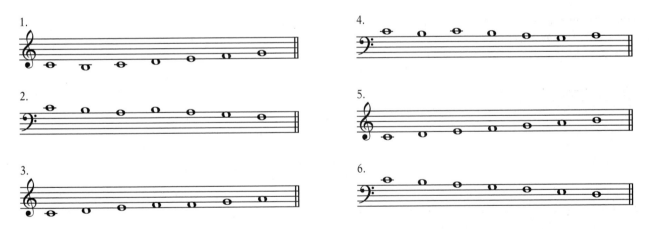

1.

4.

2.

5.

3.

6.

C. In this set of exercises only the numbers of the scale steps are indicated. The number 1 refers to the tonic (first note) of a major scale and so on. Choose any beginning pitch you wish and sing these just as you sang the exercises in the two previous sets of sight singing assignments. 8 has been used when the tonic note is to be above the seventh scale degree for these exercises.

1.	1	2	3	2	3	4	5
2.	8	7	6	5	4	5	6
3.	1	2	2	3	4	5	6
4.	8	7	7	6	5	6	7
5.	1	2	3	4	5	6	7

D. Sing the following melodies. The flats and sharps of the beginning of each tune form the key signature. Each symbol affects every note with that letter name in the line. You are given the name of the scale at the beginning of each tune.

1.

F Major   1   2   3   4   5   5   5   6   6   5   4   3   2   1

2.

D Major   1   1   1   2   1   7   6   6   7   1   2   2   2   3   2   1   1   7   7   1

3.

C Major   8   7

4.

G Major   8   8   7

5.   "Hamburg," hymn tune, arr. from Gregorian chant by Lowell Mason (1792–1872)[+]

F Major   1

6.   Johann Crüger (1598–1662), "Nun danket alle Gott" (Now Thank We All Our God)

F Major   5

7.   Lowell Mason, *Mason's Sacred Harp*, "Bealoth," hymn tune (1843)[+]

A Major   3

8.   Martin Luther (1483–1546), *German Mass*, "Gloria" (1524)

F Major Glo - ry   to   God   in   the   high - est,   and   on   earth ____ peace   to   men _   in ___ whom

He   is   well   pleas   -   ed

This melody is without a time signature—that is, it is nonmetric.

9.   Gregorian chant (medieval)

C Major Glo   -   ri - a   in   ex - cel - sis __ De - o

Notice that two of these melodies are nonmetric and have no bar lines. Sing the even quarter notes smoothly and without accent. The words are given for these examples; the Latin words in the Gregorian chant example mean the same as the first phrase of Luther's melody.

$\mathcal{W}$RITTEN ASSIGNMENT

A. *Identifying Major and Minor Seconds.* Following is a series of major and minor seconds. Identity each interval using the abbreviation M2 for major second and m2 for minor second. The example is worked correctly for you.

EXAMPLE:

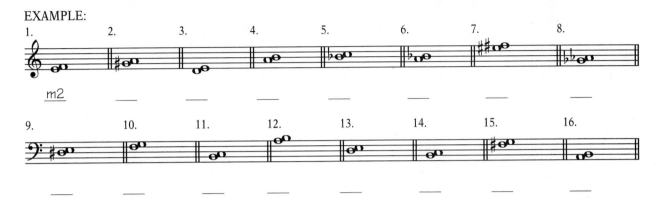

B. *Writing Major and Minor Seconds.* Following is a series of single notes. Write a major second and a minor second above each note in the spaces provided. The example is worked correctly for you.

C. *Placing Major and Minor Seconds on the Keyboard.* Using the letter names write the intervals requested on the keyboard diagrams. The example has been worked correctly for you. Play all the examples as melodic intervals on the piano in several octaves.

1. EXAMPLE: m2 up from G♯

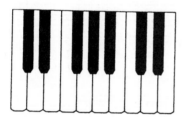

2. M2 up from C

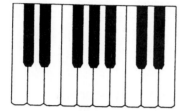

3. m2 up from E

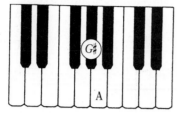

4. M2 up from A

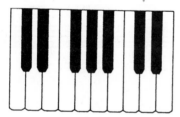

5. M2 up from G

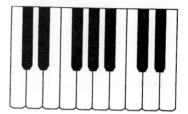

6. m2 up from C♯

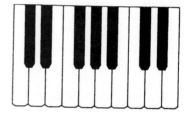

7. m2 up from F♯

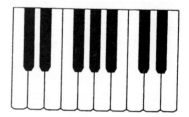

8. M2 up from D♭

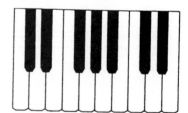

$\mathcal{E}$AR TRAINING ASSIGNMENT

A. In each of the following exercises you will hear four scales played. Only one of these scales is a *major* scale. Place a circle around the letter that indicates the *major* scale. For example, you will hear:

Answer: 1. (a.)   b.   c.   d.

2. a.   b.   c.   d.

3. a.   b.   c.   d.

4. a.   b.   c.   d.

5. a.   b.   c.   d.

6. a.   b.   c.   d.

7. a.   b.   c.   d.

8. a.   b.   c.   d.

9. a.   b.   c.   d.

10. a.   b.   c.   d.

B. In each of the following exercises you will hear a short melody played in three different ways. Only one will use the notes of the *major* scale. The other two versions will use notes of other scales. Circle the letter that indicates the version that uses the *major* scale.

1. a.   b.   c.

2. a.   b.   c.

3. a.   b.   c.

4. a.   b.   c.

5. a.   b.   c.

6. a.   b.   c.

C. In each of the following exercises you will hear three intervals.

One interval will be a *major* second (M2).

One interval will be a *minor* second (m2).

One interval will be an interval larger than a second (X).

Fill in the blank with the correct symbol for each interval you hear.

1. a. _____   b. _____   c. _____

2. a. _____   b. _____   c. _____

3. a. _____   b. _____   c. _____

4. a. _____   b. _____   c. _____

5. a. _____   b. _____   c. _____

6. a. _____ b. _____ c. _____

7. a. _____ b. _____ c. _____

8. a. _____ b. _____ c. _____

9. a. _____ b. _____ c. _____

10. a. _____ b. _____ c. _____

D. In each of the following exercises you will hear a series of four notes. The intervals created between these notes will always be either a *major second* (M2) or a *minor second* (m2).

Two of the intervals will be *major seconds*.

One of the intervals will be a *minor second*.

As you listen, mark the correct intervals in the spaces provided.

1. 1. _____ 2. _____ 3. _____ 4.

2. 1. _____ 2. _____ 3. _____ 4.

3. 1. _____ 2. _____ 3. _____ 4.

4. 1. _____ 2. _____ 3. _____ 4.

5. 1. _____ 2. _____ 3. _____ 4.

6. 1. _____ 2. _____ 3. _____ 4.

E. In each of the following exercises you will hear a melody of seven notes. You are to:

1. Mark a "+" between the numbers indicating the notes that form either a *major* or a *minor second* (M2 or m2).

2. Do not mark between the notes that form other intervals.

EXAMPLE:

Answer: 1. 1. _+_ 2. _+_ 3. _+_ 4. _+_ 5. ___ 6. ___ 7.

2. 1. ___ 2. ___ 3. ___ 4. ___ 5. ___ 6. ___ 7.

3. 1. ___ 2. ___ 3. ___ 4. ___ 5. ___ 6. ___ 7.

4. 1. ___ 2. ___ 3. ___ 4. ___ 5. ___ 6. ___ 7.

5. 1. ___ 2. ___ 3. ___ 4. ___ 5. ___ 6. ___ 7.

6. 1. ___ 2. ___ 3. ___ 4. ___ 5. ___ 6. ___ 7.

Chapter 8 ▪ Intervals: Unison, Octave, and Major and Minor Thirds

Interval Names

Interval names consist of two parts: a general name, such as **second** or **third,** and a qualifying term, such as *major, minor,* or *perfect,* that show the exact size and quality of sound of the interval. The general name is found by counting the number of scale degrees on the staff between the two tones, starting from the bottom note and counting the top note also. A summary of all the intervals is given in a chart on page 123. Each interval will be studied separately first so that you have a good opportunity to learn how each interval looks and sounds and how to sing it before moving on to the next interval.

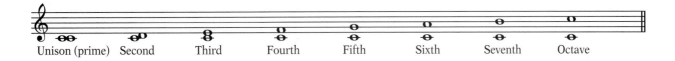

Unison (prime)   Second   Third   Fourth   Fifth   Sixth   Seventh   Octave

Perfect Intervals: The Unison

The smallest interval is formed by repeating a tone or by sounding the tone in two voices at the same time. This is called the **unison,** and it contains *no* half steps.

Perfect unison

Perfect Intervals: The Octave

The interval formed by two notes with the same letter name, eight scale degrees apart, is the octave. It contains twelve half steps. These intervals have such a close relationship between the two component tones that neither can be raised or lowered without producing a completely new quality of sound. Intervals that have only one normal size are **perfect intervals.** Perfect unison is abbreviated P1; perfect octave, P8.

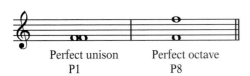

Perfect unison   Perfect octave
P1   P8

Major and Minor Thirds

Thirds are intervals that include three degrees of the scale. If the bottom note of a third is on a line, the top note will be on the next line; if the lower note is in a space, the upper will be in the next space.

Thirds are normally found in two sizes: the major third, which has four half steps (two whole steps), and the minor third, which has three half steps (one and a half whole steps). The symbol for a major third is M3; for a minor third, m3.

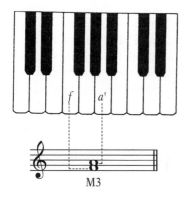
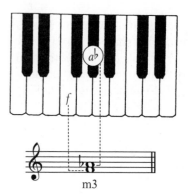

Both major and minor thirds are found in the major scale. If a third is built on each scale degree, using only the notes of the scale, major and minor thirds appear in the following order:

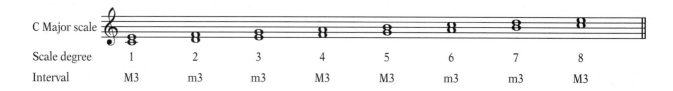

	1	2	3	4	5	6	7	8
Scale degree	1	2	3	4	5	6	7	8
Interval	M3	m3	m3	M3	M3	m3	m3	M3

Dissonance and Consonance

In playing all the intervals as harmonic intervals, you will notice a striking difference in the amount of tension in the sound. Intervals such as seconds, which have a harsh, restless quality, are called **dissonances.** Smooth-sounding intervals such as thirds and octaves are called **consonances.** The smoothest and most closely related intervals, the octave, fourth, fifth, and unison, are called **perfect consonances.**

Melodies Set with Thirds

Here are two melodies set with a parallel line of thirds. The first uses only the thirds within the G major scale, so it contains both major and minor thirds.

Antonin Dvořák (1841–1904), *Symphony No. 9 in E Minor,*
("From the New World"), Fourth Movement (1893)

The Czech composer Dvořák wrote his *New World Symphony* in 1893 while he was living in New York. Nearly fifty years later, Béla Bartók was living in New York as a refugee from the Nazis during World War II. There he wrote the *Concerto for Orchestra*. By then the musical language had changed, and although both Dvořák's *Symphony* and Bartók's *Concerto* use folklike melodies and rhythms, they sound very different. In the passage below, also for two oboes, Bartók writes two lines a third apart, but instead of keeping both lines within the same scale and thus having both major and minor thirds, he uses only one size of third. Compare both with the passage of parallel seconds at the end of the previous chapter on page 52. Try to fix the very different sounds of these intervals in your memory. What size *are* the thirds in this passage?

Béla Bartók (1881–1945), *Concerto for Orchestra*, "Giuoco delle Coppie" (Game of Pairs) (1944)

© Copyright 1946 by Hawkes & Son (London) Ltd.; Copyright Renewed.
Reprinted by permission of Boosey and Hawkes, Inc.

SIGHT SINGING ASSIGNMENT

A. Sing the following short melodies using the scale numbers as provided under the notes. If you prefer, you may use syllables (see page 52). Always be aware of the interval you are singing (M2, m2, M3, m3, and so on).

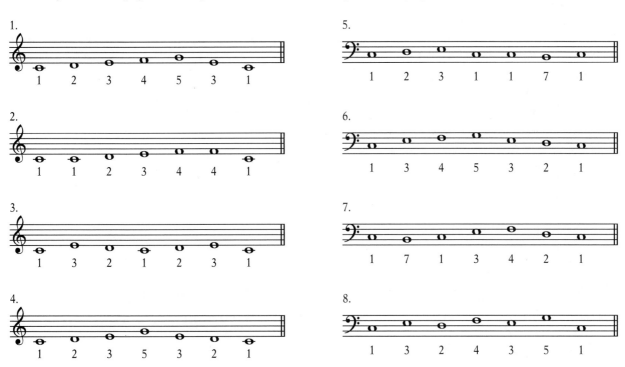

Following is a very useful exercise that can be sung in any major scale. It is shown here in C major.

1   2   1   2   3   2   3   4   3   4   5   4   5   6   5   6   7   6   7   8   7   8

B. Sing the following short melodies providing the correct scale numbers as you sing.

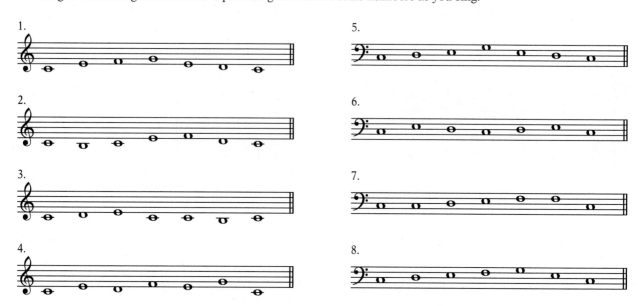

C. In this set of exercises only the numbers of the scale steps are indicated. The number 1 refers to the tonic (first note) of a major scale and so on. Choose any beginning pitch you wish and sing these just as you sang the exercises in the two previous sets of sight singing assignments.

1.	1	2	3	4	5	4	2	3	1
2.	1	3	2	3	4	5	3	2	1
3.	1	2	4	3	5	5	4	2	1
4.	1	3	5	5	2	4	3	2	1
5.	1	3	1	3	5	4	2	3	1

D. Sing the following melodies.

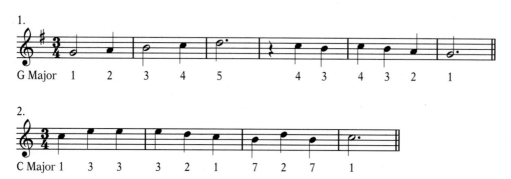

G Major   1   2   3   4   5   4   3   4   3   2   1

C Major   1   3   3   3   2   1   7   2   7   1

3.

F Major   1   3 4   5   5 5   6 4 3 2   1

4.

D Major   1   3 2   1 3   5   4 2   3 1   2 7   1

5.

F Major   1   3 2   1   7 2   5   1   5 3   1   2 7   1

6.

B♭ Major   1   7 6   5 3   5   6   7 1   2 7   1

7.

"When the Saints Go Marching In," New Orleans African-American funeral spiritual[+]

G Major   1 3 4   5

8.

"Early One Morning," English folk song

D Major   2   3 4 5 3 1

Aaron Copland used this next old hymn tune in his ballet *Appalachian Spring.* You might like to hear how it sounds in that version!

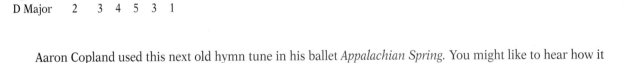

"Simple Gifts," American Shaker hymn (1848)[+]

9.

G Major   5 5   1

10.

Arnold de Lantins (ca. 1430), "Puisque je voy" (Since I Saw Her)

F Major   5   5   5

The next group of melodies are all different versions of the same succession of pitches, but very different rhythms are used. All the melodies are from a **Mass** by Palestrina, an Italian composer of the Renaissance (sixteenth-century). See how well you can read the different rhythms in which the same melodic pattern is set. The scale for all is F Major.

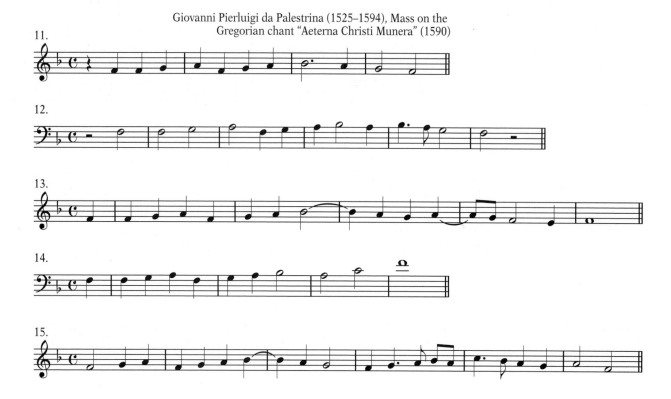

Giovanni Pierluigi da Palestrina (1525–1594), Mass on the
Gregorian chant "Aeterna Christi Munera" (1590)

$\mathcal{W}$RITTEN ASSIGNMENT

A. *Identifying Major and Minor Thirds.* Following is a series of major and minor thirds. Identify each interval using the abbreviation M3 for major third and m3 for minor third. The example is worked correctly for you.

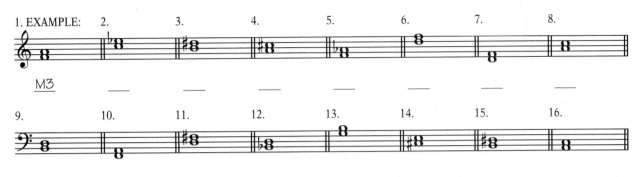

1. EXAMPLE: 2.   3.   4.   5.   6.   7.   8.

M3

9.   10.   11.   12.   13.   14.   15.   16.

B. *Writing Major and Minor Thirds.* Following is a series of single notes. Write a major third and a minor third above each note in the spaces provided. The example is worked correctly for you.

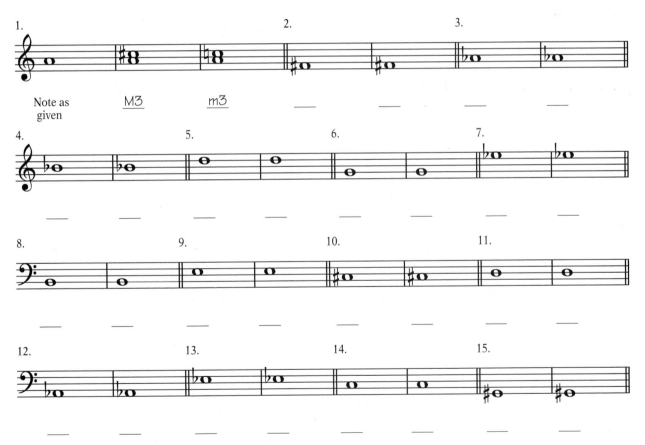

1.   2.   3.

Note as   M3   m3
given

4.   5.   6.   7.

8.   9.   10.   11.

12.   13.   14.   15.

C. *Placing Major and Minor Thirds on the Keyboard.* Using the letter names, write the intervals requested on the following keyboard diagrams. The example is worked correctly for you. Play all the examples on a piano. Play them both as melodic intervals and as harmonic intervals. Listen carefully.

1. EXAMPLE: m3 up from E

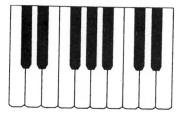

5. m3 up from C♯

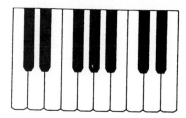

2. M3 up from A

6. m3 up from F

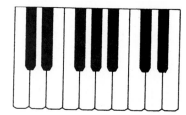

3. m3 up from G♯

7. M3 up from C

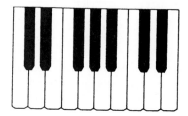

4. M3 up from F

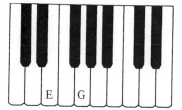

8. M3 up from G♭

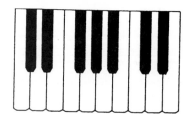

$\mathcal{E}$AR TRAINING ASSIGNMENT

A. In each of the following exercises the teacher will play an interval. This interval will be either a major or a minor third. Underline the name of the interval you hear played. See the example.

You will hear:

Answer: 1. <u>Major Third</u>   Minor Third

                    2. Major Third   Minor Third

                    3. Major Third   Minor Third

                    4. Major Third   Minor Third

                    5. Major Third   Minor Third

                    6. Major Third   Minor Third

                    7. Major Third   Minor Third

                    8. Major Third   Minor Third

                    9. Major Third   Minor Third

                  10. Major Third   Minor Third

B. In each of the following exercises the teacher will play three intervals. One of these three will be a major third. Circle the letter that shows which is the major third.

1. a.	b.	c.	6. a.	b.	c.
2. a.	b.	c.	7. a.	b.	c.
3. a.	b.	c.	8. a.	b.	c.
4. a.	b.	c.	9. a.	b.	c.
5. a.	b.	c.	10. a.	b.	c.

C. In each of the following exercises the teacher will play three intervals. One of these three will be a minor third. Circle the letter that shows which one is the minor third.

1. a.	b.	c.	6. a.	b.	c.
2. a.	b.	c.	7. a.	b.	c.
3. a.	b.	c.	8. a.	b.	c.
4. a.	b.	c.	9. a.	b.	c.
5. a.	b.	c.	10. a.	b.	c.

D. In each of the following exercises you will hear a four-note melody. Somewhere in each of these melodies you will hear the leap of a major third (between adjacent tones). Underline the phrase that describes where the major third is located in each exercise. The example is illustrated and is worked correctly for you.

EXAMPLE:

You will hear:

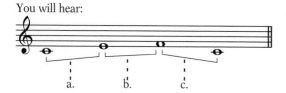

Answer: 1. a. <u>Between 1st and 2nd note</u>

b. Between 2nd and 3rd note

c. Between 3rd and 4th note

2. a. Between 1st and 2nd note

b. Between 2nd and 3rd note

c. Between 3rd and 4th note

3. a. Between 1st and 2nd note

b. Between 2nd and 3rd note

c. Between 3rd and 4th note

4. a. Between 1st and 2nd note

b. Between 2nd and 3rd note

c. Between 3rd and 4th note

5. a. Between 1st and 2nd note

b. Between 2nd and 3rd note

c. Between 3rd and 4th note

6. a. Between 1st and 2nd note

b. Between 2nd and 3rd note

c. Between 3rd and 4th note

7. a. Between 1st and 2nd note

b. Between 2nd and 3rd note

c. Between 3rd and 4th note

8. a. Between 1st and 2nd note

b. Between 2nd and 3rd note

c. Between 3rd and 4th note

9. a. Between 1st and 2nd note

b. Between 2nd and 3rd note

c. Between 3rd and 4th note

10. a. Between 1st and 2nd note

b. Between 2nd and 3rd note

c. Between 3rd and 4th note

Chapter 9 ▪ The Major Triad and the Interval of the Perfect Fifth

The Triad

Three or more different tones sounding together form a **chord.** There are many different kinds of chords, but those that form the basis for the music since the beginning of the fifteenth century are built of thirds.

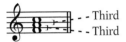

- - Third
- - Third

A chord that consists of three different tones, each a third apart, is called a *triad.*

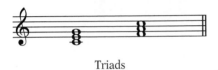

Triads

Tones of the triad may be arranged in different orders or placed in different octaves, but if the names of the notes are the same, the chord preserves its identity. It is always possible to reassemble the notes of the triad in thirds to show its construction. This arrangement of the notes of the triad is called the **simple position** of the triad.

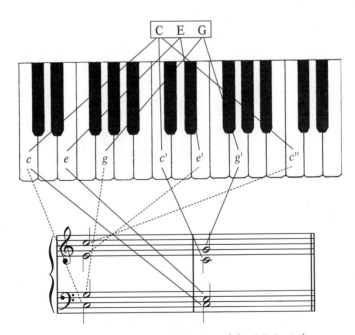

Two arrangements of the notes of the C E G triad

Simple position of the C E G triad

There are several different kinds of chords as you can hear if you play the following triads on the piano.

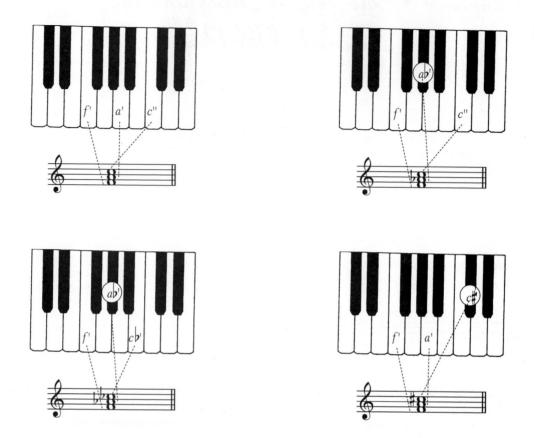

The Major Triad

A triad with a major third on the bottom and a minor third on the top is called a *major triad*.

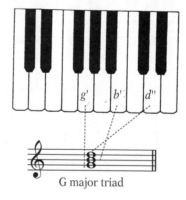

G major triad

The Perfect Fifth

The interval between the bottom and top notes of a triad is a **fifth.** In the major triad, the fifth always contains seven half steps. The fifth is an interval whose size cannot be altered without giving an entirely new character to the sound, so it belongs to the category of *perfect intervals*. A *perfect fifth* always has *seven* half steps.

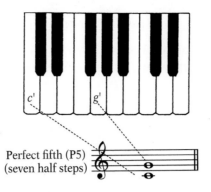

Perfect fifth (P5)
(seven half steps)

𝒯he Names of the Triad Tones

Each member of the triad is named in relation to the tone on which the chord is constructed, which is the **root** of the triad. The note a third above the root is called the **third** of the triad. The fifth above the root is the **fifth** of the triad. Triads are named by the *root* and the *quality* of sound: thus, in the following example, a major triad built on C is called the *C major triad.*

C major triad

Fifth
Third
Root
m3
M3
P5

𝒯he Diminished Fifth

If a fifth is built on each note of any major scale, all but one of the fifths will have seven half steps (perfect fifths). One fifth, however, has only six half steps. Its quality of sound is so totally different from that of the perfect fifth that it is called **diminished** (the term used for all intervals one half step smaller than the normal size of the interval).

C major								
Scale degree	1	2	3	4	5	6	7	8
Number of half steps	7	7	7	7	7	7	6	7
Name of interval	P5	P5	P5	P5	P5	P5	d5	P5

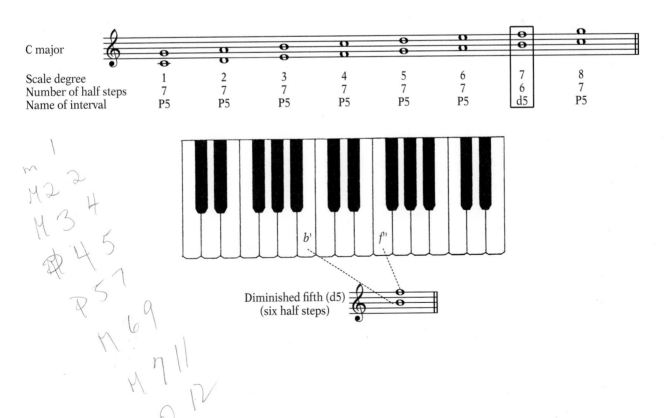

Diminished fifth (d5)
(six half steps)

How to Write Fifths

The very first harmony in Western European music was based on the interval of the perfect fifth, back in the ninth century. Here is how that music (called **organum**) sounded, in an example from one of the earliest theory textbooks.

Musica Enchiriadis (Musical Handbook) (ca. 850)

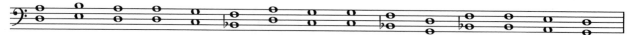

This music was for singers, so sing the example together in class, using a neutral syllable such as *la*.

In this music, *only perfect intervals could be used,* so it was necessary to alter the fifth between B and F by adding a flat. (Notice that, like Gregorian chant of the same period, this music is nonmetric.)

All fifths on the white keys except the fifth between B and F are perfect fifths. B to F has only *six half steps* and is a *diminished fifth.* If either note of any perfect fifth on the white keys is raised or lowered by a sharp or flat, the other must have the same accidental for the interval to remain perfect.

Perfect fifths (P5)
(seven half steps)

To make a perfect fifth on B, however, an F♯ must be used. B♭ to F is also a perfect fifth. These are the *only* two perfect fifths in which both notes do *not* have the same accidentals.

Perfect fifths (P5)
(seven half steps)

Music with Melodies Set with Fifths

After the Middle Ages composers avoided writing successions of perfect intervals like the fifths in the example above. However, at the end of the nineteenth century, composers such as Debussy again became fascinated with the sounds of fifths. Listen to this little passage from his piano prelude "The Engulfed Cathedral," in which the fifths are doubled by octaves (just as the medieval fifths you sang earlier were, if they were sung by both male and female voices).

Claude Debussy (1862–1918), *Preludes pour Piano,* Book I,
"La Cathédrale engloutie" (The Engulfed Cathedral)
(1910)

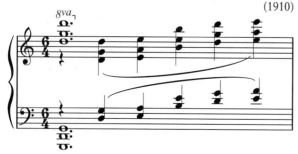

Bartók presents one melody in **parallel fifths** in his *Concerto for Orchestra*. This time the paired instruments are flutes. Does Bartók use both sizes of fifths in this passage?

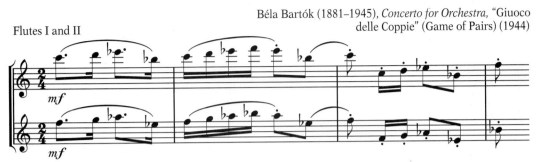

Béla Bartók (1881–1945), *Concerto for Orchestra*, "Giuoco delle Coppie" (Game of Pairs) (1944)

The Major Triads in the Major Scale

If a triad is constructed on each note of the C major scale, using only the notes of the scale, there will be three major triads in the series, on the first, fourth, and fifth degrees of the scale (C, F, and G).

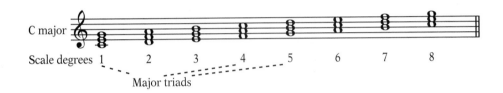

How to Construct a Major Triad

These are the only three major triads consisting entirely of white keys. These three triads are the *C major* triad, the *F major* triad, and the *G major* triad. Find these three triads on the piano and play them, listening carefully to the sound.

To construct all other major triads, sharps and flats must be used to make a major third and perfect fifth above the root of the triad.

major triad = M3 + P5 above the root

Common fingerings for playing many of the major triads on the guitar are given in Appendix 3. Those with guitars can find these fingerings and play the major triads given there. Listen carefully to all the sounds played. The common symbol for a major triad is the name of the root of the chord written as a capital letter. Thus, C means to play a C major chord on the guitar.

Following are all the major triads in simple position. First the position on the keyboard is shown, then the proper notation on the music staff. Learn to find these major triads in *all* octaves of the regular piano keyboard. The shading on the keyboard shows you which notes to play.

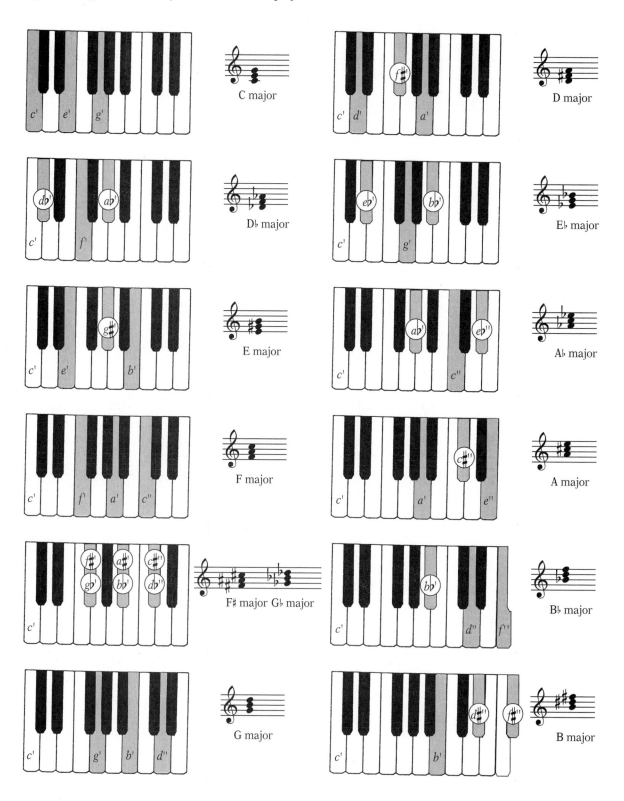

SIGHT SINGING ASSIGNMENT

A. *Sight Singing, a Warm-up Exercise.* Professional vocalists often warm up their voices before they perform. One exercise that they commonly use is a series of thirds up and down over a span of one octave and one step. This is a very useful exercise because it "tunes" the ear and exercises the vocal range.

As this text requires a good deal of singing, the student might find developing facility with this exercise to be very useful in preparing the voice to sing with accuracy. It is important for the student to remember that sight singing examples do not require a beautiful performance worthy of the stage, only vocal accuracy in relation to pitch and rhythm. When singing each note, be sure to sing the diatonic number of the note as indicated below.

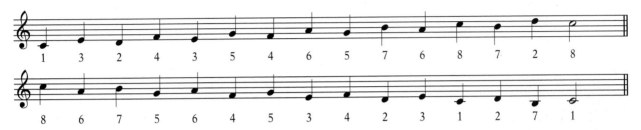

B. Sing the following short melodies using the scale numbers as provided under the notes. You will notice the melodic use of the triad. Exercises 2, 4, 6, and 8 are the same as exercises 1, 3, 5, and 7, but they are **transposed** to the key of F major. Use syllables if your teacher prefers.

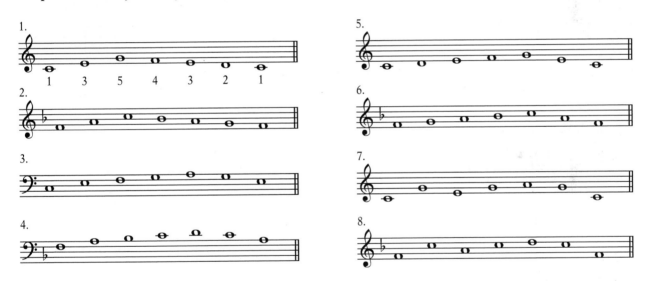

C. Sing the following short melodies, providing the correct scale numbers or syllables as you sing.

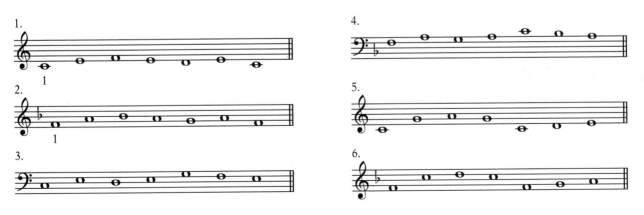

D. In this set of exercises only the numbers are indicated. The number 1 refers to the tonic (first note) of a major scale and so on. Choose any beginning pitch you wish and sing these just as you sang the exercises in the two previous sets of sight singing assignments.

1.	1	3	5	6	5	4	3	2	1
2.	1	3	3	4	5	1	3	2	1
3.	1	5	1	1	2	3	5	3	1
4.	1	3	3	4	5	6	7	8	1

E. Sing the following melodies with scale numbers, syllables, or letter names.

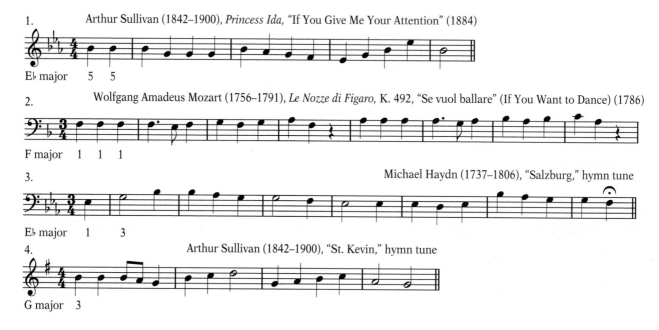

1.
Arthur Sullivan (1842–1900), *Princess Ida,* "If You Give Me Your Attention" (1884)

E♭ major   5   5

2.
Wolfgang Amadeus Mozart (1756–1791), *Le Nozze di Figaro,* K. 492, "Se vuol ballare" (If You Want to Dance) (1786)

F major   1   1   1

3.
Michael Haydn (1737–1806), "Salzburg," hymn tune

E♭ major   1   3

4.
Arthur Sullivan (1842–1900), "St. Kevin," hymn tune

G major   3

The melody below is a round. Sing it first straight through, then divide the group into three parts. The first group begins. When they get to the second line, the second group sings from the beginning. When they reach the second line, the third group joins, again from the beginning. You can continue singing until all groups have sung the melody through once. There will be other rounds later in this book.

"Oh, How Lovely Is the Evening," traditional round

G major   Oh,   how   love - ly   is   the   eve - ning,   is   the   eve - ning,

when   the   bells   are   sweet - ly   ring - ing,   sweet - ly   ring - ing!

Ding,   dong,   ding,   dong,   ding,   dong.

WRITTEN ASSIGNMENT

A. *Recognition of Triads by Sight.* Following is a series of chords. Some are triads, and some are not. Circle the chords that *are* triads. In this group of exercises, the root of each chord is the lowest (bottom) note.

B. *Rearranging Triads into Simple Root Position.* All the chords in these exercises are triads, but the triad notes are not arranged in *simple root position* (with the root as the lowest note). Rearrange the notes of each exercise into simple root position. The example is worked correctly for you.

EXAMPLE:

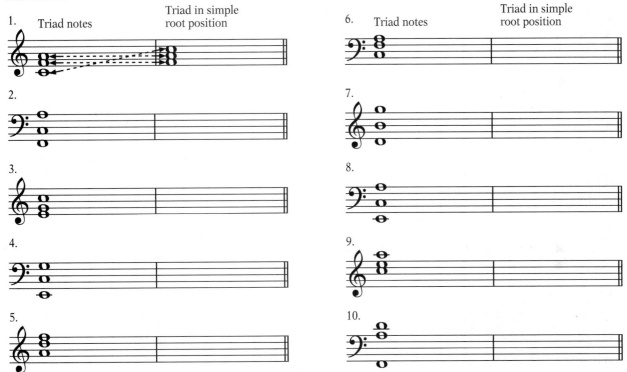

C. *Drill in Writing Perfect Fifths on the Music Staff.* Write a perfect fifth *above* each given note. The example is worked correctly for you.

D. *Recognition by Sight of Major Triads.* Circle only the triads that are *major* triads.

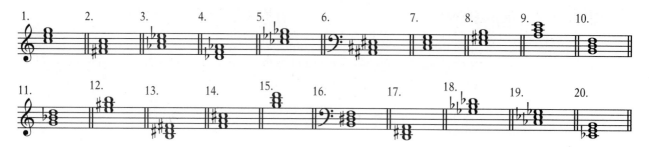

E. Choose the major triad from each pair, circle it, and then play the major triads on the keyboard.

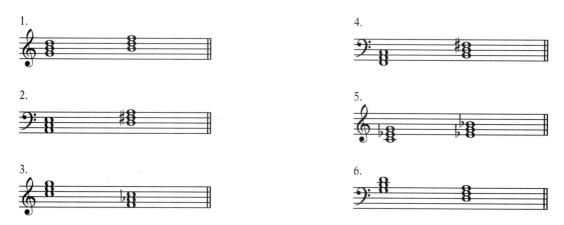

F. *Placing Triads on the Keyboard.* Using letter names with octave designation to mark the right keys, place the following triads on the keyboard. *Play* all the triads you have labeled on the piano. The example is worked correctly for you.

After labeling the diagrams and playing the triads, write each triad in bass clef in the space provided.

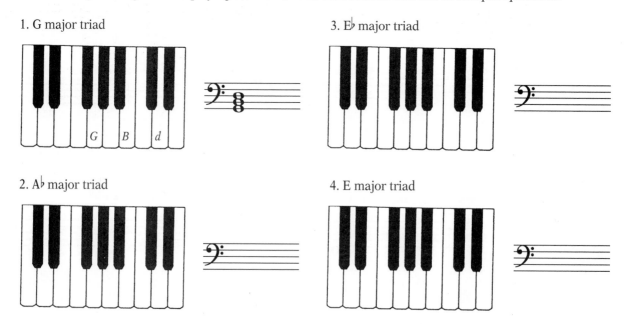

5. F major triad

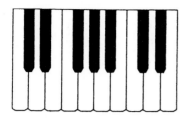 

9. A major triad

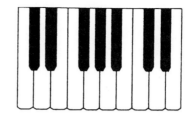 

6. C♯ major triad

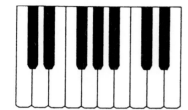 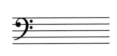

10. B major triad

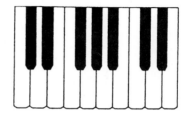 

7. D major triad

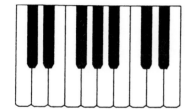 

11. F♯ major triad

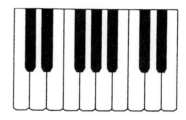 

8. D♭ major triad

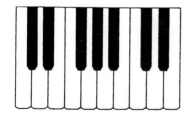 

12. B♭ major triad

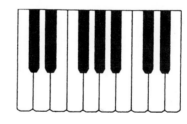 

$\mathcal{E}$AR TRAINING ASSIGNMENT

A. *Major Triads in Simple Position.* In each of the following exercises one of the four triads played will be a major triad. Circle the letter that represents the major triad.

You will hear:

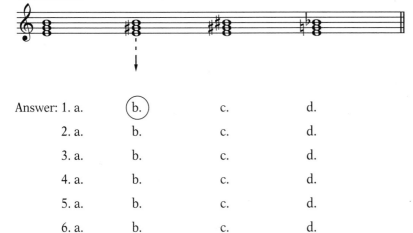

Answer: 1. a.   (b.)   c.   d.

      2. a.   b.   c.   d.

      3. a.   b.   c.   d.

      4. a.   b.   c.   d.

      5. a.   b.   c.   d.

      6. a.   b.   c.   d.

B. *Major Triads in Four-Part Harmony.* In each of the following exercises one of the three triads (this time in four-part harmony) is a major triad. Circle the letter that represents the major triad.

You will hear:

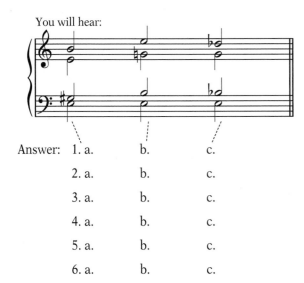

Answer: 1. a.   b.   c.

       2. a.   b.   c.

       3. a.   b.   c.

       4. a.   b.   c.

       5. a.   b.   c.

       6. a.   b.   c.

C. *Recognition of the Perfect Octave, Perfect Fifth, and Major Third.* In each exercise you will hear three harmonic intervals.

1. One will be a perfect fifth (P5).
2. One will be a perfect octave (P8).
3. One will be a major third (M3).

Mark each interval you hear with the proper symbol. Each exercise will be played twice.

You will hear:

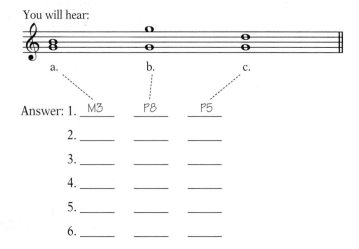

Answer: 1. __M3__   __P8__   __P5__

2. _____   _____   _____

3. _____   _____   _____

4. _____   _____   _____

5. _____   _____   _____

6. _____   _____   _____

D. *Recognition of the Perfect Fifth in Melodic Context.* In each of the following exercises you will hear four notes of a melody. Somewhere in each of these melodies you will hear the leap of a *perfect fifth* (between adjacent tones). Underline the phrase that describes where the perfect fifth is located in each exercise. Each exercise will be played twice.

You will hear:

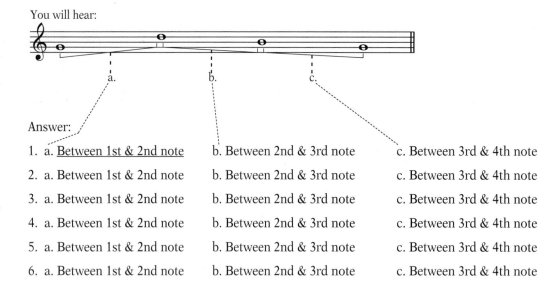

Answer:

1. a. <u>Between 1st & 2nd note</u>   b. Between 2nd & 3rd note   c. Between 3rd & 4th note

2. a. Between 1st & 2nd note   b. Between 2nd & 3rd note   c. Between 3rd & 4th note

3. a. Between 1st & 2nd note   b. Between 2nd & 3rd note   c. Between 3rd & 4th note

4. a. Between 1st & 2nd note   b. Between 2nd & 3rd note   c. Between 3rd & 4th note

5. a. Between 1st & 2nd note   b. Between 2nd & 3rd note   c. Between 3rd & 4th note

6. a. Between 1st & 2nd note   b. Between 2nd & 3rd note   c. Between 3rd & 4th note

Chapter 10 ▪ The Circle of Fifths and the Key Signatures of the Major Scales

The Pattern of the Major Scale

When major scales begin on notes other than C, sharps or flats must be used to produce the correct pattern of whole steps and half steps—half steps between the third and fourth and the seventh and eighth degrees.

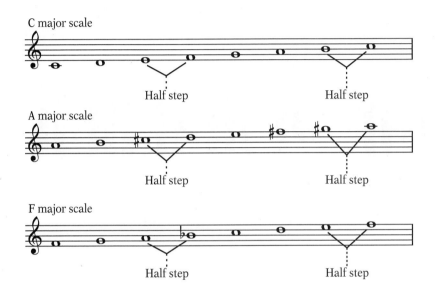

The Keys with Sharps

The only scale among the major keys with no sharps or flats is C major. If a scale begins a perfect fifth higher than C (on G), it will have one sharp on its seventh degree (F sharp).

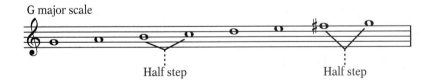

To find the next scale, begin a fifth above G on the note D. This scale will keep the F♯ of the preceding scale and add one more sharp (on *its* seventh degree). Thus, it has two sharps, F♯ and C♯.

This process may be continued until all the notes of the scale are sharped. The order of the scales with sharps follows. The first few scales are written out completely, but space is left for you to complete the rest. Play the scales you have written, using the piano and/or any other instrument or instruments you play.

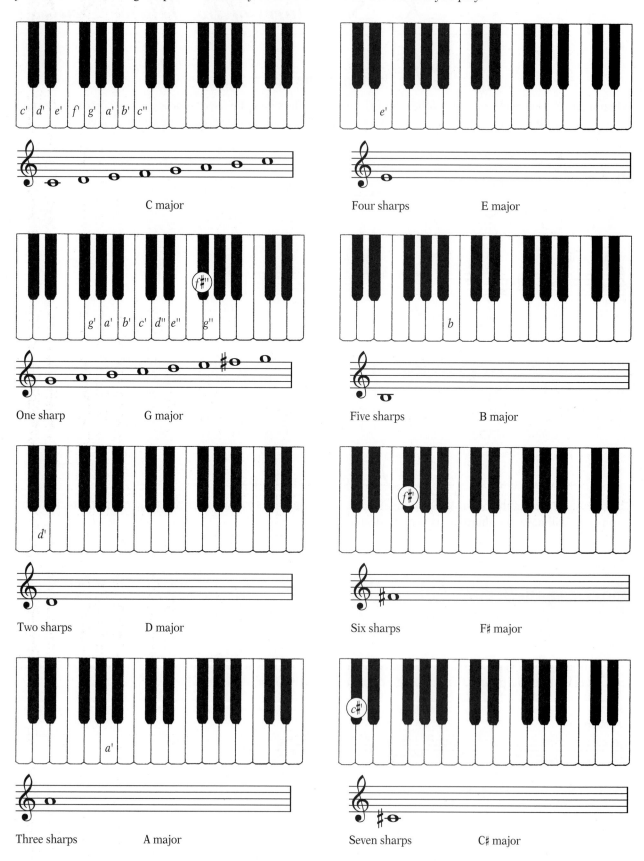

C major

One sharp   G major

Two sharps   D major

Three sharps   A major

Four sharps   E major

Five sharps   B major

Six sharps   F♯ major

Seven sharps   C♯ major

The Keys with Flats

The major flat scales are found by beginning each scale a fifth lower than the preceding scale, beginning with the fifth below the C major scale.

This process is continued until all the notes of the scale are flats.

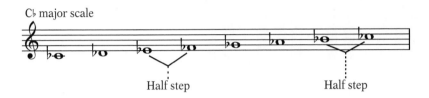

The order of the scales is given here. The first two scales are written out completely. Space is left for you to complete the rest.

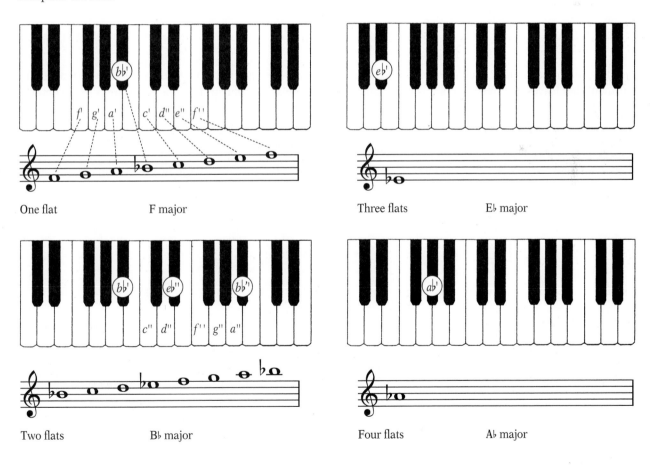

One flat   F major   Three flats   E♭ major

Two flats   B♭ major   Four flats   A♭ major

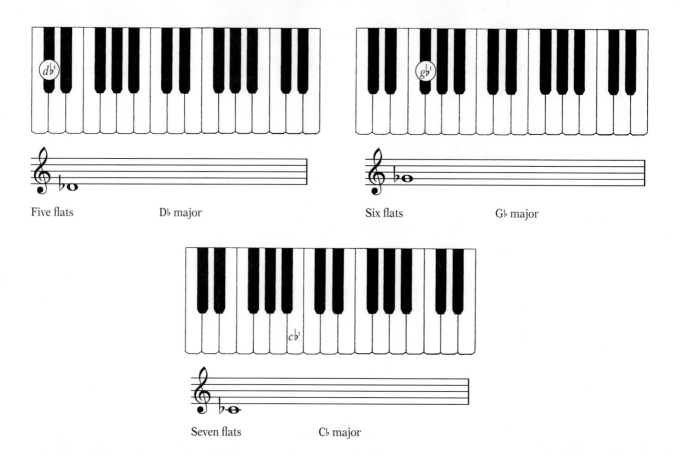

Five flats   D♭ major

Six flats   G♭ major

Seven flats   C♭ major

Play all the scales that you have written on a piano and/or other instrument or instruments. If you play an instrument that leaves you free to do so, say the name of each note as you play it. Play the scales in as many octaves as you can.

The Circle of Fifths

The order of all the sharp and flat scales can be shown by a circle because by moving in either direction in perfect fifths, you eventually return to the starting key. The **circle of fifths** here illustrates this return.

Flat keys   Sharp keys

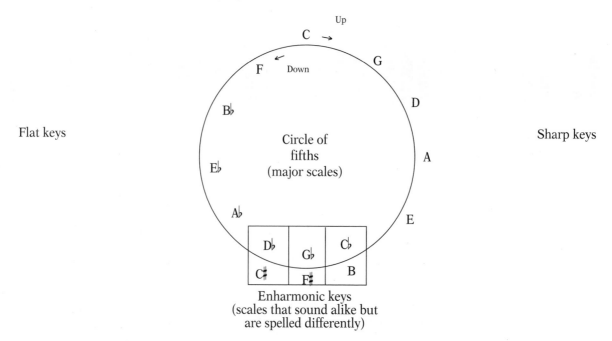

Enharmonic keys
(scales that sound alike but
are spelled differently)

The Key Signature

Music using the notes of a particular scale is said to be *in the key of the first note of that scale.*

Anonymous (formerly attributed to Henry Carey), "My Country 'Tis of Thee" (As "God Save the King," this tune dates back to about 1744); also known as "America"

"America" in the key of G major

When a composer writes music in keys that have sharps or flats, it would be quite cumbersome to have to write a sharp or flat sign in front of every affected note, so a **key signature** (sharps or flats showing the notes of the key) is used at the beginning of every staff to show which sharps or flats are in the key. In effect, the F lines and spaces are made into F♯ lines and spaces by the G major key signature. The sharp or flat need appear only once in the signature to affect all octaves.

Key signature

"America" with a key signature (G major)

The conventional pattern of arrangement of sharps or flats in the key signature shows the order of introduction of the sharps or flats. Because the pattern never varies, it is easy to tell at a glance what the sharps or flats of the key will be.

| G major | D major | A major | E major | B major | F♯ major | C♯ major |

Key signatures of the sharp keys in treble and bass clef

To remember the order of the sharps, memorize the signature for C♯ major. To find the signature for the other keys, subtract the proper number of sharps from the right side of the key signature to find which sharps are left in the key you need.

The order of the flats in the key signature follows the order of introduction of the flats in the circle of fifths. As with the sharps, it is easy to memorize the key signature of C♭ major, which contains all the flats, and subtract from the right side the proper number to find the flats remaining in the key desired.

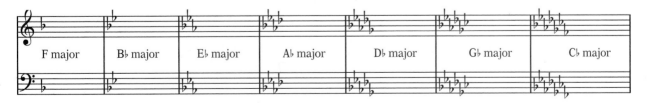

| F major | B♭ major | E♭ major | A♭ major | D♭ major | G♭ major | C♭ major |

Key signatures of the flat keys in treble and bass clef

You can remember which major scale belongs to each key signature by keeping in mind that in sharp keys, the seventh note of the scale is always the last sharp, whereas in flat keys, the fourth note of the scale is always the last flat. Thus, if the last sharp is A♯, go up one half step to B, which will be the tonic of the key; if the last flat is E♭, count down four notes to find the tonic note, B♭. Remember that the name of the scale *must* include the sharp or flat if there is one on the tonic note.

When you notate key signatures, allow sufficient space so that none of the sharps or flats is directly above or below another and the proper order is kept clear.

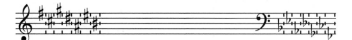

Key signatures showing spacing of symbols

$\mathcal{A}$ccidentals

When sharps, flats, or naturals that are not part of the key signature are used, they are placed to the left of the note that they affect. They are called **accidentals.** When an accidental occurs, it affects all notes of that pitch that follow it in the same measure. The effect of an accidental is canceled by the bar line. If a sharp or flat has been used at the beginning of a measure, and a note without accidental is needed later in the measure, a natural sign must be used.

G sharp,
from previous
accidental

G natural

Natural sign required to
cancel sharp within the bar

$\mathcal{S}$IGHT SINGING ASSIGNMENT

A. *Singing Scales and Intervals above the Tonic Note.* Sing the following exercise in all the major sharp scales using scale step numbers first and then letter names of the notes. The example is given in C major. It may be *transposed* (that is, *exactly duplicated beginning on a different pitch*) to all the other major sharp keys. It is very useful to sing *each* scale with the names of the notes as well as with numbers or syllables. Use the scales you have written out in this lesson.

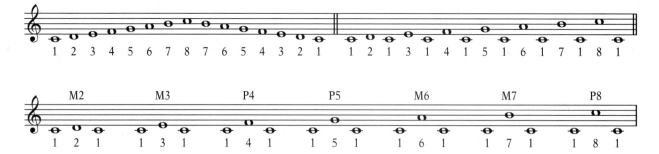

Sing the intervals in all major scales, using the names of the notes.

B. The more you practice *singing* intervals, the easier they will be to hear. When you hear the white note, respond by singing the black notes.

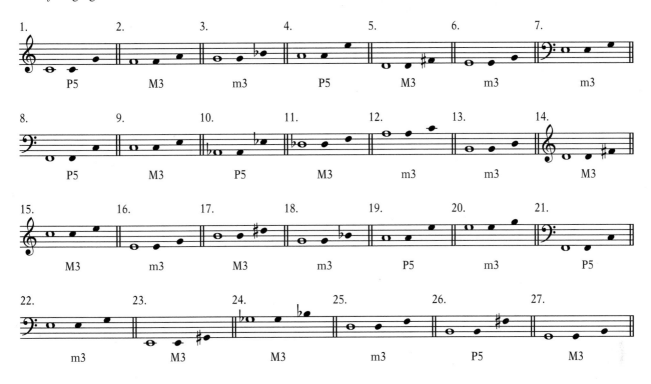

C. Here the intervals are *descending* instead of *ascending*.

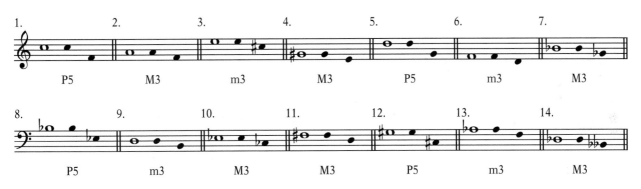

D. Do you know any melodies that begin with thirds or fifths (ascending or descending)? Make a collection in your class of such melodies to help you remember the sounds of the intervals.

E. Close your books for this exercise.
   1. Your teacher will play the exercise on the piano, as shown in whole (white) notes.
   2. Then you sing the exercise back using scale numbers, note names, or syllables. This is shown in black notes.
   3. The teacher will then give the beginning note (only) of another key. This is shown by the single white note.
   4. Sing the same exercise in the new key using the same numbers, note names, or syllables, as shown in black notes.

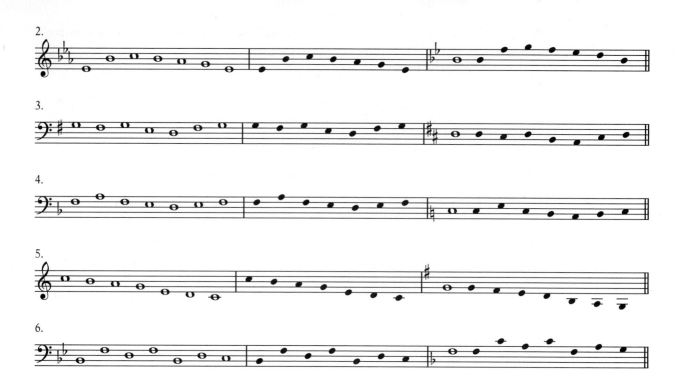

F. The following exercises are for rhythm. Sing or say the regular meter beat (as indicated) and at the same time clap the note values as shown.

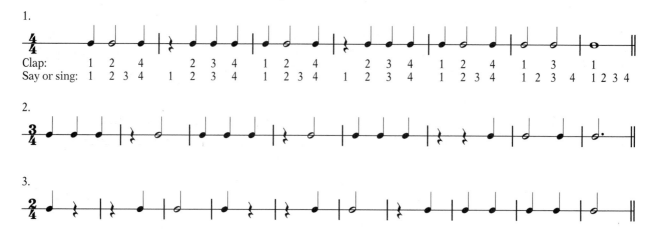

G. Sing the following melodies with the syllables, scale numbers, or texts where these are given.

"Michael, Row the Boat Ashore," spiritual[+]

Mi - chael, row the boat a - shore, Hal - le - lu - jah! Mi - chael, board the gos - pel

boat, Hal - le - lu - jah!

2.

John Frederik Peter (1746–1813), "Glory Be to Him"[+]

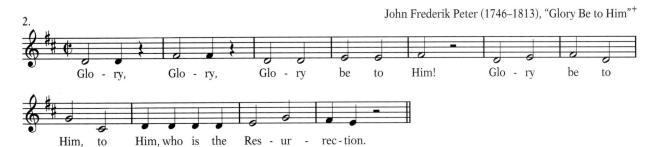

Glory, Glory, Glo - ry be to Him! Glo - ry be to

Him, to Him, who is the Res - ur - - rec - tion.

3.

Vincent Persichetti (1915–1987), *Divertimento for Band*, March (1951)[+]

H. A useful exercise is to sing a melody in major key and then sing it again in another scale beginning on the same note, in a minor key. Use scale step numbers or syllables to sing the following. You will learn more about the minor keys in the next chapter.

1. a.

1   3   5

b.

1   3   5

2. a.

b.

3. a.

b.

WRITTEN ASSIGNMENT QUIZ

It is very important to *memorize* the scales and key signatures, that is, to be able to write each scale from memory and to write the key signature for each major key, with the sharps or flats in the correct order. The best way to be sure you can do this is for your teacher to give you a quiz on them.

$\mathcal{E}$AR TRAINING ASSIGNMENT

A. *Further Drill on Major and Minor Thirds and Major and Minor Seconds.* In each exercise you will hear a series of four harmonic intervals. Two intervals will be seconds (major or minor); two intervals will be thirds (major or minor). Mark the correct symbol in the space provided, using M3 for major third, m3 for minor third, M2 for major second, and m2 for minor second. The example is worked correctly for you.

EXAMPLE:
You hear:

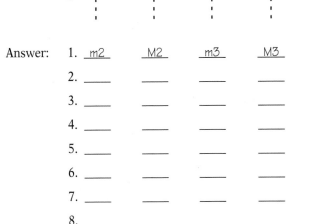

Answer: 1. _m2_   _M2_   _m3_   _M3_

            2. ____   ____   ____   ____

            3. ____   ____   ____   ____

            4. ____   ____   ____   ____

            5. ____   ____   ____   ____

            6. ____   ____   ____   ____

            7. ____   ____   ____   ____

            8. ____   ____   ____   ____

B. *Recognition of Major Triads.* In each of the following exercises, one of the three triads played will be a *major triad.* Circle the letter that represents the major triad. The example is worked correctly for you.

EXAMPLE:
You hear:

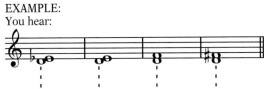

Answer: 1. (a.)   b.   c.

            2. a.   b.   c.

            3. a.   b.   c.

            4. a.   b.   c.

            5. a.   b.   c.

            6. a.   b.   c.

            7. a.   b.   c.

            8. a.   b.   c.

C. *Recognition of Major and Minor Thirds and Perfect Fifths in Melodies.* In each of the following exercises you will hear four notes of a melody. The only intervals used in the melodies will be major and minor thirds and perfect fifths. Each melody may contain *any combination* of these intervals. Label each interval in the space provided, using M3 for a major third, m3 for a minor third, and P5 for a perfect fifth.

EXAMPLE:

Answer: 1. 1 _P5_ 2 _m3_ 3 _M3_ 4

2. 1 _____ 2 _____ 3 _____ 4

3. 1 _____ 2 _____ 3 _____ 4

4. 1 _____ 2 _____ 3 _____ 4

5. 1 _____ 2 _____ 3 _____ 4

6. 1 _____ 2 _____ 3 _____ 4

7. 1 _____ 2 _____ 3 _____ 4

8. 1 _____ 2 _____ 3 _____ 4

D. *Recognition of Parallel Lines in Thirds, Seconds, and Fifths.* In each exercise you will hear a short melody. It will be set with a parallel line a second, a third, or a fifth away. Underline the correct interval.

1. Second   Third   Fifth

2. Second   Third   Fifth

3. Second   Third   Fifth

4. Second   Third   Fifth

5. Second   Third   Fifth

Chapter 11 ▪ The Minor Scales

The Minor Scale

The scales studied so far have been major scales, which have half steps between the *third and fourth* and *seventh and eighth* degrees of the scale. When the arrangement of half steps and whole steps is changed, the aesthetic effect of the music is profoundly altered. For example, if a familiar tune such as "My Country 'Tis of Thee" has the third degree of the scale lowered one half step, a completely new tonal feeling results.

Lowering the third degree in this manner produces a *minor third* between the first and third degrees of the scale. Many scales have this characteristic interval between the first and third degrees, but by far the most common one is the **minor scale,** which has half steps between the *second and third* and *fifth and sixth* degrees of the scale.

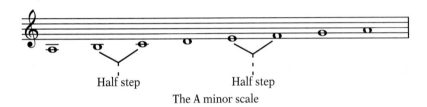

Half step   Half step
The A minor scale

This scale is often altered by accidentals, but the basic form shown above is called the **natural,** or *pure,* minor scale.

The Circle of Fifths for Minor Scales

The order of sharps and flats in minor key signatures is the same as for major scales. Like the major scales, minor keys follow the circle of fifths, with *a minor* rather than *C major* as the starting point.

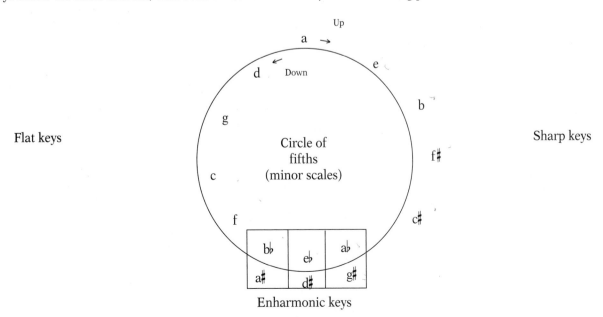

Enharmonic keys

Relative Scales

Major and minor scales that share the same key signature are called **relative scales.** G major and e minor both have a key signature of one sharp (F sharp); therefore, G major is the *relative major* of e minor, and e minor is the *relative minor* of G major. The relative minor scale always begins a *minor third* below the major scale with the same key signature.

MAJOR	KEY SIGNATURE	RELATIVE MINOR
C Major	No sharps or flats	a minor
G Major	F♯	e minor
D Major	F♯, C♯	b minor
A Major	F♯, C♯, G♯	f♯ minor
E Major	F♯, C♯, G♯, D♯	c♯ minor
B Major	F♯, C♯, G♯, D♯, A♯	g♯ minor
F♯ Major	F♯, C♯, G♯, D♯, A♯, E♯	d♯ minor
C♯ Major	F♯, C♯, G♯, D♯, A♯, E♯, B♯	a♯ minor
F Major	B♭	d minor
B♭ Major	B♭, E♭	g minor
E♭ Major	B♭, E♭, A♭	c minor
A♭ Major	B♭, E♭, A♭, D♭	f minor
D♭ Major	B♭, E♭, A♭, D♭, G♭	b♭ minor
G♭ Major	B♭, E♭, A♭, D♭, G♭, C♭	e♭ minor
C♭ Major	B♭, E♭, A♭, D♭, G♭, C♭, F♭	a♭ minor

Parallel Scales

Major and minor scales that share the same *tonic note* are called **parallel scales.** *C major,* with no sharps or flats, and *c minor,* with three flats, are parallel scales. The key signature for the *parallel minor scale* is the same as that of the major key a minor third above the tonic of the major scale.

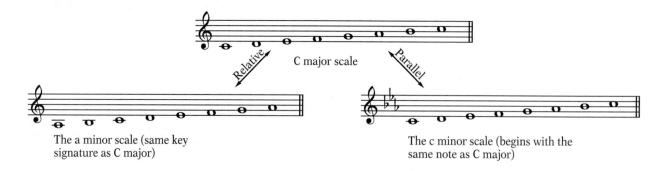

The a minor scale (same key signature as C major)

C major scale

The c minor scale (begins with the same note as C major)

SIGHT SINGING ASSIGNMENT

A. *Natural Minor.* Sing the following short melodies in the natural minor mode. Use syllables or scale numbers on all exercises.

   1. The scale numbers are provided for you in the first two exercises.
   2. In the other six exercises figure out the scale numbers or syllables for yourselves.

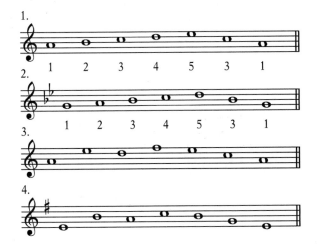

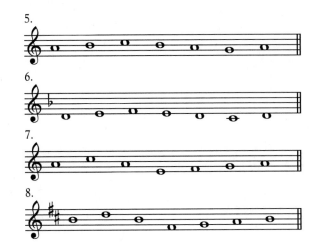

B. *Natural Minor.* In this set of exercises only the numbers are indicated. The number 1 refers to the tonic (first note) of the natural minor scale. Choose any beginning pitch you wish and sing these just as you sang the previous exercises.

   (a) 1 3 5 6 4 5 3 1
   (b) 1 2 3 4 3 8 7 8

   (c) 1 5 6 7 8 6 4 1
   (d) 1 4 3 5 2 4 7 8

   (e) 1 3 2 4 2 3 1 7 1
   (f) 1 5 3 1 7 1 3 2 1

C. Close your books for this exercise.

   a. The teacher plays the exercise on the piano, as shown in whole (white) notes.
   b. The student then sings the exercise back to the teacher using scale numbers. This is shown in black notes.
   c. The teacher gives the first note of a new key, and the student sings the same exercise using the same scale numbers.

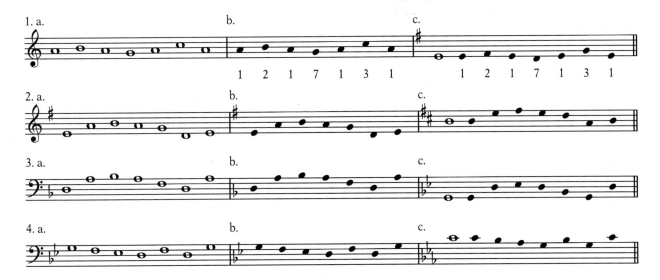

D. *Melodies to Sing.* Sing the melodies below with syllables, with scale step numbers, or with the texts.

1. Gabriel Fauré (1845–1924), *Requiem (Mass for the Dead),* "Libera me" (Set Me Free) (1877)

From death __ e - ter - nal, _____ O set me free, Lord my God. _____

2. John H. Hopkins, Jr. (1820–1891),
    "We Three Kings of Orient Are" (1857)+

We three kings of O - ri - ent are,

3. Béla Bartók (1881–1945), *Mikrokosmos (Little Universe),* Vol. V,
    "New Hungarian Folk Song" (1940)

Oh, how high, green for - est, spread your high - est tree?

© Copyright 1946 by Hawkes & Son (London) Ltd.; Copyright Renewed.
Reprinted by permission of Boosey and Hawkes, Inc.

4. Antonin Dvořák (1841–1904), *Symphony No. 9 in E Minor (From the New World),* First Movement (1893)

5. "St. Patrick," traditional Irish hymn

6. "O Come, O Come, Emmanuel," carol based on Gregorian chant

7. "The Birch Tree," Russian folk song

O - ver on the hill stands a birch tree, Grow-ing tall and white in yon - der mead - ow.

The Russian composer Tchaikovsky used the melody you just sang as the basis for a theme and variations in his fourth symphony (1877). You might like to hear how he treated this old folk tune by listening to the symphony.

8. John Merbecke (ca. 1505–1585), "Agnus Dei" (Lamb of God), from *The Book of Common Prayer Noted* (1550)

Notice that the above example, like those from Gregorian chant, is nonmetric. Read the rhythm carefully and sing it smoothly without accent.

9.

Anne L. Miller (20th century), "Give Peace, O God, the Nations Cry" (1941)[+]

E. The preceding melodies all used the natural minor scale. Sing the following three melodies, which are in major, using scale step numbers, syllables, or texts if they are given.

1. Johannes Brahms (1833–1897), "Vergebliches Ständchen" (False Serenade) (1882)

Good ev' - ning, my treas - ure, Good ev' - ning, my dear.

2. "We Gather Together," Dutch folk song

We gath - er to - geth - er to ask the Lord's bless - ing;

3. James Sanderson (18th century), "Hail to the Chief" (before 1812)

F. The following melody is a dance tune that was always accompanied by a repeated drum-beat pattern. Sing the melody with scale step numbers, syllables, or the text while tapping the drum-beat pattern or playing it on a drum. The piece is a **pavan,** a popular Renaissance dance.

Thoinot Arbeau (ca. 1519–1595), *Orchesorgraphie,* "Pavan" (1588)

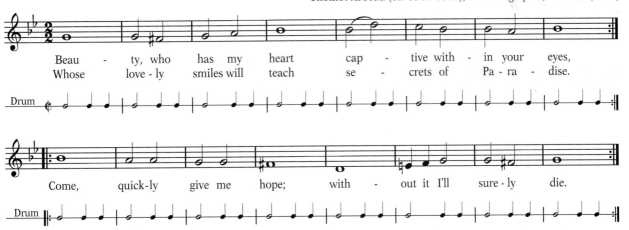

Beau - ty, who has my heart cap - tive with - in your eyes,
Whose love - ly smiles will teach se - crets of Pa - ra - dise.

Drum

Come, quick-ly give me hope; with - out it I'll sure - ly die.

Drum

Although this piece is in g minor, it is not natural minor. What makes it different? You will learn more about this in a later chapter!

$\mathcal{W}$RITTEN ASSIGNMENT

Placing Minor Scales in Position on the Keyboard. Place the following natural minor scales on the keyboard by writing the letter names of the notes on the proper keys. Then place the proper key signature on the staff at right. Then indicate the relative major key in the space provided. The example is worked correctly for you. After writing out the scale and giving the name of the relative major, write the name and signature for the parallel major.

1. EXAMPLE: Scale of E natural minor

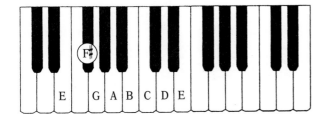

Key signature

Relative major

G

What is the *parallel* major scale and signature?

E major

2. Scale of D natural minor

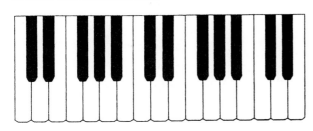

Key signature

Relative major

_____

Parallel major scale name and signature

_____

3. Scale of C♯ natural minor

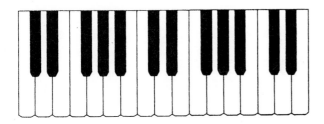

Key signature

Relative major

_____

Parallel major scale name and signature

_____

4. Scale of G natural minor

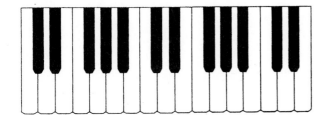

Key signature

_____

Relative major

_____

Parallel major scale name and signature

_____

5. Scale of B natural minor

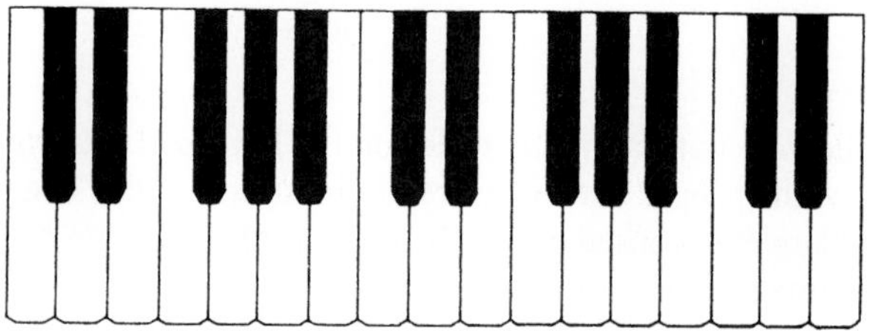

Key signature

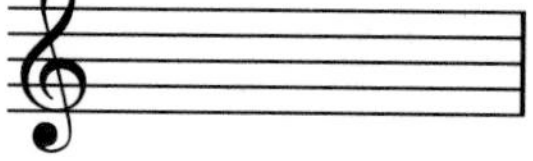

Relative major

_____

Parallel major scale name and signature

_____

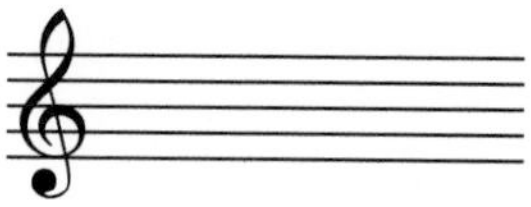

6. Scale of F♯ natural minor

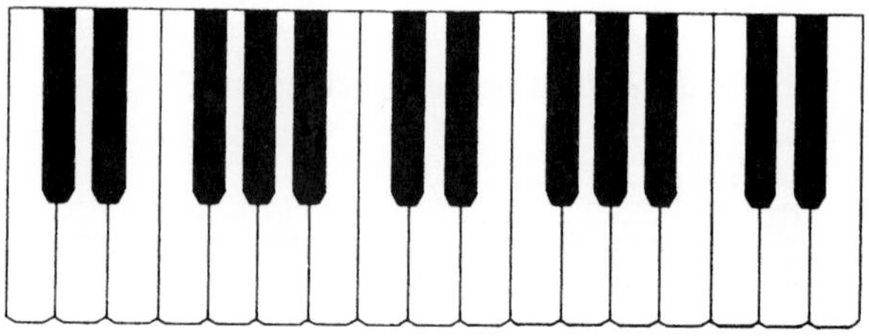

Key signature

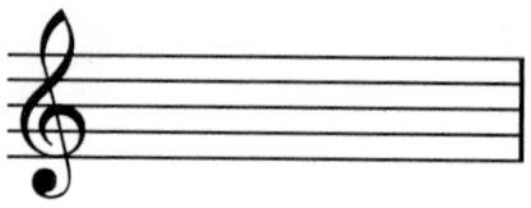

Relative major

_____

Parallel major scale name and signature

_____

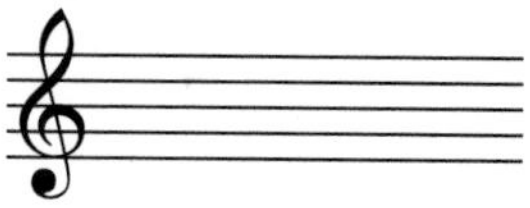

7. Scale of G♯ natural minor

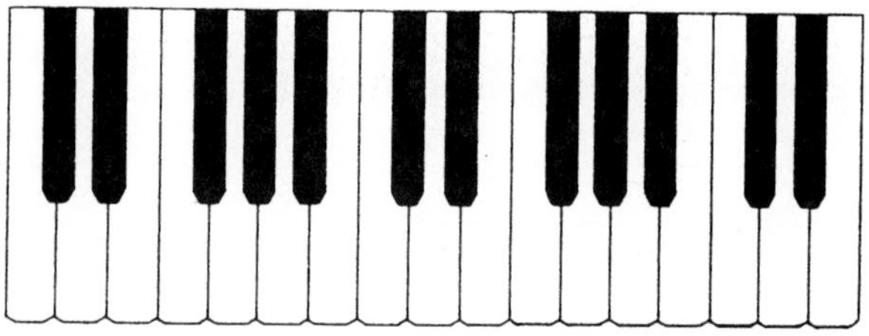

Key signature

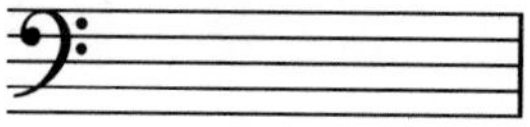

Relative major

_____

Parallel major scale name and signature

_____

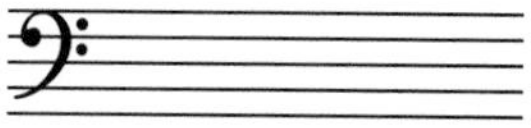

8. Scale of C natural minor

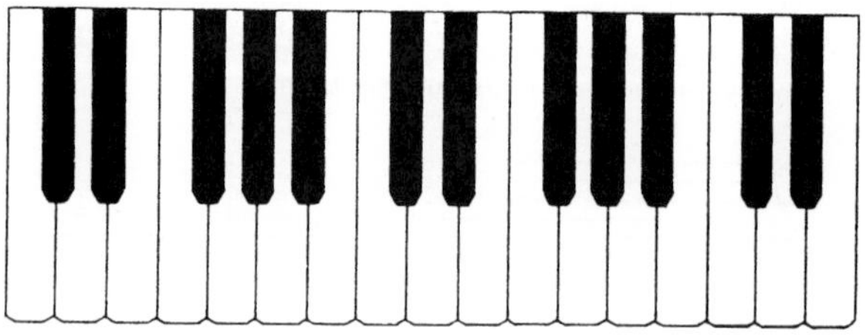

Key signature

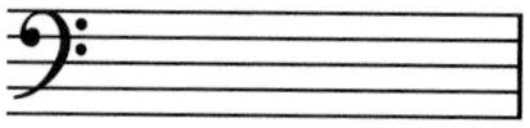

Relative major

_____

Parallel major scale name and signature

_____

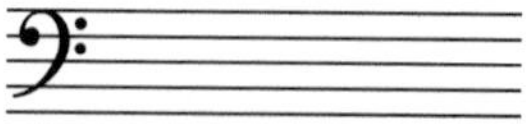

Play all the scales you have written on the piano and/or any other instrument.

$\mathcal{E}$AR TRAINING ASSIGNMENT

A. *Melodies Using the Minor Scale.* In each of the following exercises you will hear six notes of a melody in the minor mode. The first three notes of the melody are written on the staff for you. Write the other notes of the melody on the staff in whole notes. Each melody will be played twice. See the example.

1. EXAMPLE:

B. *Hearing Major and Minor Modes in Musical Examples.* You will hear six phrases of music. Some will be in major, and some will be in minor mode. Underline the correct mode for each example.

1. Major   Minor

2. Major   Minor

3. Major   Minor

4. Major   Minor

5. Major   Minor

6. Major   Minor

C. *Recognition of Major and Minor Thirds, Major and Minor Seconds, and Perfect Fifths.* In each of the following exercises you will hear four notes of a melody. The intervals used in the melodies will be major and minor thirds, major and minor seconds, and perfect fifths. In each exercise you will be told whether the intervals will include thirds, seconds, or fifths. You are to determine how many of each are used and whether the thirds and seconds are major or minor. Label each interval in the space provided, using M3 for major thirds, m3 for minor thirds, M2 for major seconds, m2 for minor seconds, and P5 for perfect fifths. The example is worked correctly for you. Each exercise will be played twice.

EXAMPLE: Teacher plays:

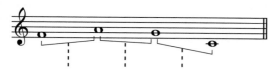

Answer:
1. 1 _M3_   2 _M2_   3 _P5_ 4   second, third, fifth

2. 1 ____   2 ____   3 ____ 4   second, third, third

3. 1 ____   2 ____   3 ____ 4   second, third, fifth

4. 1 ____   2 ____   3 ____ 4   second, third, fifth

5. 1 ____   2 ____   3 ____ 4   second, second, fifth

6. 1 ____   2 ____   3 ____ 4   second, third, fifth

7. 1 ____   2 ____   3 ____ 4   second, second, fifth

8. 1 ____   2 ____   3 ____ 4   second, third, fifth

D. *More Drill on Major Triad Patterns in a Melodic Context.* A group of three triad patterns will be played as broken chords. One triad pattern will be a major triad. Circle the letter that indicates the major triad. The example is worked correctly for you. Each exercise will be played twice.

EXAMPLE: Teacher plays:

Answer:
1. (a.)   b.   c.

2. a.   b.   c.

3. a.   b.   c.

4. a.   b.   c.

5. a.   b.   c.

6. a.   b.   c.

7. a.   b.   c.

8. a.   b.   c.

Chapter 12 • Intervals: Fourths, Fifths, and the Tritone

The Perfect Fourth

The perfect intervals studied so far include the perfect unison (no half steps), the perfect octave (twelve half steps), and the perfect fifth (seven half steps). There is one other perfect interval, the *perfect fourth*, which has five half steps. Following is a perfect fourth on the keyboard. The strings on the guitar are tuned in perfect fourths (except for the major third), as you see on the tablature.

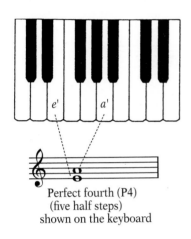

Perfect fourth (P4)
(five half steps)
shown on the keyboard

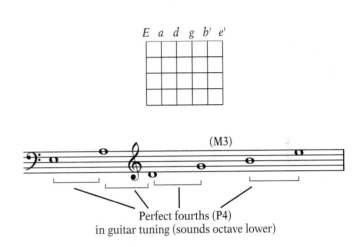

Perfect fourths (P4)
in guitar tuning (sounds octave lower)

The Fourths in Major

When all the fourths of the major scale are arranged in order, all but one are perfect fourths.

C major								
Scale degree	1	2	3	4	5	6	7	8
Number of half steps	5	5	5	6	5	5	5	5
Size of interval	P4	P4	P4		P4	P4	P4	P4

The Augmented Fourth (the Tritone)

Because the fourth built on the fourth degree of the major scale is one half step larger than a perfect fourth, it is called an **augmented fourth.** Because the six half steps equal *three whole steps,* it is also called the **tritone** (meaning "three tones"). In the medieval era, when harmonies were all based on perfect fourths or perfect fifths, the tritone was a forbidden interval. The old name for it was *diabolus in musica*—"the devil in music"—because it had such a restless sound.

The augmented fourth between F and B is the only augmented fourth played only on white keys. All other fourths on the white keys are perfect fourths. If one note of any fourth (other than that between F and B) is sharped or flatted, the other note must have the same accidental to be a perfect fourth.

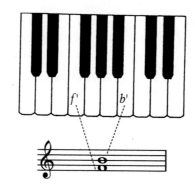

Augmented fourth (A4)
tritone
(six half steps or
three whole steps)

F-B, the only augmented fourth
using only white keys

To make the augmented fourth F to B a perfect fourth, either sharp the F or flat the B. Play the intervals below on a keyboard instrument and/or any other instruments played by members of the class.

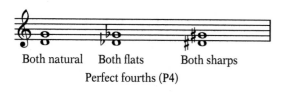

Both natural Both flats Both sharps

Perfect fourths (P4)

Perfect fourths (P4)

𝒯he Diminished Fifth (Also a Tritone!)

The interval of the augmented fourth contains the same number of half steps as the **diminished fifth.** On the piano, they have an identical sound and are distinguished by the context in which they are used. Unlike the perfect fourth and perfect fifth, the augmented fourth and diminished fifth have a restless, unstable quality of sound and are classed as **dissonant** intervals. A4 is the abbreviation for an augmented fourth; d5 is the symbol for a diminished fifth. Both are the tritone (three whole steps) sound.

Ways of writing the tritone sound

When you hear the interval *G to C♯ (D♭)* in isolation, you might hear it either as an augmented fourth (G to C♯) or as a diminished fifth (G to D♭). For this reason, both intervals are referred to as the *tritone* (that is, the interval with three whole tones) in the ear training drills.

𝒜ncient Harmony Using Fourths

In the ninth century harmony could be based on the interval of the fourth, so if you sing the following example in class, you will be hearing a use of the fourth that is eleven centuries old.

"Rex caeli" (King of Heaven), 9th century

King of Heav - en, Lord of O - cean's sound - ing waves __

Modern Music Using Fourths

At the beginning of the twentieth century, composers again became fascinated by the sound of melodies set with the perfect intervals—fourths, fifths, and octaves. Play the following passage on the piano and listen to the fourths with an occasional third!

Claude Debussy (1862–1918), *Préludes pour Piano,* Book I, "La fille aux cheveux de lin" (The Girl with the Flaxen Hair) (1910)

Twentieth-century composers have also been interested in the way fourths can be used to build melodies. This example is from the opening of Bartók's *Concerto for Orchestra* and is played by the low strings of the orchestra—violas, cellos, and string basses.

Béla Bartók (1881–1945), *Concerto for Orchestra,* Introduzione (1944)

Compare the sound of this melody built of *melodic fourths* with Beethoven's similarly shaped melody based on a *chord built of thirds (triad)* and written a century and a half ago.

Ludwig van Beethoven (1770–1827), *Symphony No. 5 in C Minor,* Third Movement (1807–08)

Sight singing assignment

A. By practicing the interval of the fourth you will learn to hear it better and to use it in singing melodies. Play the whole note and sing the black notes.

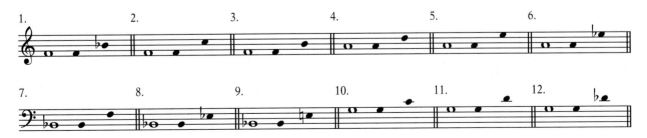

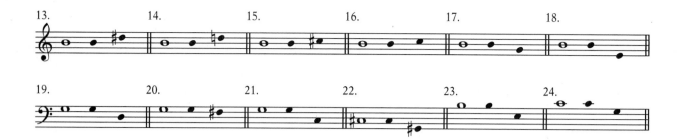

B. "Here Comes the Bride" (Bridal Chorus from *Lohengrin* by Wagner) begins with a *perfect fourth* up. Can you think of some more tunes you know that begin with a perfect fourth up or down? Collect a list of the tunes your class knows that could help you remember the sound of the perfect fourth.

C. Close your book for this exercise, which uses many intervals you have learned.
   1. The teacher plays the exercise on the piano, as shown in whole notes.
   2. Then sing the exercise back to the teacher using the scale numbers. This is shown by the black notes.
   3. The teacher gives the first note of a new key (the whole note shown), and the student sings the same exercise using the same scale numbers.

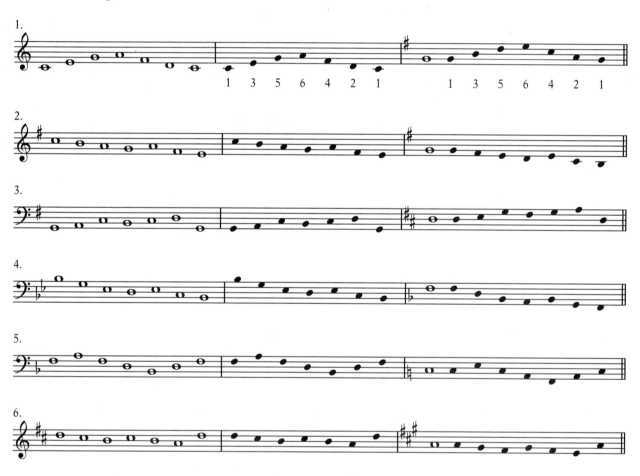

D. *Melodies That Use Fourths.* These melodies can be sung with words, syllables, or scale step numbers.

Engelbert Humperdinck (1854–1921), *Hansel and Gretel,* "Children's Prayer"
(1893) (the *original* musician by this name!)

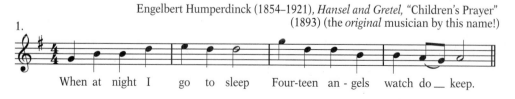

When at night I go to sleep   Four-teen an-gels watch do __ keep.

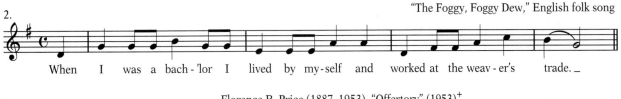

2.

"The Foggy, Foggy Dew," English folk song

When   I   was a bach-'lor I   lived by my-self and   worked at the weav-er's   trade. _

3.

Florence B. Price (1887–1953), "Offertory" (1953)[+]

From *The Organ Portfolio*, vol. 17/130, © Copyright 1953. Used by permission of Lorenz Publishing Co., Dayton, OH.

E. *Review of the Circle of Fifths.* Of all the pedagogical tools for learning music, the circle of fifths is one of the most important to learn well. The circle of fifths contains information that virtually every musician must be able to use instinctively. Therefore, it is important to commit to memory all the information contained in the circle of fifths. Use this page to practice the circle of fifths until it is committed to memory. Duplicate this page (making several copies) and practice filling in the circle.* Outside the circle, place the key signature. Practice this with both bass and treble clefs, placing the sharps or flats correctly for the clef used. Inside the circle, place the name of each key as indicated (M = major, m = minor). Time yourself and practice until you can do the exercise very quickly.

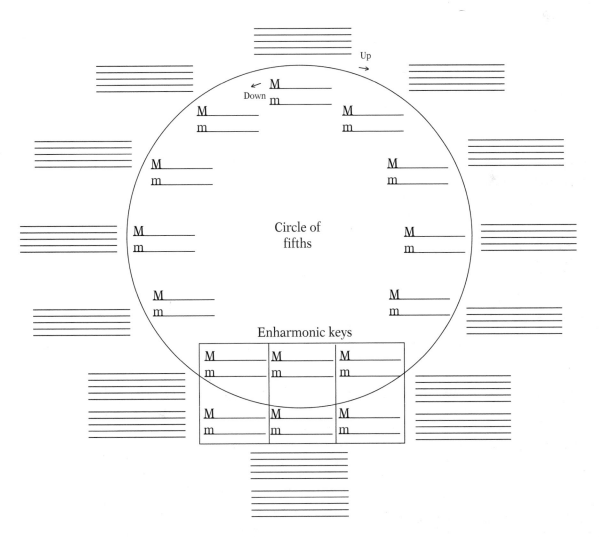

*This page may be duplicated.

WRITTEN AND KEYBOARD ASSIGNMENT

Play all the examples on the keyboard after writing them.

A. *Recognition of the P4, P5, A4, and d5.* Each exercise contains four intervals, one each of the following:

Interval	Abbreviation Symbol	Half Steps	Whole Steps
Perfect fourth	P4	5	2½
Perfect fifth	P5	7	3½
Augmented fourth	A4	6	3
Diminished fifth	d5	6	3

Name the intervals in each exercise and place the answers in the blanks beneath the staff. The example has been worked correctly for you. Remember, each exercise will contain one each of the four intervals listed above. Keep in mind that accidentals occurring in a measure retain the alteration until the bar line unless altered again. Be able to play these intervals.

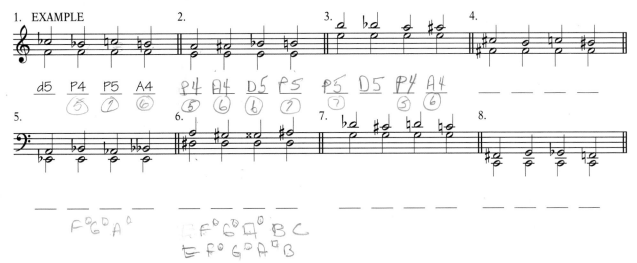

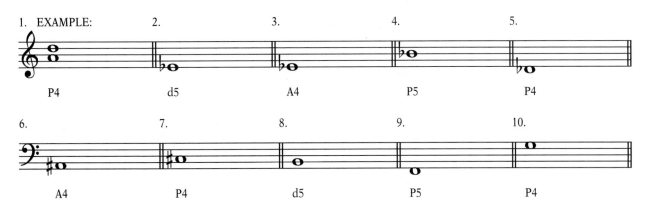

B. *Placement of Intervals on the Music Staff.* In each exercise place the interval on the staff above the given note as directed and then play it. See the example.

1. EXAMPLE: 2.   3.   4.   5.

    P4   d5   A4   P5   P4

6.   7.   8.   9.   10.

    A4   P4   d5   P5   P4

C. *Recognition of Melodic Intervals.* Each exercise consists of a short melody. Name the intervals between the successive notes of the melody and write them in the blanks provided. The example is begun for you. Use these abbreviations:

Perfect octave	P8	Major third	M3		
Perfect unison	P1	Minor third	m3	Augmented fourth	A4
Major second	M2	Perfect fourth	P4	Diminished fifth	d5
Minor second	m2	Perfect fifth	P5		

EXAMPLE:

1.
John Philip Sousa (1854–1932), "Semper Fidelis March" (1888)[+]

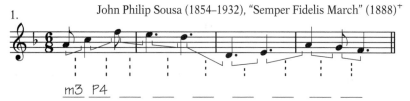

2.
Wolfgang Amadeus Mozart (1756–1791), *Symphony No. 39 in E-flat Major,* K. 543, First Movement (1788)[*]

X : Half step, but *not* a minor second.

3.
Modest Musorgsky (1839–1881), *Pictures at an Exhibition,*
"Promenade Theme" (1874)

4.
Felix Mendelssohn (1809–1847), *Symphony No. 4 in A Major* (Italian), Op. 90, Second Movement (1833) (Note that not all movements of the symphony may be in the main key of the work. This part is in d minor!)

5.
Johann Sebastian Bach (1685–1750), *Sonata for Violin and Continuo,*
BWV 1021, Third Movement (about 1720)[**]

Play all the examples and listen carefully to the sounds of the intervals you have named.

[*] Not all composers marked their works with *opus numbers.* Mozart's works were put in chronological order after his death by a man named Köchel, so we refer to Mozart's compositions by *K. numbers,* thus showing the order in which it is thought they were composed. The symphony quoted here was his 543rd work, *K. 543,* written late in his life—just three years before his death.

[**] The numbering system used for Bach's works is indicated by the abbreviation BWV, for *Bach Werke-Verzeichnis,* the German words for *Bach's Works Index.*

$\mathcal{E}$AR TRAINING ASSIGNMENT

A. *Recognition of P5 and Tritone in Melodic Intervals.* In each example you will hear three melodic intervals. One interval will be a perfect fifth, and one will be a tritone. The other interval will be something else. Place an X in the space for the melodic perfect fifth and a ✓ in the space for the melodic tritone. Leave the space for the other interval blank. You will hear each exercise only once.

EXAMPLE: You hear:

P5   Tritone

Answer: 1. _____   X   ✓

2. _____ _____ _____

3. _____ _____ _____

4. _____ _____ _____

5. _____ _____ _____

6. _____ _____ _____

7. _____ _____ _____

B. *Recognition of Tritone, P4, P5, P8, M3, and M2.* In each exercise you will hear three harmonic intervals played. The *order of playing* of these intervals will be different from the order that you see. Rearrange the order (as given) so that the intervals are in the order played. The example is illustrated and is worked correctly for you. Each exercise will be played twice.

Intervals used
(not in proper order):

Proper order of intervals:

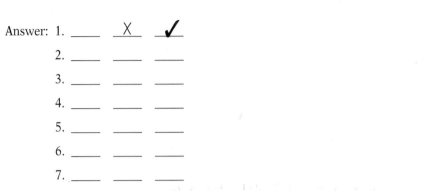

		Intervals used					
EXAMPLE:	1.	M3	P4	P5	P4	P5	M3
	2.	P8	P5	P4	___	___	___
	3.	P8	Tritone	P5	___	___	___
	4.	P5	P4	P8	___	___	___
	5.	P5	M3	P4	___	___	___
	6.	M3	P8	P4	___	___	___
	7.	P4	P5	Tritone	___	___	___
	8.	P8	Tritone	P5	___	___	___
	9.	P4	Tritone	M3	___	___	___
	10.	M3	P4	M2	___	___	___

C. *Recognition of the Tritone in a Melody.* In each exercise a six-note melody will be played. Some of the melodies include a tritone; others do not. Underline the proper answer. The example is illustrated and worked correctly for you. Each melody will be played twice.

EXAMPLE:

Answer:

1. a. <u>Includes tritone</u>   b. No tritone

2. a. Includes tritone   b. No tritone

3. a. Includes tritone   b. No tritone

4. a. Includes tritone   b. No tritone

5. a. Includes tritone   b. No tritone

6. a. Includes tritone   b. No tritone

Chapter 13 ▪ The Minor Triad

Introduction to the Minor Triad

The triad with a perfect fifth between the root and fifth and a minor third between the root and third is called a **minor triad.** In the minor triad, the interval between the third and fifth is a major third.

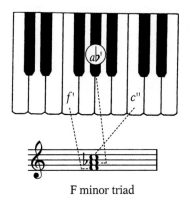

F minor triad

Minor Triads in the Major Scale

There are three minor triads in the major scale.

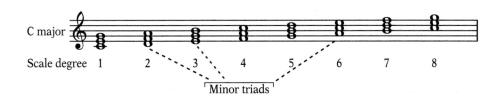

Minor Triads in the Minor Scale

In the natural minor scale, there are minor triads on the first, fourth, and fifth degrees. Because these are the most important chords in the key, the predominance of minor triads imparts a characteristic color to harmonies in a minor key.

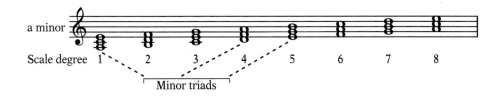

The Minor Triads on the White Keys

There are only three minor triads that are played entirely on white keys. These three triads are the *a minor* triad, the *d minor* triad, and the *e minor* triad. Find these three triads on the piano and play them, listening carefully to the sound.

To construct all other minor triads, use sharps or flats to make a minor third and a perfect fifth above the root of the triad.

Guitar Chords

Common fingerings for playing many of the minor triads on the guitar are given in Appendix 3. Those with guitars can find these fingerings and play the minor triads given there. Listen carefully to all the sounds you play. The common **chord symbol** for a minor triad is the name of the root (capitalized) followed by the letters *m* or *mi*. Thus, *Cmi* or *Cm* means a *c minor* triad on the guitar. In this book, *m* is used for minor triads on the guitar.

SIGHT SINGING ASSIGNMENT

A. *Minor Triad Drill.* Sing the black notes after hearing the whole note. You may give yourself the first note or it may be played for you by your teacher.

B. *Minor Triad Drill.* You will hear the whole note played, then sing the broken chords from the fifth or the third.

C. *Drill on Major and Minor Triads.* A good exercise to improve triad singing is to sing major and minor triads in succession, going up diatonically.

KEYBOARD ASSIGNMENT

A. Following are all the minor triads in simple position. First the position on the keyboard is shown and then the proper notation on the music staff. Learn to find these minor triads on *all* octaves of the keyboard. Play all examples using the right hand for treble clef and left hand for bass clef.

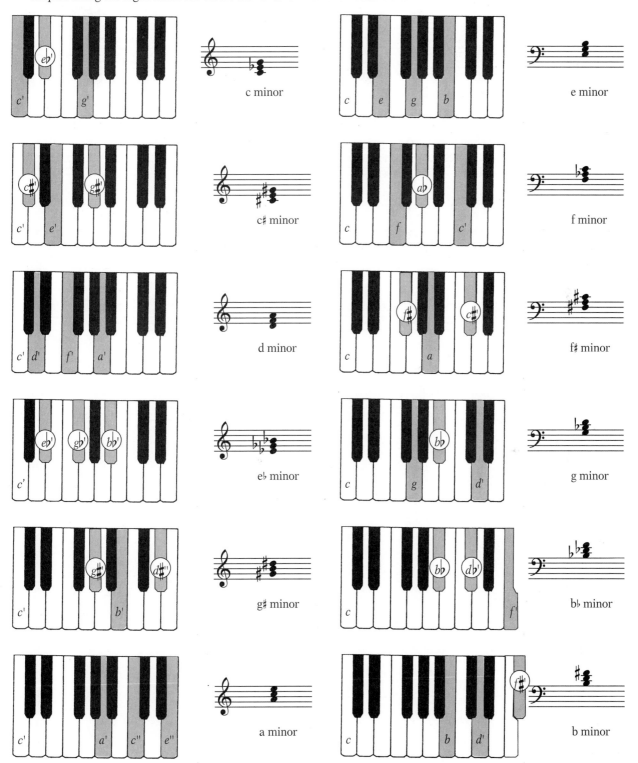

B. *Keyboard and Written Assignment for Triads.* In the following eleven examples triads are present in close position (examples 1–5) and open position (examples 6–11). First identify the chord quality of each (major or minor), then write the chord of the opposite chord quality. That is, if the chord is minor, write it in the same voicing in major. If you want to put the open position chords into close position, you may do so in the space provided. Play each example you have written on a keyboard.

$\mathcal{E}$AR TRAINING ASSIGNMENT

A. *Recognition of the Major and Minor Triads.* In each exercise you will hear four chords. Of the four, one will be a minor triad, and one will be a *major triad.* The other two will be chord formations not yet studied. Mark the *major triad* with an "M," the *minor triad* with an "m," and leave the other chords blank. See the example. Each exercise will be played twice.

EXAMPLE: You will hear:

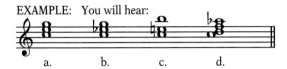

a.   b.   c.   d.

Answer: 1.   __M__   __m__   _____   _____

2.   _____   _____   _____   _____

3.   _____   _____   _____   _____

4.   _____   _____   _____   _____

5.   _____   _____   _____   _____

6.   _____   _____   _____   _____

B. *Recognition of Minor Triads in a Phrase of Music.* A chord progression will be played in each exercise; it will include one or more minor triads. Place an X in the blank for each minor triad. Leave the other spaces blank. See the example. Each exercise will be played twice.

EXAMPLE: You will hear:

Answer: 1. _X_   _X_   ___   ___   _X_   ___   _X_

2. ___   ___   ___   ___   ___   ___   ___

3. ___   ___   ___   ___   ___   ___   ___

4. ___   ___   ___   ___   ___   ___   ___

5. ___   ___   ___   ___   ___   ___   ___

6. ___   ___   ___   ___   ___   ___   ___

Chapter 14 ▪ More Intervals: Major and Minor Sixths and Sevenths, More Augmented and Diminished Intervals

Sixths and Sevenths

Sixths and **sevenths** come in two normal sizes. Sixths contain either eight or nine half steps. A sixth with *nine* half steps (4½ whole steps) is a *major sixth* (M6); with *eight* half steps (4 whole steps), a *minor sixth* (m6).

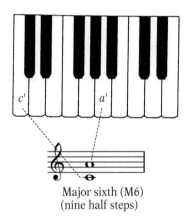

Major sixth (M6)
(nine half steps)

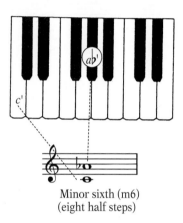

Minor sixth (m6)
(eight half steps)

Major sevenths have eleven half steps (5½ whole steps), just one half step less than an octave. The symbol for this interval is M7. *Minor sevenths* (m7) have ten half steps (5 whole steps), one whole step less than an octave.

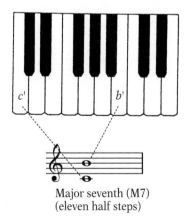

Major seventh (M7)
(eleven half steps)

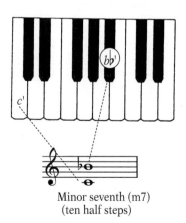

Minor seventh (m7)
(ten half steps)

The Sixths in a Major Key

There are four major sixths and three minor sixths in a major scale. Major and minor sixths have a bland, smooth quality, like thirds, and are *consonances*.

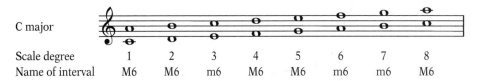

C major								
Scale degree	1	2	3	4	5	6	7	8
Name of interval	M6	M6	m6	M6	M6	m6	m6	M6

The Sevenths in a Major Key

There are two major sevenths and five minor sevenths in the major scale. Sevenths, like seconds, have a harsh, restless quality and are *dissonances*.

C major								
Scale degree	1	2	3	4	5	6	7	8
Name of interval	M7	m7	m7	M7	m7	m7	m7	M7

Melodies Set with Sixths and Sevenths

The Bartók movement that was used previously to find examples of melodies set with various different intervals also contains themes set in sixths and sevenths.

One sixth is not the same size as the rest. Which one is it, and what size is it? What size are the rest? Are all these sevenths the same size?

Now listen to a recording of the whole movement to see how these themes are used and in what order they appear. Listen carefully to the interval sounds in the pairs of instruments.

Parallel Sixths:

Béla Bartók (1881–1945), *Concerto for Orchestra*, "Giuoco delle Coppie,"
(Game of Pairs) (1944)

Parallel Sevenths:

Béla Bartók (1881–1945), *Concerto for Orchestra*, "Giuoco delle Coppie," (Game of Pairs) (1944)

The following table summarizes the intervals.

CONSONANT		CONSONANT		DISSONANT		DISSONANT	
Perfect Intervals	Half Steps	Major and Minor Intervals	Half Steps	Major and Minor Intervals	Half Steps	Augmented and Diminished Intervals	Half Steps
Unison	0	Major third	4	Major second	2		
Octave	12	Minor third	3	Minor second	1	Augmented fourth	6
Fourth	5	Major sixth	9	Major seventh	11		
Fifth	7	Minor sixth	8	Minor seventh	10	Diminished fifth	6

Other Augmented and Diminished Intervals

The chart above summarizes the *interval sounds* within the octave. There is also a group of intervals that are formed by different spellings of the sounds. Intervals are always named on the basis of the *written* appearance of the interval, which means that f' to a', f' to a♭', f' to a♯', and f' to a𝄪' are all thirds.

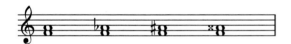

Obviously, some of these thirds are neither major nor minor thirds because all do not have the proper number of half steps. If a written third is one half step smaller than a minor third, it is called a *diminished third.* If it is a half step larger than a major third, it is an *augmented third.* In the unlikely event that it is a half step larger than an augmented third, it is called a *doubly augmented third,* and so forth. Doubly augmented and doubly diminished intervals are rarely used.

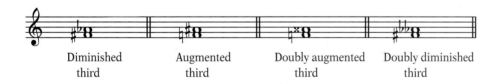

| Diminished third | Augmented third | Doubly augmented third | Doubly diminished third |

The same principle applies to all other intervals. A *written* sixth, seventh, second, or third that is a half step larger than the major interval is called an *augmented interval.* A *written* second, third, sixth, or seventh that is a half step smaller than a minor interval is called a *diminished interval.* Intervals a half step larger than perfect intervals are also augmented; those a half step smaller than perfect intervals are diminished.

The chart below summarizes the relationship of intervals of various qualities:

Diminished ◄──► Perfect ◄──► Augmented

Diminished ◄──► Minor ◄──► Major ◄──► Augmented

Made larger by one half step for each change in size ──►

Made smaller by one half step for each change in size ◄──

*S*IGHT SINGING ASSIGNMENT

A. *Major Sixth Interval Drill.* The teacher will play the whole note; after hearing it, sing the black notes. (You may play the first note yourself and then sing the black notes.)

1 2 3 4 5 6 1 6

B. *Major Sixth Identification Drill.* This simple pattern will help you to identify and sing the major sixth.

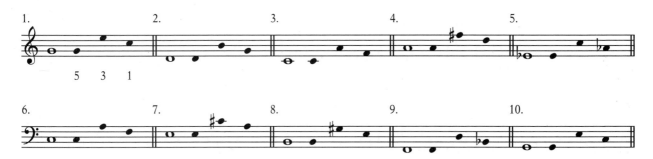

5 3 1

C. *Minor Sixth Interval Drill.* The whole note will be played; sing the black notes.

D. *Minor Sixth Identification Drill.* The first interval in this simple melody is a *minor sixth*. You can use this tune to help you identify and sing the minor sixth easily.

"Go Down, Moses," spiritual[+]

5   3 3 2 2 3 3 1   5 5 7 7   1

Major Sixth Identification Drill. The first interval in this well-known melody is a *major sixth*. Thus, it can also be used as a memory device to fix the sound of the major sixth in your mind easily.

Charles Pratt (pseudonym H.J. Fuller), "My Bonnie Lies over the Ocean" (1881)[+]

Perhaps you know some tunes that begin with other intervals. For example, "A Bicycle Built for Two" begins

Dai - sy

with a minor third down. "Swing Low, Sweet Chariot," on the other hand, begins with a major third down. Make a collection for yourself (and to share with the class) of tunes you know well that begin with different intervals and that you could use to help you remember the sound of the interval.

Other melodies containing sixths:

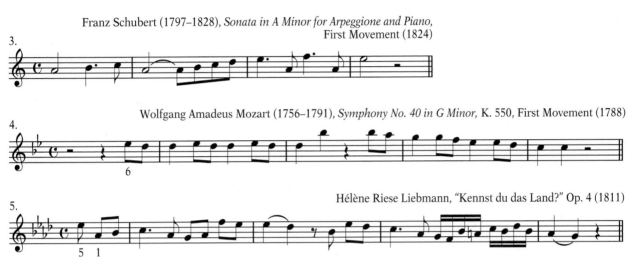

Franz Schubert (1797–1828), *Sonata in A Minor for Arpeggione and Piano,*
First Movement (1824)

3.

Wolfgang Amadeus Mozart (1756–1791), *Symphony No. 40 in G Minor,* K. 550, First Movement (1788)

4.

Hélène Riese Liebmann, "Kennst du das Land?" Op. 4 (1811)

5.

From *Lieder by Women Composers of the Classical Era,* vol. 1, © 1987. ClarNan Editions, Fayetteville, AR. Used by permission.

E. *Melody Using the Tritone.* Before singing the melody, sing the following pattern of whole steps that uses the scale on which the melody is based. This will help you to fix the sound of the tritone in your ear. Note that the melody is not major or minor but uses another, more exotic sounding scale called the Lydian mode.

Lydian scale

Béla Bartók (1881–1945), *Mikrokosmos,* Vol. VI, "Ostinato" (1940)

© Copyright 1940 by Hawkes & Son (London) Ltd.; Copyright Renewed.
Reprinted by permission of Boosey and Hawkes, Inc.

F. *Continued Practice of Intervals Already Studied.* By continuing to practice intervals you have already learned, your facility in singing all intervals will improve. When you hear the whole note played, sing back the black notes to review the intervals you studied in previous chapters.

Sing up: uses notes of C major

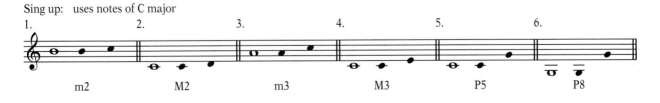

1.   2.   3.   4.   5.   6.

m2   M2   m3   M3   P5   P8

Sing up: uses notes of D major

7.
8.
9.
10.
11.
12.

m3   P5   M3   m2   P4   P8

Sing down: uses notes of A major

13.
14.
15.
16.
17.
18.

M3   P5   P8   m3   m2   M2

Sing up: uses notes of D major

19.
20.
21.
22.
23.
24.

M2   m2   P4   P5   P8   m3

WRITTEN AND KEYBOARD ASSIGNMENT

A. *Writing Sixths and Sevenths.* Below are several intervals of sixths or sevenths. Some are major and some are minor. Label each interval. Then, if it is major, write the minor form of the interval in the space provided. If the given interval is minor, write the major form of the interval in the space. Play all the intervals you have written.

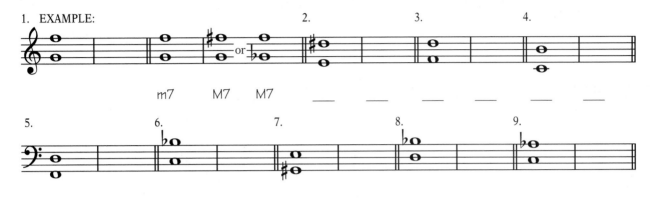

1. EXAMPLE: 2.   3.   4.

m7   M7   M7   ____   ____   ____

5.   6.   7.   8.   9.

____   ____   ____   ____   ____

B. *Placing the M6, m6, M7, and m7 on the Keyboard and Music Staff.* Using the letter names of the notes, write the intervals requested on the keyboard, then place the same interval on the staff at the right of the keyboard. Play all of the intervals on the piano (or on any other instrument you play).

1. m7 up from F

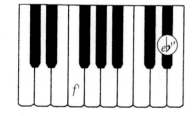

4. M6 up from C

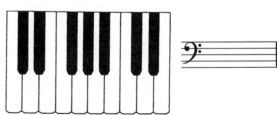

2. m6 up from D

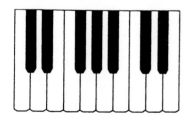

5. m6 up from C♯

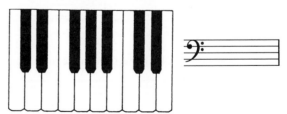

3. m7 up from E♭

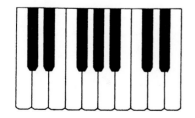

6. m7 up from F♯

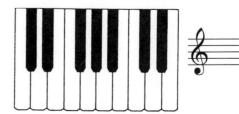

C. *Changing Perfect Intervals to Diminished and Augmented Intervals.* In each of the following eight exercises you are to change the perfect interval by altering the upper note so that (1) the interval is augmented and (2) the interval is diminished. The example is worked correctly for you.

EXAMPLE:

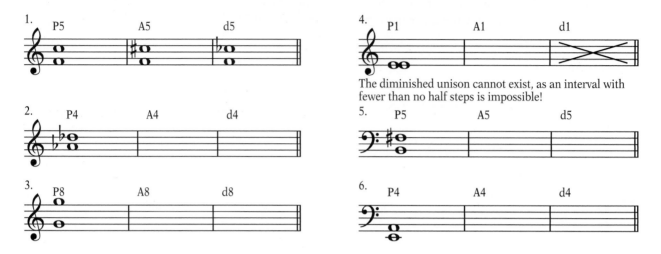

The diminished unison cannot exist, as an interval with fewer than no half steps is impossible!

D. *Drill in Enharmonic Spelling.* Following are two very familiar tunes. They are difficult to read and sing because of the way the notes are spelled. Beneath each melody rewrite the tune and spell the notes so they can be read easily in the key suggested. *Remember that the sound of the melody will not be changed—only the spelling of the notes.*

1. Melody with notes spelled enharmonically:

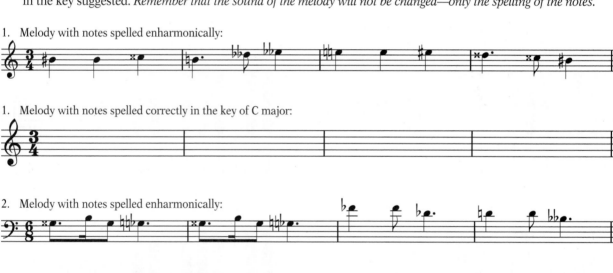

1. Melody with notes spelled correctly in the key of C major:

2. Melody with notes spelled enharmonically:

2. Melody with notes spelled correctly in the key of D major:

What are the names of the tunes?

ℰAR TRAINING ASSIGNMENT

A. *Recognition of All Intervals.* In each exercise you will hear a melody of four notes. The intervals used between the notes of the melody are listed in incorrect order in a column at the left. After listening to the melody, re-arrange the intervals in the order in which they are heard in the melody. The example is illustrated and is worked correctly for you. Each melody will be played twice.

Proper order of intervals:

1. Teacher plays:

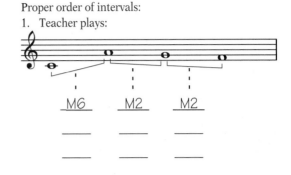

Intervals used
(not in proper order):

EXAMPLE:	1.	M2	M6	M2	M6	M2	M2
	2.	m3	M2	P4	___	___	___
	3.	M3	P5	M2	___	___	___
	4.	m7	m2	Tritone	___	___	___

Now a similar melody of four notes will be played. See if you can identify the intervals you hear and place the interval name in the space provided. Each melody will be played twice.

5. ____   ____   ____

6. ____   ____   ____

7. ____   ____   ____

8. ____   ____   ____

9. ____   ____   ____

10. ____   ____   ____

B. *Recognition of Errors in Simple Melodies.* In each of the following exercises you will hear and see a melody of four notes. The first written note is correct. Three of the written notes are correct as played, but *one* is incorrect in each exercise. Circle the note that is written incorrectly. The example is worked correctly for you. Each melody will be played twice.

1. EXAMPLE:

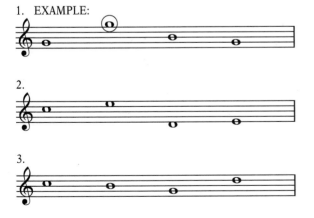

4.

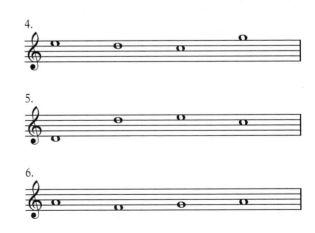

C. *Recognition of All Intervals.* In each exercise you will hear three harmonic intervals. In the column at the left are listed the intervals played in each exercise, but they are not arranged in proper order. Rearrange the order of the intervals to conform to the order you hear and write your answers in the right column. The example is illustrated and is worked correctly for you. Each exercise will be played twice.

Teacher plays:

EXAMPLE:	1.	M3	m7	P5	P5	m7	M3
	2.	P4	M6	M2	___	___	___
	3.	M6	m7	P8	___	___	___
	4.	P4	A4	M3	___	___	___

In the following exercises you will again hear three intervals in each exercise, but the names of the intervals played will not be given to you. See if you can identify the intervals you hear and place the interval name in the space provided. Each exercise will be played twice. The first time each interval will be played as a harmonic interval, the second time as a melodic interval.

5. ___ ___ ___

6. ___ ___ ___

7. ___ ___ ___

8. ___ ___ ___

9. ___ ___ ___

10. ___ ___ ___

11. ___ ___ ___

12. ___ ___ ___

Chapter 15 ▪ Harmonic and Melodic Minor Scales

In addition to *natural minor,* two other forms of the minor scale are in common use. These scales use sharps, flats, and naturals that are not part of the key signature (*accidentals*) to change the interval structure of the scale.

The Harmonic Minor Scale

The **harmonic minor scale** contains one accidental, the raised seventh degree. This makes a half step between the seventh note (called the **leading tone**) and the **tonic.** This half step increases the tendency of the seventh note of the scale to move toward the tonic, thereby strengthening the feeling of the tonal center.

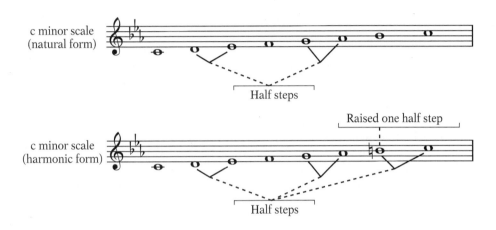

This accidental not only changes the interval between the seventh and eighth degrees of the scale but also creates a new interval between the sixth and seventh degrees. This interval, which had been a major second, is now one and one-half steps. Thus, it has become an *augmented second.* The harmonic minor scale has *three half steps* between the second and third, fifth and sixth, and seventh and eighth degrees of the scale; *one augmented second* between the sixth and seventh degrees of the scale; and *three whole steps* between the first and second, third and fourth, and fourth and fifth degrees of the scale.

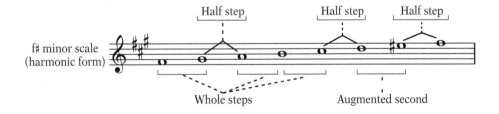

The Melodic Minor Scale

The **melodic minor scale** uses one more accidental to smooth out the "awkward" interval of the augmented second and *raises both the sixth and seventh degrees one half step.* Harmonic minor scales are the same both ascending and descending. In melodic minor, however, the alterations are used in the *ascending scale only,* and the *descending scale is like natural minor.*

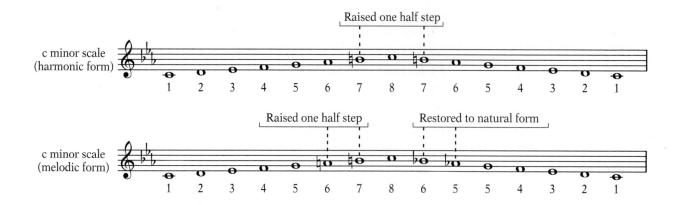

Because the ascending and descending forms of melodic minor are *not* the same, written examples of that scale must always include both.

The Minor Key

These scales are actually summaries of the tones normally used in compositions in a *minor key*. A piece in a minor key could use only the notes of one form of the minor scale, but composers commonly use notes from all forms of the minor scale in extended works, so we speak of Beethoven's *Symphony No. 5 in C Minor*, designating that it is in the *minor key*. In passages within the symphony, however, Beethoven might use patterns drawn from *any* of the normal minor scales. Thus, we never speak of a piece of music as being in a melodic minor key or a harmonic minor key, although we might find particular passages that use melodic or harmonic minor scale materials. In an earlier chapter, you sang Thoinot Arbeau's "Pavan," which used alterations in a minor key. Turn back to page 99 and sing it again.

Musicians practice scales in all these forms to develop facility on their instruments and to train their ears to hear and play these patterns accurately. Learn to play all the scales that you have learned both on your own instrument and on the keyboard.

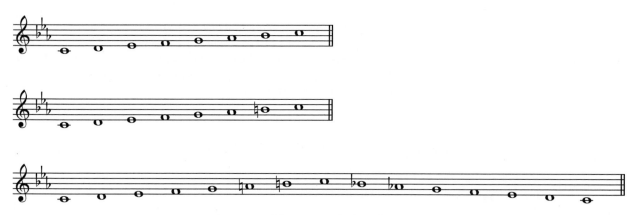

Summary of the notes in the key of c minor

SIGHT SINGING ASSIGNMENT

A. *Harmonic and Melodic Minor Drill.* When you hear the white note, respond with the black notes.

B. *Compositions Using the Notes of the Minor Scales.*

Johann Sebastian Bach (1685–1750), "Schwing' dich zu deinen Gott" (Soar Upwards to Thy God) (1713)

"Hatikvah," traditional melody, arr. Sam Cohen (1888)

Edward Grieg (1843–1907), *Peer Gynt* (1876)

Fanny Mendelssohn Hensel (1805–1847), *Trio in D Minor,* Op. 11, Finale (1847)

Felix Mendelssohn (1809–1847), *Concerto in E Minor for Violin and Orchestra,* Op. 64, Third Movement (1844)

6.

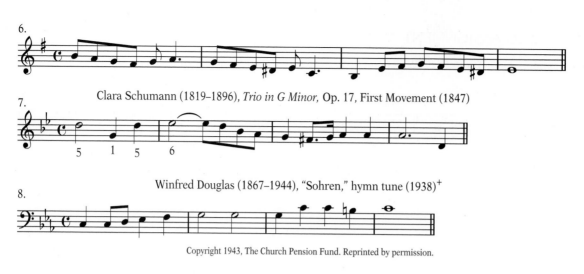

Clara Schumann (1819–1896), *Trio in G Minor,* Op. 17, First Movement (1847)

7.

8.

Winfred Douglas (1867–1944), "Sohren," hymn tune (1938)[+]

9.

Wolfgang Amadeus Mozart (1756–1791), *Symphony No. 40 in G Minor,* K. 550, Third Movement (1788)

10.

Adapted from George Frideric Handel (1685–1759), "Capriccio"

11.

Adapted from William Byrd (1543–1623), "Hugh Ashton's Ground"

12.

"Greensleeves," English folk song

*W*RITTEN ASSIGNMENT

A. *Writing Harmonic, Melodic, and Natural Minor Scales.* Write the scale called for in each exercise. Use the proper key signature for each scale. Play all the scales you have written both from your book and from memory.

1. D melodic minor

2. E harmonic minor

3. F♯ harmonic minor

4. G melodic minor

5. C♯ harmonic minor

6. F harmonic minor

7. B melodic minor

8. A harmonic minor

9. C melodic minor

10. G♯ harmonic minor

11. A♭ melodic minor

12. B♭ harmonic minor

13. C natural minor

14. D natural minor

15. F♯ natural minor

16. D harmonic minor

17. E natural minor

18. G natural minor

B. On a separate piece of paper write the relative and parallel major scales of each of the minor scales just shown. Play all the scales you have written.

ℰAR TRAINING ASSIGNMENT

A. *Recognition of the Major, Natural Minor, Harmonic Minor, and Melodic Minor Scales.* In each exercise you will hear three scales (*ascending only*). The scales used are listed in the left column but are not in the proper order. Rearrange the names of the scales into the order in which they are played. The example is illustrated and is worked correctly for you. Each exercise will be played twice.

Teacher plays:

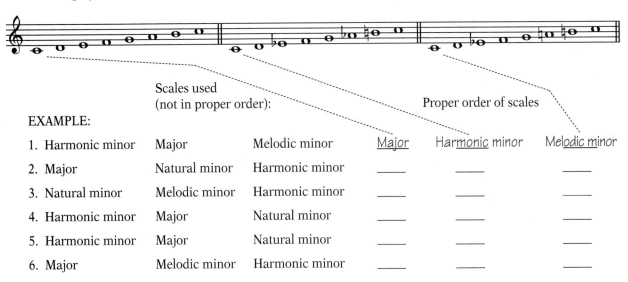

	Scales used (not in proper order):		Proper order of scales		
EXAMPLE:					
1. Harmonic minor	Major	Melodic minor	<u>Major</u>	Har<u>monic</u> minor	Mel<u>odic minor</u>
2. Major	Natural minor	Harmonic minor	_____	_____	_____
3. Natural minor	Melodic minor	Harmonic minor	_____	_____	_____
4. Harmonic minor	Major	Natural minor	_____	_____	_____
5. Harmonic minor	Major	Natural minor	_____	_____	_____
6. Major	Melodic minor	Harmonic minor	_____	_____	_____

Chapter 16 ▪ Augmented and Diminished Triads, The Whole-Tone Scale

Review of Major and Minor Triads

Both major and minor triads contain the interval of a perfect fifth and differ from each other only in the arrangement of their major and minor thirds.

Perfect fifth

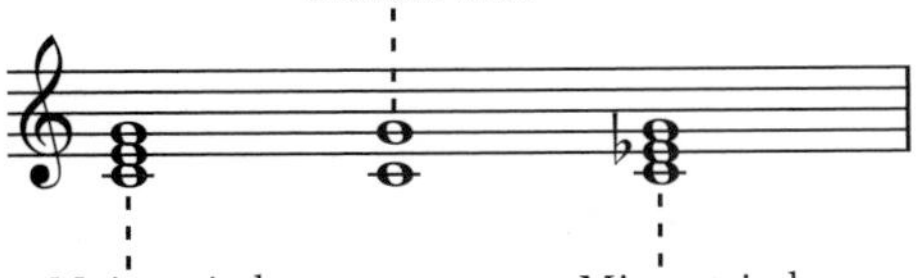

Major triad   Minor triad

Diminished and Augmented Triads

There are two triads that do not contain the interval of the perfect fifth: the diminished triad, which contains a diminished fifth, and the augmented triad, which contains an augmented fifth.

Diminished fifth   Augmented fifth

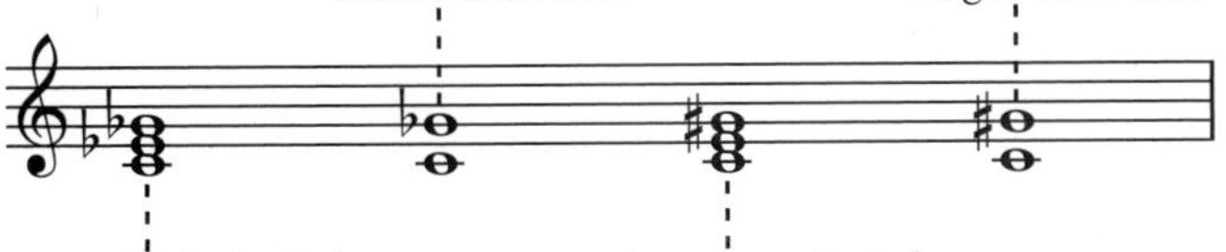

Diminished triad   Augmented triad

In the diminished triad both the thirds are minor thirds.

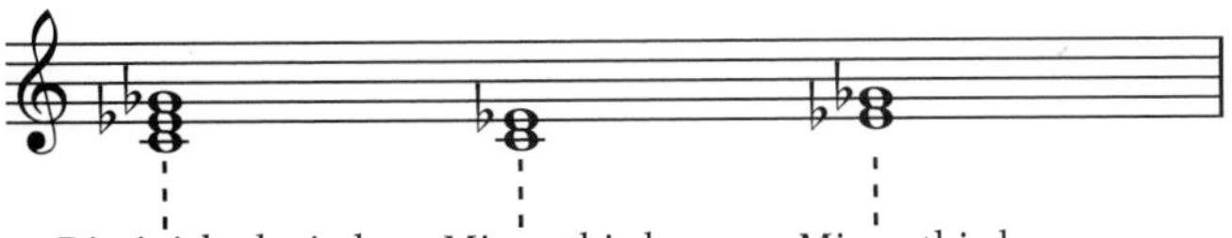

Diminished triad   Minor third   Minor third

In the augmented triad both thirds are major thirds.

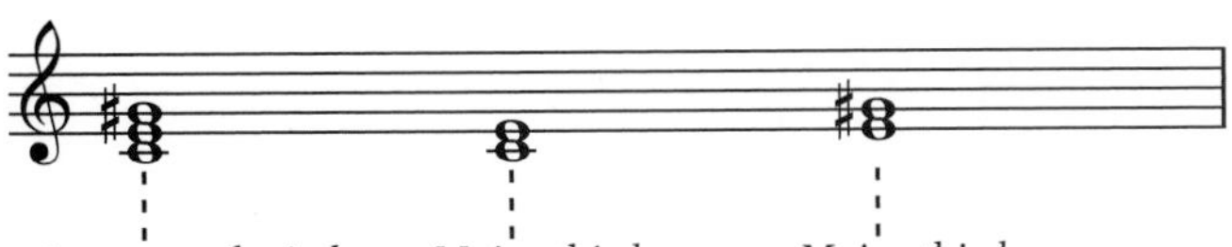

Augmented triad   Major third   Major third

M 3 - 4

C D E F G G#

Aug triad
2 Major 3rd

There is only one diminished triad using only white keys on the piano because there is only one diminished fifth on the white keys.

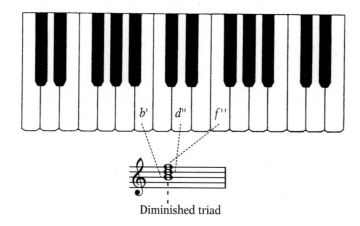

Diminished triad

The Diminished Triad in a Major Key

The triad on the seventh degree of the major scale is the only diminished triad in major.

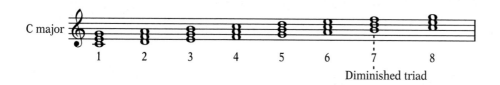

C major
1 2 3 4 5 6 7 8
Diminished triad

The Diminished Triad in the Minor Scales

In natural minor there is a diminished triad on the second degree of the scale.

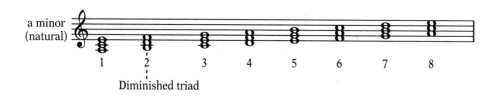

a minor
(natural)
1 2 3 4 5 6 7 8
Diminished triad

In harmonic minor, there are diminished triads on the second and seventh degrees.

a minor
(harmonic)
1 2 3 4 5 6 7 8
Diminished triad   Diminished triad

In the ascending form of the melodic minor scale there are two diminished triads on the sixth and seventh degrees of the scale.

The following short piece was written to demonstrate the wonderful sounds created by the diminished triad. More complicated harmonies, which you will learn about in Chapters 28 and 30, are also used. The piece is written so that one student can play the melody and another the harmony. The chords marked with an asterisk are the diminished triads.

Bruce R. Jackson (1951–   ), *Dimentoz* (1998)[+]

* Indicates diminished triad.

The Augmented Triad in Minor Scales

The augmented triad does not exist in the *major scale* or in *natural minor*. The only scales in which it can be found are harmonic and ascending melodic minor, in both of which there is an augmented triad on the third degree of each scale. The augmented triad *cannot* be played with white keys alone.

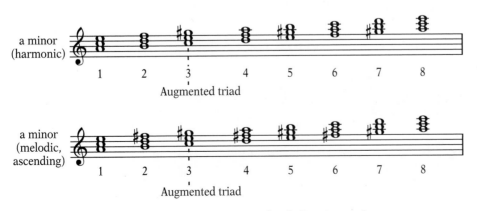

Augmented triads in harmonic and melodic minor scales

The following piece has many augmented chords as well as other harmonies you will learn about in Chapters 28 and 30. The piece is written so that one student can play the melody and another the harmony. The chords with an asterisk are the augmented triads.

Bruce R. Jackson (1951–   ), *Augmentoz* (1998)[+]

* Indicates an augmented triad.

The Scale That Has Only Augmented Triads

There is one twentieth-century scale that can produce *only* augmented triads. It is called the **whole-tone scale** and is made up entirely of whole tones. There are only two possible groups of pitches on the keyboard that can produce a whole-tone scale.

The two whole-tone scales

Most composers who use this scale use it only for portions of larger compositions. One of the most famous examples using the whole-tone scale is the Debussy piano **prelude** "Voiles" (Sails). The whole-tone scale is used in the first and last sections of the piece, although the middle section uses a different scale.

Claude Debussy (1862–1918), *Préludes pour Piano,* Book I, "Voiles" (Sails) (1910)

Guitar Chords and Their Symbols

Common tablature guitar fingerings of many of the major and minor triads and some diminished triads are given in Appendix 3. Although this appendix covers only some of the more common placement of notes on the fingerboard of the guitar (more properly referred to as *chord voicing*), there are many more *voicings* of the common chords than are indicated in this section. It is important to remember that chord symbols indicate three elements:

1. The capitalized letter always indicates the root of the triad. If the chord symbol is a "B♭," the root of the chord is B♭ even though the octave placement of the pitch is not indicated.
2. The quality of the chord is indicated as follows:
   a. Major triads use the capital letter alone. For example, A♭ is an A♭ major triad.
   b. Minor triads include a "mi" after the chord. For example, Cmi indicates a C minor triad.
   c. Diminished triads are usually indicated by °.
   d. Augmented triads are indicated by ⁺.
3. Extensions of the chord beyond the triad are indicated by numbers that represent the interval above the root. This material is covered in Chapter 28.

SIGHT SINGING ASSIGNMENT

A. *Augmented and Diminished Triad Drill.* You will hear the whole note played; sing back the black notes. These exercises associate the augmented triad with the major triad and the diminished triad with the minor triad.

B. *Compositions Using the Notes of the Minor Scale.*

Antonin Dvořák (1841–1904), theme from *Dmitri*, Op. 64 (1894–95)

"Is That So?" Polish folk song

"God Rest Ye Merry Gentlemen," 18th century English carol

C. *Melodies Using Diminished and Augmented Triads.*

Franz Schubert (1797–1828), *Octet* (1824)

*W*RITTEN ASSIGNMENT

Placing Augmented and Diminished Triads on the Keyboard and on the Music Staff. Using the letter names of the notes to mark the proper keys of the keyboard, write the augmented and diminished triads requested. Write the same triads on the music staff at the right of each printed keyboard. See the example.

EXAMPLE:

1. Augmented triad on D

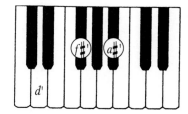 

Diminished triad on D

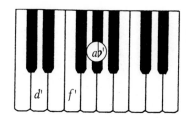 

2. Augmented triad on A♭

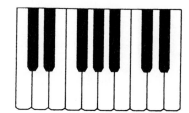 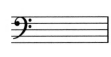

Diminished triad on A♭

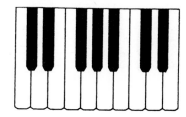 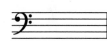

3. Augmented triad on F♯

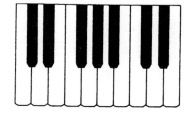 

Diminished triad on F♯

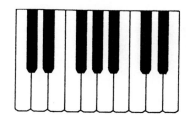 

4. Augmented triad on C

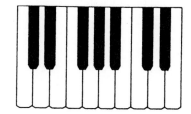 

Diminished triad on C

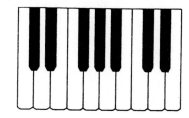 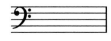

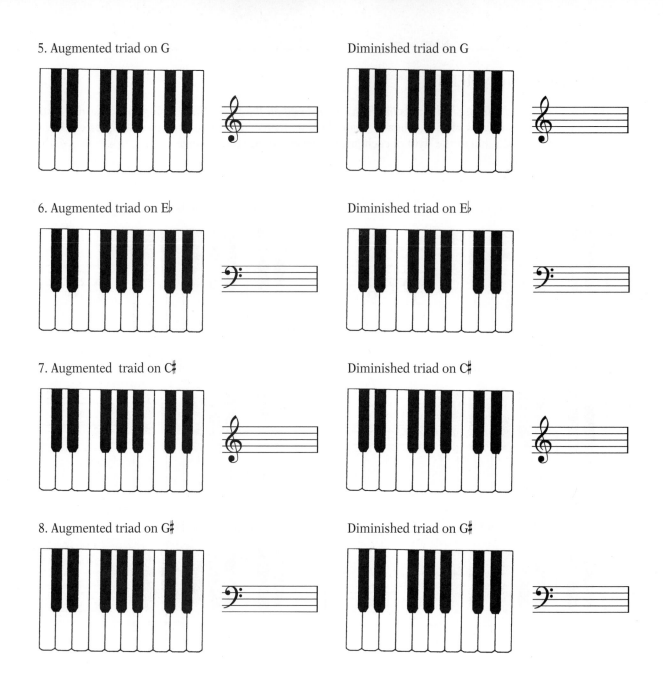

5. Augmented triad on G   Diminished triad on G

6. Augmented triad on E♭   Diminished triad on E♭

7. Augmented traid on C♯   Diminished triad on C♯

8. Augmented triad on G♯   Diminished triad on G♯

Play all the triads you have written. Be able to play an augmented or diminished triad on any note!

$\mathcal{E}$AR TRAINING ASSIGNMENT

A. *Recognition of Major, Minor, Diminished, and Augmented Triads.* In each of the following exercises you will hear three triads played in simple position. The species of triads used in each exercise is found in the left column, but the order of playing is not correct. Place the proper symbol showing the order of the triads in the column at the right. You will hear each exercise twice.

Triad Species	Symbol for Identification
Major triad	M
Minor triad	m
Diminished triad	d
Augmented triad	A

The example is illustrated and is worked correctly for you.

These triad species
are used
(not in proper order):

Rearrange in
proper order
here:

EXAMPLE:	1.	m	M	A		M	A	m
	2.	m	A	M		___	___	___
	3.	A	m	M		___	___	___
	4.	d	M	m		___	___	___

The remaining exercises will be similar, except that you will not be given the names of the triad species used. Place the names of the triads (using the abbreviations above) in the blanks. You will hear each exercise twice.

5. ___ ___ ___	9. ___ ___ ___
6. ___ ___ ___	10. ___ ___ ___
7. ___ ___ ___	11. ___ ___ ___
8. ___ ___ ___	12. ___ ___ ___

B. *Recognition of Scale Numbers.* In each exercise you will hear a four-note melody. Four possible combinations of scale numbers are given for each four-note melody. Only one answer is correct. Underline this answer. The example is illustrated and is worked correctly for you. Each exercise will be played twice.

EXAMPLE: 1.   Teacher plays:

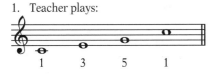

1   3   5   1

Answer:

	1. a.	<u>1 3 5 1</u>	b. 1 2 3 4	c. 1 2 4 1	d. 1 4 3 2
	2. a.	1 4 3 2	b. 1 5 6 7	c. 1 5 4 3	d. 1 6 5 4
	3. a.	1 5 3 1	b. 1 6 4 2	c. 1 5 2 1	d. 1 4 5 1

4. a. 1 3 4 4   b. 1 4 5 5   c. 1 2 3 4   d. 1 2 3 3

5. a. 1 5 5 1   b. 1 4 4 1   c. 1 4 5 6   d. 1 6 6 4

6. a. 1 7 6 7   b. 1 5 3 5   c. 1 4 2 1   d. 1 6 4 6

7. a. 1 2 3 4   b. 1 3 5 1   c. 1 7 6 5   d. 1 3 4 5

8. a. 1 1 5 3   b. 1 1 2 3   c. 1 1 7 6   d. 1 1 5 1

Chapter 17 ▪ Inversion of Intervals, Compound Intervals

*I*nversion of Intervals

If the lower note of an interval is raised an octave or the upper note lowered an octave, the new interval formed is called the **inversion** of the first interval.

Some intervals and their inversions

When an interval is inverted, the sum of the interval and its inversion will always be *nine.* This is because, in combining the two intervals, one note within the octave is counted twice.

$$1 + 8 = 9 \quad 2 + 7 = 9 \quad 3 + 6 = 9 \quad 4 + 5 = 9 \quad 5 + 4 = 9 \quad 6 + 3 = 9 \quad 7 + 2 = 9 \quad 8 + 1 = 9$$

Every *major* interval inverts to a *minor* interval; every *minor* interval becomes *major;* every *diminished* interval becomes *augmented;* every *augmented* interval becomes *diminished. Perfect intervals* alone do not change their quality in inversion and *remain perfect.*

Major → minor   Minor → major   Perfect → perfect   Augmented → diminished   Diminished → augmented

*S*imple and Compound Intervals

Intervals that encompass more than an octave are called **compound intervals;** those of an octave or less, **simple intervals.**

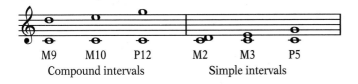

M9   M10   P12   M2   M3   P5
Compound intervals   Simple intervals

Compound intervals can be described in terms of their actual size, such as *tenth, eleventh, twelfth,* and so forth, but for most purposes it is more convenient to reduce them to the octave span and make them equivalent to the simple interval with the same letter names for some types of analysis. However, in *chords* that involve more notes than a triad, the compound names of intervals such as ninth, eleventh, and thirteenth are used.

10th   =   3rd   9th   =   2nd   12th   =   5th

SIGHT SINGING ASSIGNMENT

A. *Interval Inversion Drill.* These exercises may be done two different ways:
1. *For the classroom:* The teacher plays the whole notes, and the student immediately sings the black notes.
2. *For individual drill:* Play the whole notes (outside class) and immediately sing the black notes. Play the black notes on the piano *after* singing them. This acts as a final check on the accuracy of singing.

B. *Melodies for Sight Singing.* Sing all melodies in the octave register comfortable for your own voice range.

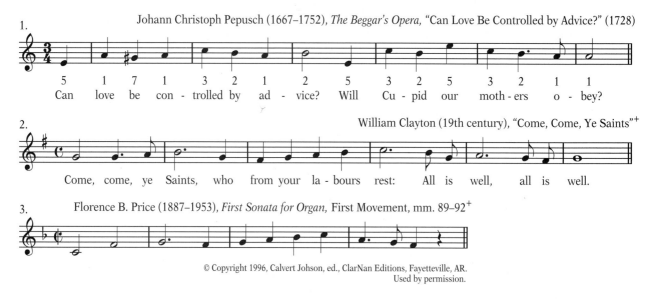

Anonymous traditional round

4.

Row, row, row your boat gent - ly down the stream; Mer-ri - ly, mer-ri - ly, mer-ri - ly, mer-ri - ly,

life is but a dream.

"Sumer Is Icumen In" (ca. 1240)

5.

Sum - mer is a - com - in' in, _____ Loud - ly sing cuck - oo. Grow - eth seed, and

blow - eth mead - ows, Woods are grow - ing new. Sing cuck - oo, Ewes are bleat - ing

at their lambs, At calf the cow doth moo. Bull - ock leap - ing, bucks are run - ning, Mer - ry sing cuck -

oo, cuck - oo, cuck - oo, Well sing-est thou cuck - oo, _ Who sor - row nev - er knew.

This is the oldest known **round** and can be sung like "Row, Row, Row Your Boat." (English text has been modernized)

* Marks the spot where the next voice begins to sing the tune from the beginning.

*W*RITTEN ASSIGNMENT

Interval Inversion. Find the interval asked for on the keyboard diagram and mark the notes with an X. Write an O on the notes for the inversion of that interval. Then write both intervals on the staff and name each inverted interval. See the example.

1. P4 and above *c'*

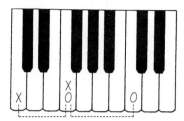

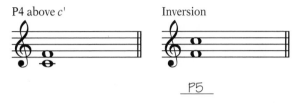

P4 above *c'*   Inversion

P5

2. m6 above *c*

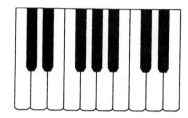

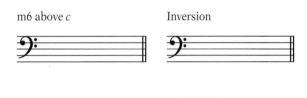

m6 above *c*   Inversion

_____

3. M7 above *d'*

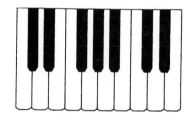

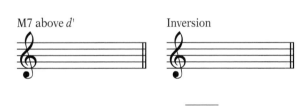

M7 above *d'*   Inversion

_____

4. m3 above *C♯*

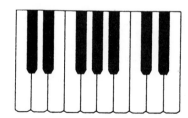

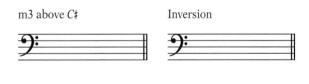

m3 above *C♯*   Inversion

_____

5. P5 above *e"*

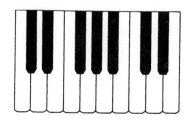

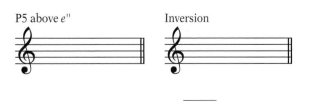

P5 above *e"*   Inversion

_____

6. M6 above C♯

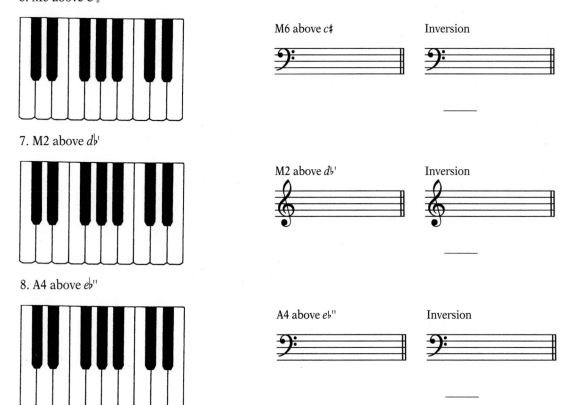

M6 above c♯   Inversion

7. M2 above d♭'

M2 above d♭'   Inversion

8. A4 above e♭"

A4 above e♭"   Inversion

Play and sing all intervals you have written.

ℰAR TRAINING ASSIGNMENT

A. *Recognition of All Simple Intervals.* In each exercise you will hear four harmonic intervals. In the answers given three are correct, but one interval is not the same as the interval you hear. Circle the incorrect interval in each exercise. Each exercise will be played twice. See the example.

EXAMPLE: 1. Teacher plays:

Answer:	1.	M6	P4	(M2)	M3
	2.	P8	M2	m6	m3
	3.	M3	P5	P4	A4
	4.	M6	M2	M3	M7
	5.	P8	M6	P8	P5
	6.	m3	P5	M2	M6
	7.	m6	P5	m6	P4
	8.	M3	P5	m3	m2

B. *Recognition of Triads in Chord Progressions.* In each exercise you will hear a chord progression of four chords. The progressions will use all four types of triads: major (M), minor (m), diminished (d), and augmented (A), although all four might not occur in every exercise. Put the abbreviation for the triad you hear in each of the spaces provided. Each progression will be played three times. See the example.

EXAMPLE:

Answer:	1.	m	d	M	m
	2.	___	___	___	___
	3.	___	___	___	___
	4.	___	___	___	___
	5.	___	___	___	___
	6.	___	___	___	___

PARTS III, IV, AND V · Rhythm and Meter, Melody, and Harmony

In Part I of this book you learned to recognize (by sight and sound), to write, and to sing the basic musical building materials. You learned how pitch, rhythm, and other musical qualities are organized and notated and how they are related to the keyboard and guitar. You also had experience in hearing them, performing simple rhythms, and singing short patterns.

In Part II you saw how these basic elements could be combined to create a tonal center and to produce intervals, triads, and scales. You also learned to listen to these basic combinations. You sang some melodies that displayed the qualities of the intervals and scales and learned how to write these basic combinations on the staff.

Now you are ready for more lengthy and complicated combinations of rhythms together with systematic practice in using different meters. You can also now see how **melody** is created from the two dimensions of movement—*movement from pitch to pitch* and *movement in time.* And you now have the materials to consider how to relate chords to each other—the study of **harmony.**

Suggested Order of Study of These Parts

Parts III through V of this book can be studied just in the order they appear in the text, or you can study a chapter of each part and then move on to the next chapter in each part. The advantage of the second approach is that you will continue to sing and practice rhythms even when you are working with chords. Likewise, when you are studying melody, you will have in mind its relation to harmony and rhythm. Keep in mind that these aspects of music are all interrelated!

PART III · Rhythm and Meter

Chapter 18 · Simple Duple, Triple, and Quadruple Meters

Duple Meter

In duple meters the musical pulse is grouped in *twos*. The first pulse is somewhat *accented* and serves as a point of arrival in the measure. The second pulse has less stress. The conductor beats all duple meters by moving the baton down for the first beat (the **downbeat**) and up for the second beat (the **upbeat**).

1 2

Various note values may serve as the note that receives the beat (the *beat unit*). As you remember, the value of the beat unit is shown by the bottom number of the time signature. In **simple meter,** the beat unit is a note value that normally subdivides into two parts. Common simple duple meters are:

Half-note beat unit

Quarter-note beat unit

Although the preceding examples look quite different in notation, the sound of both is identical because the beat is the same tempo for each one. *The tempo must always be set on the basis of the tempo marking rather than from the appearance of the note values* because *tempo* is determined by the *speed of the beat,* not by the notation of the beat unit.

Triple Meter

In triple meters the musical pulse is grouped in *threes.* Simple triple meters have beat units subdivided into two parts.

Eighth-note beat unit

Quarter-note beat unit

Although these examples look quite different, they sound exactly alike because it is the *tempo marking,* not the appearance of the note values, that determines the speed.

The conductor's beat for triple meters is:

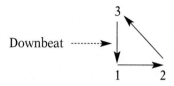

In triple meter the first beat is the stressed beat:

```
>
1   2   3
```

Quadruple Meter

Quadruple meter is a combination of two duple groups in one measure. The first beat receives the primary accent, and the third beat receives a secondary accent:

```
>       >
1   2   3   4
```

The conductor's beat pattern for quadruple meter is:

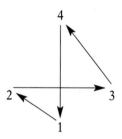

Note that 1 is a downbeat in every meter. Quadruple meters use the same beat unit values as duple meters.

$\frac{4}{4}$ meter is also called **common time** and sometimes has the sign **C** in place of $\frac{4}{4}$ as a time signature.

If a vertical line is drawn through the **C**, the time becomes **alla breve** ¢, which means that the half note becomes the beat unit. This is actually the equivalent of the $\frac{2}{2}$ time signature.

Divisions within the Beat in Simple Meters

In $\frac{2}{4}$, $\frac{3}{4}$, and $\frac{4}{4}$ time, for which the beat unit is a quarter note, the half-beat note value is an eighth note. In the following examples, the beats are divided into half-beat values, with two notes per beat.

Ludwig van Beethoven (1770–1827), *Symphony No. 7 in A Major*, Op. 42, Second Movement (1816)*

Half-beat values in $\frac{2}{4}$ meter

Eighth notes are counted as shown:

When you count half-beat values, it is very important to keep the tempo of the beat *steady* and to divide the beats *evenly*. In the following examples, the half-beat values are counted with *rhythmic syllables* (*1 and 2 and* or *1 te 2 te*).

"Song of the Volga Boatmen," Russian folk tune

In $\frac{2}{8}$, $\frac{3}{8}$, and $\frac{4}{8}$ time, the half-beat value is a sixteenth note. The same syllables are used for counting sixteenth notes in these meters as for eighth notes in meters with a quarter-note beat unit.

Felix Mendelssohn (1809–1847), *Midsummer Night's Dream*, Op. 21, Scherzo (1842)

In $\frac{2}{2}$, ₵, $\frac{3}{2}$, and $\frac{4}{2}$ time, the half-beat value is a quarter note.

Johannes Brahms (1833–1897), *Trio for Violin, Cello, and Piano in B Major*,
Op. 8, First Movement (1853–54)

* Note that some movements of a symphony may be in keys that contrast with the main key of the work.

Half-beat values in rhythms with dotted notes or ties are notated in the various meters:

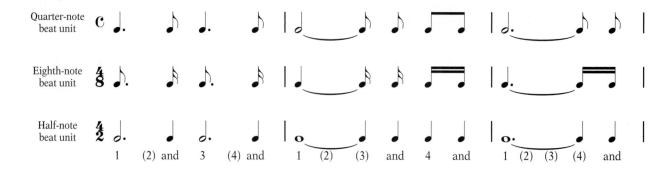

The most common dotted-note pattern is the dotted quarter and eighth note.

"Auld Lang Syne," Traditional Scottish song

We'll take a cup of kind - ness yet for __ auld __ lang __ syne.

The same pattern could be notated with ties.

Georges Bizet (1838–1875), *Carmen,* "Fate Motive" (1873–74)

1   (2) and 3 and

Half-beat values for rests produce rhythms similar to dotted notes or ties when the rest is used on the first half of the beat.

John Philip Sousa (1854–1932), "The Stars and Stripes Forever" (1896)[+]

1   (2) and 3   4

Half-beat value rests on the first half of the beat

In meters with a quarter note beat unit ($\frac{2}{4}$, $\frac{3}{4}$, and $\frac{4}{4}$), division of the beat into four equal parts produces sixteenth notes. When the beat is divided into four equal parts, the following syllables shown are used in counting:

1   a   and du 2   a   an du
or 1   ta te ta 2   ta te ta

Two sixteenths can combine with an eighth note to produce two normal patterns within beats.

1 (a) an du 2 a an (du)
or 1 (ta) te ta 2 ta te (ta)

One sixteenth note is needed to fill the beat following a dotted eighth note.

1 (a an) du 2 (a an) du

Reversing the pattern and placing the short note on the first quarter beat produces a lively rhythm called the "Scotch Snap." It is used in some Scottish folk dances (thus the name), jazz, Hungarian folk tunes, and other music. The short note is usually accented strongly. It often occurs in connection with a language pattern, reflecting the emphatic rhythm of the words.

"Hello, Girls!", American folk tune[+]

Hel-lo, girls! . . .

Scotch snap

In meters that have a half note for the beat unit ($\frac{2}{2}$, ¢, $\frac{3}{2}$, and $\frac{4}{2}$), the four equal parts of the beat are eighth notes.

1 a an du 2 a an du   1 (a) an du 2 a an (du) 2 a(an) du 2

Typical quarter-beat value patterns with a half-note beat unit

Meters with eighth-note beat units have thirty-second notes as quarter-beat values.

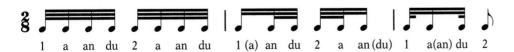

1 a an du 2 a an du   1 (a) an du 2 a an (du) 1 a(an) du 2

Typical quarter-beat value patterns with eighth-note beat units

SIGHT SINGING ASSIGNMENT

A. *Duple and Quadruple Meter Drill.* Sing or say the regular meter beat (1, 2 or 1, 2, 3, 4) and at the same time clap the note values as shown. You may conduct while you sing instead of clapping, or you may use a metronome. All ways of doing sight singing should be practiced.

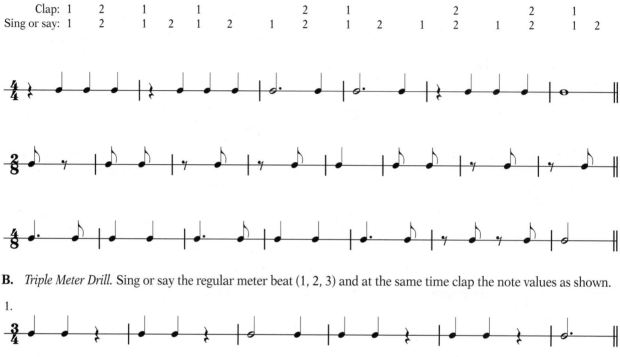

Clap: 1   2   1   1   2   1   2   2   1
Sing or say: 1   2   1   2   1   2   1   2   1   2   1   2   1   2   1   2

B. *Triple Meter Drill.* Sing or say the regular meter beat (1, 2, 3) and at the same time clap the note values as shown.

1.

2.

3.

4.

C. *Half-Beat Values in Simple Time.* Each exercise is taken from a well-known melody. Perhaps you will be able to recognize the tune from the rhythm alone as given here. Practice these values as you did for A and B.

1.

2.

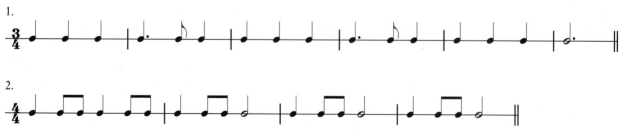

3.

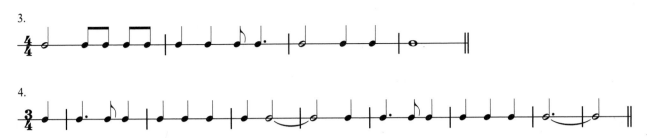

4.

D. *Rhythm Drill: Exercises in Accents.* The following four exercises show each melody in $\frac{2}{4}$, $\frac{3}{4}$, and $\frac{4}{4}$ meter. Practice singing these exercises in each of the three different meters listed. In some meters the melodies sound natural; in others they sound awkward. Try to sing the melodies accurately in all meters given.

1.

E. *Quarter-Beat Values in Simple Time.* Do these exercises in the same manner as for A, B, and C. You can also sing all these exercises up and down major or minor scales.

1.

2.

3.

4.

*W*RITTEN ASSIGNMENT

A. *Completion of Measures in Duple and Quadruple Meters.* Following is a series of short exercises in which each measure of the exercise is incomplete rhythmically. Complete each measure with *only one note* of the proper value. The example is worked correctly.

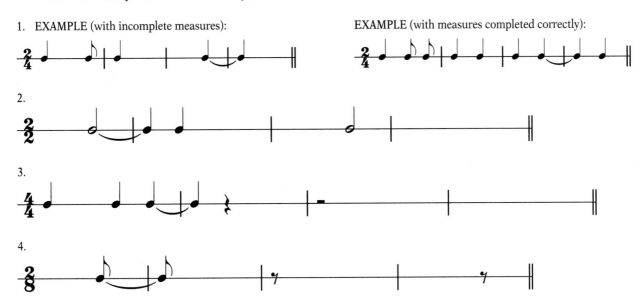

1. EXAMPLE (with incomplete measures):   EXAMPLE (with measures completed correctly):

2.

3.

4.

B. *Unit Value Drill.* Following is a series of short melodies. Each one is written out using a certain value of note per beat. Beneath each melody rewrite the melody using the new time signature provided. You will need to use a new note value for the beat in each case. The example is worked correctly.

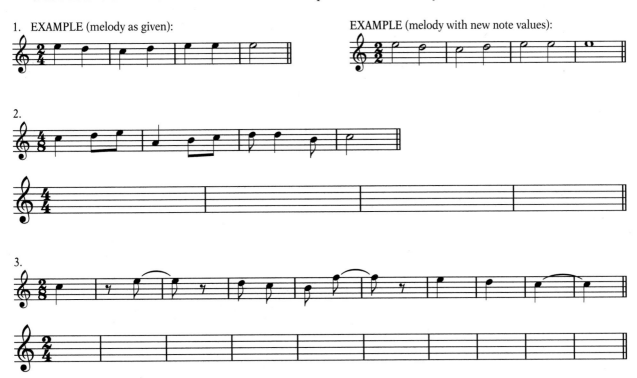

1. EXAMPLE (melody as given):   EXAMPLE (melody with new note values):

2.

3.

ℰAR TRAINING ASSIGNMENT

A. In each exercise you will hear a short melody with the same rhythm in each measure. Circle the letter indicating the correct rhythm. The first exercise is worked correctly for you.

EXAMPLE (teacher plays this):

Answer:

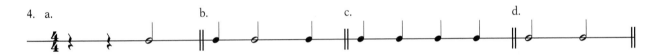

B. *Simple Rhythmic Patterns in Duple and Quadruple Meters.* In each exercise you will hear a rhythmic pattern of one measure length repeated several times in a melodic context. Three possible rhythmic patterns are given. Choose from among these the one which is played. Circle the letter indicating the correct rhythmic pattern played.

C. *Simple Rhythmic Patterns in Triple Meter.* In each exercise you will hear a rhythmic pattern of one measure length repeated several times in a melodic content. Three possible rhythmic patterns are given. Choose from among these the one which is played. Circle the letter indicating the correct rhythmic pattern played.

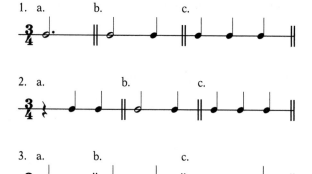

D. *Dictation of Half-Beat Rhythmic Values in Simple Time.* Following is a series of incomplete rhythmic exercises. You will hear the exercises in their completed form. Write in the missing rhythmic values in note values on the single line—disregard the pitches in this series of exercises. The example is illustrated and has been worked correctly for you. Each exercise will be played twice.

EXAMPLE:

E. *Dictation of Quarter-Beat Values in Simple Time.* Following is a series of incomplete rhythmic exercises. You will hear the exercises in their completed form. Write in the missing rhythmic values in note values on the single line. The example is illustrated and has been worked correctly for you. Each exercise will be played twice.

EXAMPLE:

1. Example completed correctly:

2.

3.

4.

5.

6.
Presto

Chapter 19 ▪ Syncopation

When the accent in music is shifted so that the stress falls on a weak beat instead of on the expected strong beat, the effect is called **syncopation.** There are three ways to emphasize a weak beat: (1) by beginning a note on a weak beat and tying it to a strong beat, (2) by placing rests on the strong beats so that the only notes heard are on weak beats, or (3) by placing dynamic accents on weak beats instead of strong beats.

Examples of Syncopations

In the following phrase, the syncopated note begins on the weak second beat and is held through the strong third beat of the measure. The exciting effect of this rhythm comes from the suppression of the expected accent on the third beat and the unexpected stress on the second beat, due to its position in the rhythmic pattern, even though it receives no special dynamic accent. When the rhythm returns to the normal accent pattern in the second measure, a great release of tension results. Play all the musical examples, counting them aloud. Sing the examples too!

Ludwig van Beethoven (1770–1827), *Leonore Overture No. 3* (1810)

Syncopation by beginning a note on a weak beat
and continuing it through the next strong beat

Ludwig van Beethoven (1770–1827), *Sonata No. 5* ("Spring") *for Violin and Piano,* Op. 24, Scherzo (1801)

Syncopation with rests on strong beats

The rests on the first beats of the above example delay the beginning of the staccato melodic fragments until the second beat. This gives a breathless, jesting quality to the rhythm, made more pronounced by the rapid tempo. Beethoven loved to use syncopation and other surprising rhythmic effects in his **scherzo** ("joke") movements!

Johannes Brahms (1833–1897), *Symphony No. 2,* Third Movement (1878)

Syncopation by accent

The preceding example uses both a dynamic *accent* and a *grace note* to emphasize the third beat. **A grace note** is a note printed in small type that takes part of the time normally allotted to an adjacent note. A small line running diagonally through the stem indicates that the note comes slightly before the beat and is very rapid. Grace notes give a melodic decoration to the note and add rhythmic stress and spice to the beat.

Ludwig van Beethoven (1770–1827), *Sonata No. 10 in F Major for Violin and Piano*, Op. 96, Scherzo (1812)

Syncopation by accents in another Beethoven scherzo

Syncopation by accent often requires vivid contrasts between the stressed and unstressed notes of the pattern. It is not unusual to find such extreme markings as **fp** (*forte piano*—loud, then suddenly soft), **sfz** (*sforzando*—strong accent), or even **sfp** (*sforzando piano*—strong accent, then immediately soft).

Not all syncopation involves strong accents. In much music of the sixteenth century in which a smooth performance is called for, syncopation is often found in the cadences (the closing part of a phrase).

Giovanni Pierluigi da Palestrina (1525–1594), *Pope Marcellus Mass*, "Kyrie eleison" (Lord, Have Mercy) (1567)

Syncopation within the Beat

Syncopation, emphasis on a weak beat and suppression of a strong beat, is also used with sub-beat values.

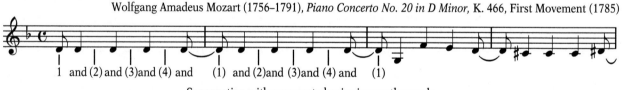

Wolfgang Amadeus Mozart (1756–1791), *Piano Concerto No. 20 in D Minor*, K. 466, First Movement (1785)

Syncopation with every note beginning on the weak
half of the beat after the first eighth note

This kind of syncopation may continue for a long time. It may be used for a melody, as above, or as an accompaniment pattern.

Syncopation with rests produces a detached version of the same rhythm.

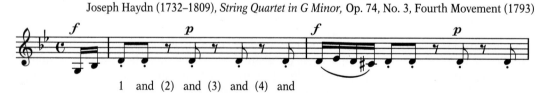

Joseph Haydn (1732–1809), *String Quartet in G Minor*, Op. 74, No. 3, Fourth Movement (1793)

Rests on the first half-beat and eighth notes
on the second half-beat

Folk tunes, spirituals, and jazz often use syncopation with half beats or even smaller values. In jazz, it is an important means of making the tune "swing." The most common type of syncopation in jazz style is the type with the beginning of the syncopation anticipating the next beat of the tune. The note to which the short note is tied is sometimes very long.

"Joshua Fit de Battle of Jericho," spiritual

By putting one eighth note between two sixteenth notes, a syncopated pattern at a lower sub-beat level is created.

Franz Schubert (1790–1828), "Frülingsglaube" (Spring Joy)

Syncopation at the *sixteenth-note level* is the characteristic syncopation of **ragtime.** It derives part of its effect from the contrast between the syncopated right hand of the piano and the regular eighth-note striding bass in the left. Ragtime was intended to be played in a *slow march tempo* (often the tempo indication in Scott Joplin's **rags**), so the syncopations could be savored fully. As Joplin said in many of his publications, "It is never right to play 'Ragtime' fast."

Scott Joplin (1868–1917), "Maple Leaf Rag" (1899)[+]

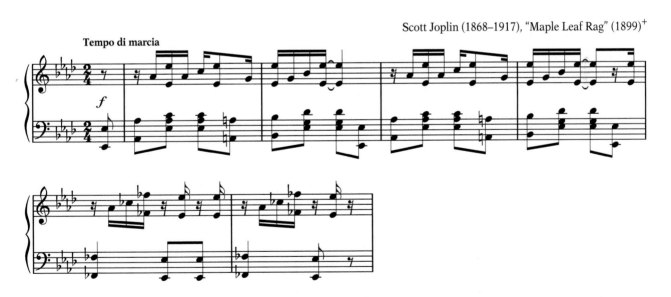

Sight singing assignment

A. *Syncopated Rhythm Drill.* Sing or say the meter (1, 2; 1, 2, 3; *or* 1, 2, 3, 4) and at the same time clap the rhythm as notated. You may conduct while you sing instead of clapping. You may also sing major scales with syllables or note names, using the rhythms of the exercises given.

B. *Syncopation with Half-Beat Values.* Sing or say the meter and at the same time clap the notated rhythm. You may conduct while you sing instead of clapping. You may also sing the rhythms using major scales.

C. *Syncopation with Quarter-Beat Values.* These exercises are to be practiced in the same manner as the preceding ones, except that the beat should be tapped with the foot and the eighth notes tapped with the left hand while the rhythm is said, sung, or tapped with the right hand. These exercises can also be done with a metronome. The rhythms in this exercise are those used by Scott Joplin (1868–1917) in his *School of Ragtime* (1908).[+]

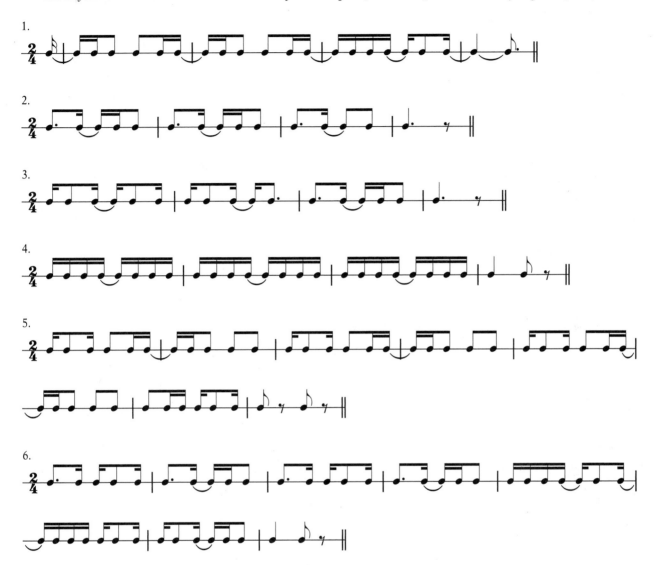

*W*RITTEN ASSIGNMENT

A. *Completion of Measure.* Complete the following measures with *one* note of proper value. The example is worked correctly for you.

EXAMPLE:

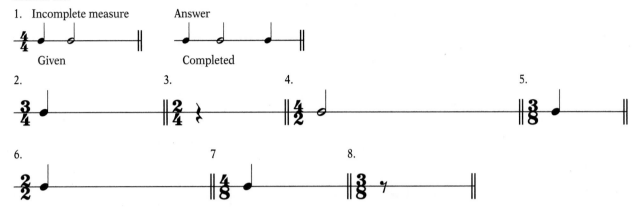

B. *Unit Value Drill.* Rewrite each of the following measures using the new time signature given at the right. The example is worked correctly for you.

EXAMPLE:

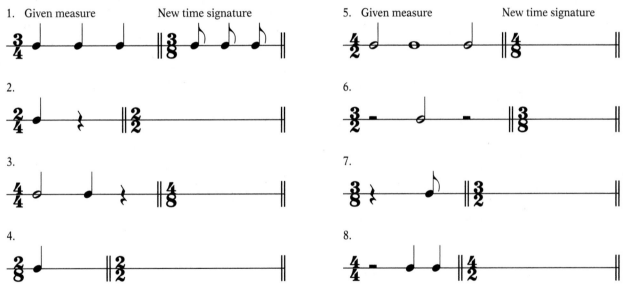

C. *Above* the exercises indicate the regular beats of the measure. *Below* the same exercises write the rhythmic syllables for each note (the syllables you would recite in rhythmic reading drill). The first exercise is written correctly for you.

EXAMPLE:

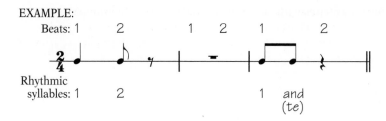

Beats: 1   2   1   2   1   2

Rhythmic
syllables: 1   2   1   and
                                            (te)

2. Beats:

Rhythmic
syllables:

3. Beats:

Rhythmic
syllables:

4. Beats:

Rhythmic
syllables:

5. Beats:

Rhythmic
syllables:

D. Clap or sing on a single pitch all the rhythms in the above exercises, using the rhythmic syllables you have written when you sing. These exercises may also be sung by applying the rhythms to a scale (major or melodic minor).

E. You probably know some tunes that use syncopation. Make a collection of syncopated tunes known by the class.

$\mathcal{E}$AR TRAINING ASSIGNMENT

A. *Simple Rhythm Patterns with Syncopations.* In each exercise you will hear a rhythmic pattern of one measure in length repeated several times in a melodic context. Four possible rhythmic patterns are given. You are to choose from among these the one that is played. Circle the letter indicating the correct rhythmic pattern played. *Your teacher will beat two measures of meter before beginning each exercise.* Each exercise will be played twice.

Teacher plays:

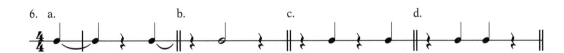

B. *Recognition of Errors in Rhythms Using Syncopations.* Following is a series of four-measure rhythmic exercises and one six-measure exercise. In each exercise the notation you see agrees with the dictated version you hear *except in one measure.* Determine which measure is played different rhythmically from the notated version and circle the number that represents that measure. Not all the exercises are syncopated. Each exercise will be played twice. The example is illustrated and is worked correctly.

Chapter 20 • Triplets

What Triplets Are

As you remember, when a group of three equal notes takes the place of two even notes of the same kind, the group of three notes is called a **triplet.** In this chapter we will see more examples of triplet use and more exercises to practice them.

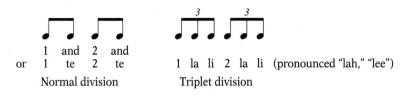

1 and 2 and
or 1 te 2 te
Normal division

1 la li 2 la li (pronounced "lah," "lee")
Triplet division

Cécile Chaminade (1857–1944), *Concertino for Flute and Orchestra*, Op. 107, First Movement (1902)

Melody using both normal and triplet division of beats

How to Write Triplets

If the triplets require beams, the notes are connected so that they show the rhythmic grouping, and the number 3 is placed on the stem side of the group, opposite the notehead.

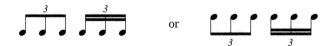

Examples of Triplets in Different Meters

These examples show various triplet groups lasting one beat.

Unit · Normal division · Triplet

Eighth-note beat unit

Gioachino Rossini (1792–1868), Overture from *William Tell* (1804)

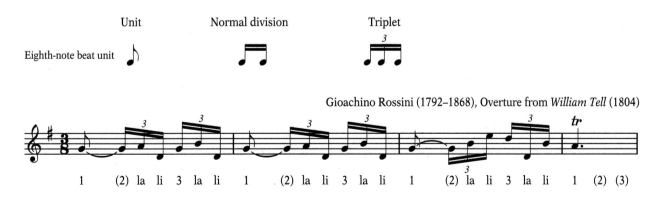

1 (2) la li 3 la li 1 (2) la li 3 la li 1 (2) la li 3 la li 1 (2) (3)

	Unit	Normal division	Triplet
Quarter-note beat unit			

Felix Mendelssohn (1809–1847), *Symphony No. 4 in A Major* ("Italian"), Fourth Movement (1833)

2 la li 3 la li 4 la li 1 la li 2 la li 3 la li 4 la li 1 la li

If the notes of the triplet are not beamed, the triplet grouping is shown by a numeral with gapped brackets.

	Unit	Normal division	Triplet
Half-note beat unit			

Edward Lalo (1823–1892), *Symphonie Espagnole for Violin and Orchestra,* Op. 21, First Movement (1875)

1 la li 2 and 1 and (2) la li 1 la li 2 la 1
      te   te   te

The long-short pattern within the triplet group is notated as follows:

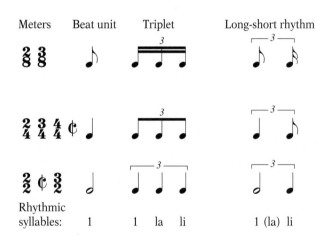

Meters	Beat unit	Triplet	Long-short rhythm

Rhythmic
syllables: 1   1 la li   1 (la) li

SIGHT SINGING ASSIGNMENT

A. *Triplets in Simple Meter*

As you count the meter, clap the notated rhythm. Then do the exercises again, clapping the beat (or using a conductor's beat with your hand), and sing or say the rhythm using the rhythmic syllables you have learned (*1 la li, 2 la li,* and so on).

B. Apply the above rhythms to scales you sing or play on an instrument. Use the major scale or any of the three forms of the minor scale.

C. Sing or play all the examples in the text of this lesson.

*W*RITTEN ASSIGNMENT

A. Rewrite the four sight singing assignments on the preceding pages in the meters indicated.

1.

2.

3.

4.

B. Write the correct syllables under each note in the following exercises.

1. EXAMPLE:

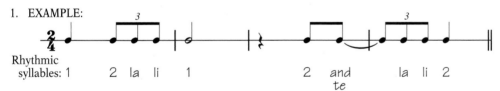

Rhythmic
syllables: 1   2 la li   1   2 and   la li 2
                                        te

2.

Rhythmic
syllables:

3.

Rhythmic
syllables:

4.

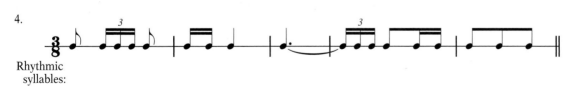

Rhythmic
syllables:

Then perform the exercises by saying the syllables while clapping or tapping the beat.

$\mathcal{E}$AR TRAINING ASSIGNMENT

You will hear exercises with triplet figures on various beats of the measure. Circle those beats of the measures where triplets occur. The example is illustrated and worked correctly for you. Each exercise will be played twice.

EXAMPLE: Teacher plays this:

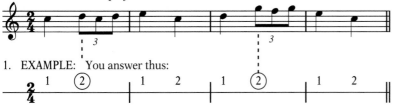

1.   EXAMPLE: You answer thus:

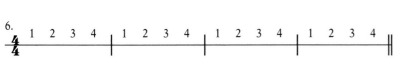

2.

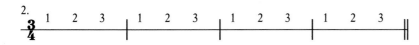

3.

4.

5.

6.

What Is Compound Meter?

In **compound meters** the beat unit has *three* normal subdivisions. The beat unit in compound meter is *always a dotted note*. The effect of compound meter is that of having a triplet on every beat; thus, some melodies could be notated equally well in simple time with triplets or compound time with normal note values. The bottom number of the time signature is *not* the beat unit but is the sub-beat note value, and the top number is the number of those notes in the measure rather than the number of beats. In compound time the top number is divisible by *three*.

"Down in the Valley," American folk tune[+]

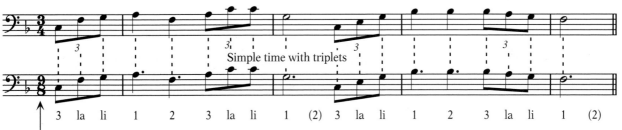

Simple time with triplets

3 la li 1 2 3 la li 1 (2) 3 la li 1 2 3 la li 1 (2)

Nine eighth notes in the measure, but three dotted-quarter-note beat units.

The Compound Meters with a Dotted-Quarter-Note Beat Unit

The most common compound meters are those with a *dotted quarter note* as the beat unit and eighth note divisions of the beat. The time signatures are $\frac{6}{8}$, $\frac{9}{8}$, and $\frac{12}{8}$. The example shows a normal pattern.

Joseph Haydn (1732–1809), *Symphony No. 94 in G Major ("Surprise"),* First Movement (1791)

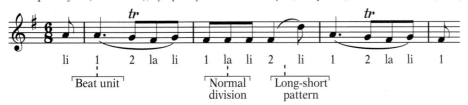

li 1 2 la li 1 la li 2 li 1 2 la li 1

Beat unit   Normal division   Long-short pattern

Note that the divisions of the beat unit are beamed together.

Other Dotted Notes as Beat Units

Compound meters using the dotted half note or the dotted eighth note as the beat unit are also used. They are counted in the same manner.

$\frac{6}{4}$ 𝅗𝅥. 𝅗𝅥. $\frac{9}{4}$ 𝅗𝅥. 𝅗𝅥. 𝅗𝅥. $\frac{12}{4}$ 𝅗𝅥. 𝅗𝅥. 𝅗𝅥. 𝅗𝅥.

1   2   1   2   3   1   2   3   4

Counting Subdivisions in Compound Meter

Subdivisions of the beat in compound time are counted as shown here. The syllable *ta* placed between the syllables further divides the beat. Triplets can also be counted *1 ta la ta li ta* if the notes of the triplet are further divided.

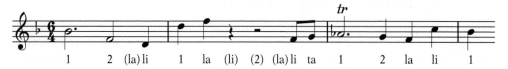

Johannes Brahms (1833–1897), *Piano Concerto No. 1 in D Minor*, Op. 15, First Movement (1854–58)

Frédéric Chopin (1810–1849), *Nocturne*, Op. 9, No. 1 (1830–31)

$\mathcal{E}$xamples of Subdivisions of the Beat in Compound Meters

One of the most common ways to use these values in compound time is in dotted note patterns like these:

Wolfgang Amadeus Mozart (1756–1791), *Sonata in A Major for Piano*, K. 300i, First Movement (1781–83)

Johann Sebastian Bach (1685–1750), *Orchestra Suite No. 1*, Forlane (about 1720)

Sometimes the third note of the group is divided as well. Syncopation patterns are sometimes used at this level.

Johannes Brahms (1833–1897), *Symphony No. 4*, Op. 98, Second Movement (1884–85)

The long note in dotted note patterns is usually on the first part of the beat. If it is on the second part of the beat instead, it gives an unusual stress to this part of the rhythm.

Johannes Brahms (1833–1897), *Sonata in G Major for Violin and Piano*, Op. 78, First Movement (1878–79)

Another interesting rhythm is produced by tying the beginning of a dotted pattern to the preceding beat.

Ludwig van Beethoven (1770–1827), *Symphony No. 7 in A Major,* Op. 92, First Movement (1811–12)

1   (2 la)ta li

$\mathcal{A}$ Special Rhythm—Hemiola

A very interesting effect can be produced by shifting the accent in a measure with six eighth notes from two groups of three eighth notes (compound duple) to three groups of two eighth notes (simple triple) or the reverse. This effect is called **hemiola.**

Gilles Binchois (ca. 1400–60), *De plus en plus* (More and More)

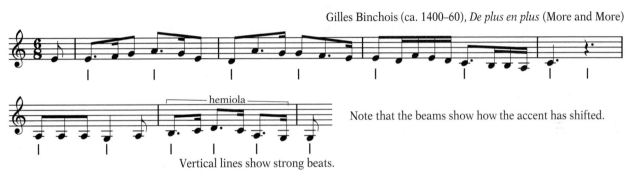

Note that the beams show how the accent has shifted.

Vertical lines show strong beats.

Johannes Brahms (1833–1897), *Liebeslieder Waltzer* (Love-Song Waltzes), Op. 52, No. 6 (1868–69)

Vertical lines show strong beats.

The example above could have been barred as follows to show the change in metrical grouping produced by the *hemiola.*

Look for more examples of hemiola in other music.

$\mathcal{S}$IGHT SINGING ASSIGNMENT

A. *Compound Meters.* Count the meter and clap the rhythm. Then clap or beat the meter and sing or say the rhythm, using the rhythmic syllables. Remember that when the beat is divided into three equal parts in compound meter, you use the same syllables as for the triple division of the beat in simple meter.

1. EXAMPLE:

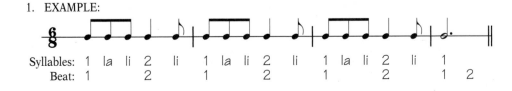

Syllables: 1 la li 2   li   1 la li 2   li   1 la li 2   li   1
Beat: 1   2   1   2   1   2   1 2

B. *Various Rhythm Patterns in Simple and Compound Time.* Count the meter and clap the rhythm for each of the patterns below, just as you did in the previous exercises, but this time repeat each example *six times continuously.*

Then clap or beat the meter and sing or say the rhythm using rhythmic syllables, again repeating each example *six times continuously.*

Finally, apply the rhythm to scales—major or melodic minor—and repeat the rhythms as many times as are required to sing up and down the scale (one octave).

For instrumentalists, rhythmic scale studies like this are *very useful* ways to practice scales on your instrument, using a metronome to give the beat.

$\mathcal{W}$RITTEN ASSIGNMENT

You can sing or clap these, too!

A. *Above* the exercise write the regular beats of the measure. Then *below* the same exercise write the proper rhythmic syllables for each note. The example is worked correctly for you.

1. EXAMPLE:

2.

3.

4.

B. Sing, say, and clap all the examples you have written. Also apply the rhythms to scales you sing or play.

C. Match the column of rhythmic syllables on the right with the notated rhythms on the left. The example is worked correctly for you. Add rest signs between the syllables where rests occur.

1. EXAMPLE: ___i___

2. ____

3. ____

4. ____

5. ____

6. ____

7. ____

8. ____

9. ____

10. ____

a. 1 2

b. 1 (2) an du

c. 1 ta la 2 li

d. 1 la li 2 la li

e. 1 ta la ta li ta 2 a an du

f. 1 ta la ta li ta 2 la li ta

g. 2

h. 1 (2) la li ta

i. 1 and 2 la li

j. 1 and 2 an du

k. 1 2 li ta

l. 1 li la

m. 1 ta la ta li ta 2 du

n. 1

o. 1 (2) li ta

D. Play, sing, or clap all the rhythms above, repeating each measure four times. Use a single pitch and then sing or play the rhythms using scales.

$\mathcal{E}$AR TRAINING ASSIGNMENT

A. *Repeated Compound Rhythm Patterns.* In each exercise you will hear a rhythmic pattern one measure in length repeated several times in a melodic context. Four possible rhythmic patterns are given. Choose the one you hear and circle the letter indicating the correct rhythmic pattern. *Your teacher will beat two measures of meter before beginning each exercise.* Each example will be played twice. See the example.

1. EXAMPLE:

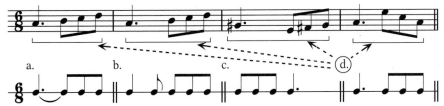

2.

3.

4.
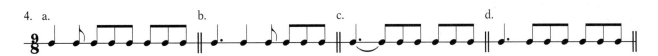

5.

6.
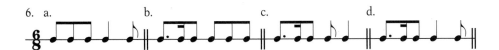

B. *Recognition of Errors in Compound Meters Using Sub-beat Values.* Following is a series of four-measure rhythmic exercises. In each exercise the notation you see agrees with the dictated version *except in one measure*. Determine which measure is rhythmically different from the notated version and circle the letter of that measure. Each exercise will be played twice.

C. *Recognition of Simple and Compound Meter.* In each of the exercises you will hear a short melody. Determine whether the melody is in simple or compound time and underline the correct answer. Each exercise will be played twice.

1. Simple	Compound		5. Simple	Compound
2. Simple	Compound		6. Simple	Compound
3. Simple	Compound		7. Simple	Compound
4. Simple	Compound		8. Simple	Compound

PART IV · Melody

What Is Melody?

Melody is a series of single musical tones, sounded successively. Because each tone has both pitch and duration, melody has two dimensions of movement: movement in time (*rhythm*) and movement in pitch (**melodic contour**).

Chapter 22 · Movement and Rest in Melody

The Phrase

Melody is divided into **phrases,** which are the "*sentences*" of musical speech. Phrases may vary greatly in length, but they are usually from two to eight measures long. The normal phrase of music of the eighteenth and nineteenth centuries is four measures, although many patterns can be found.

Johann Crüger (1598–1662), "Jesu, meine Freude" (Jesus, My Joy) (1653)
(This melody was often used by later composers, among them J.S. Bach.)

Two-measure phrases

"O Come, O Come, Emmanuel," carol based on Gregorian chant

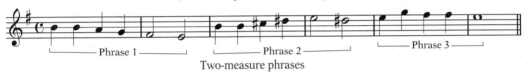

Three-measure phrases

Lady John Scott, "Annie Laurie" (18th century)

Four-measure phrases

The Cadence

Every phrase has a beginning, a middle, and an end. Throughout the phrase, the rhythm and the shape of the melodic line (*melodic contour*) combine to create a feeling of movement toward a goal that is a *point of rest*. The moment of arrival, with the melodic progression leading to it, is called the **cadence.**

Mrs. Dorothea Jordan (1762–1816), "The Blue Bell of Scotland" (1800)

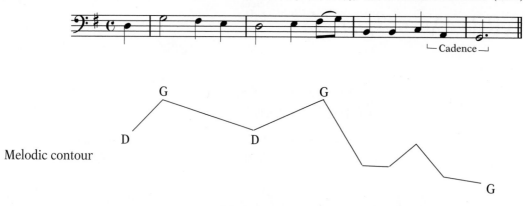

Melodic contour

Strong and Weak Cadences

When the last note of the phrase falls on a strong beat of the measure, the cadence is *strong*. A cadence in which the last note falls on a weak beat is called *weak*.

Aaron Copland (1900–1990), *Billy the Kid* (1941)[+]

Beginning the Phrase

A melody may begin on the first beat of a measure.

Joseph Haydn (1732–1809), "Gott, erhalte Franz den Kaiser!" (*Austrian Hymn*) (1796)

A tune may begin with a melodic movement into the first beat of a measure. The note or notes that move to the first strong beat are called the **anacrusis.** The terms *pickup* or *upbeat* are sometimes used for describing this type of phrase beginning.

George Frideric Handel (1685–1759), *Messiah*, "I Know That My Redeemer Liveth" (1742)

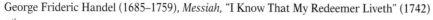

Anacrusis

An anacrusis is *not* a measure but a rhythmic and melodic movement *toward* a measure. In melodies with an anacrusis, the *first measure* is the metric unit with the *first strong beat.*

George Frideric Handel (1685–1759), *Messiah,* "He Shall Feed His Flock" (1742)

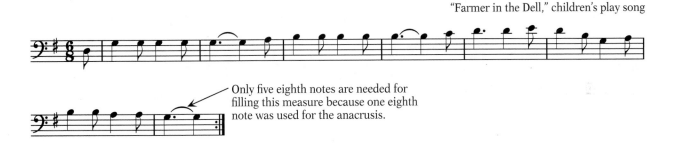

Anacrusis — First measure — Second measure —

If the first phrase of a melody begins with an anacrusis, it is likely that the following phrases will also. Thus, it is customary for the last measure of a tune with an anacrusis to subtract the beats or portions of beats used in the anacrusis at the beginning from the end of the last measure. This makes it possible to repeat the tune from the beginning without any adjustment between stanzas. This rule is not followed strictly in long, complex works in which many different kinds of phrases might be used.

"Farmer in the Dell," children's play song

Only five eighth notes are needed for filling this measure because one eighth note was used for the anacrusis.

The Names of the Notes in a Scale

Each note of the scale has a name describing its function in melodies and harmonies built from the notes of the scale.

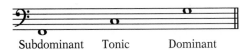

Tonic   Supertonic   Mediant   Subdominant   Dominant   Submediant   Leading tone   Tonic

The most important notes of the scale are the *tonic* (tonal center), the **dominant** (the fifth above the tonic), and the **subdominant** (the fifth below the tonic).

Subdominant   Tonic   Dominant

Halfway between the tonic and the dominant is the **mediant** (derived from a Latin word meaning *middle*); halfway between the tonic and the subdominant is the **submediant.**

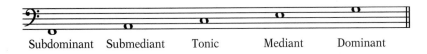

Subdominant   Submediant   Tonic   Mediant   Dominant

The two remaining notes of the scale are those just above and below the tonic note—the **supertonic** and **leading tone,** respectively. The supertonic, of course, means the note above the tonic. The term *leading tone* describes the tendency of a note a half step below the tonic to move melodically up to the tonic note.

Leading tone   Tonic   Supertonic

The same names are given to scale steps in minor, except for the seventh degree in natural minor and descending melodic minor. In these forms of the minor scale, the seventh note is a whole step below the tonic, and the term **subtonic** is used. In melodic and harmonic minor, which have a raised seventh degree, the relationship is again a half step, and the raised seventh degree is called a *leading tone.*

The following table summarizes the various names by which we refer to the notes of the scale.

MAJOR SCALE FUNCTION NAME	SCALE DEGREE NUMBER	MINOR SCALE FUNCTION NAME
Tonic	1	Tonic
Supertonic	2	Supertonic
Mediant	3	Mediant
Subdominant	4	Subdominant
Dominant	5	Dominant
Submediant	6	Submediant
	6 (raised)	Submediant
Leading tone	7	Subtonic
	7 (raised)	Leading tone
Tonic	8	Tonic

$\mathcal{A}$ctive and Rest Tones in a Key

Some notes of the scale have a strong tendency to move melodically in predictable directions. The leading tone tends to move toward the tonic, and the raised sixth in melodic minor tends to move to the raised seventh and from there to the tonic. Tones with a strong feeling of movement toward a goal can be called *active tones.* The notes to which they move, especially the notes of the tonic chord, can be described as *rest tones.*

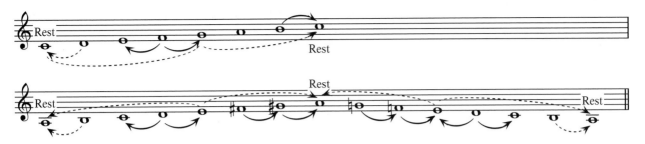

Common tendencies of melodic movement in major and minor

The most prominent of the active tones is the *leading tone.* When you sing the following melody and stop on the leading tone, you feel a strong urge to continue to the following note—the tonic toward which the leading tone is attracted. This strong sense of direction makes the pattern from the leading tone up to the tonic a strong and important melodic cadence pattern.

William Steffe (19th century), "Battle Hymn of the Republic" (1852)[+]

In the following tune, the final cadence moves *down* to the tonic from the supertonic, another very common cadence pattern.

Johann Sebastian Bach (1685–1750), "Herr, straf mich nicht" (Lord, Punish Me Not)

Descending form, down from tonic   Ascending form, up to tonic

Notice how the raised tones tend to move toward the tonic in this tune in a minor key.

Some Melodic Patterns in Cadences

If a melodic cadence skips to the tonic, it usually moves from the dominant note to the tonic, with either a skip up of a fourth or a skip down of a fifth.

"Frère Jacques," French folk tune

Dominant   Tonic

Skip from dominant *up* to tonic in the cadence

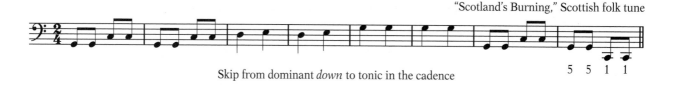

Skip from dominant *down* to tonic in the cadence

5 5 1 1

A way of decorating at a cadence is to *anticipate* the tonic on the strong beat of the cadence with the tonic note before the bar line.

George Frideric Handel (1683–1759), *Messiah,* final cadence of Overture (1742)

Anticipation

Tonic approached by supertonic, strong beat anticipated

Some Melodic Patterns in the Anacrusis (Upbeat)

The anacrusis also has several characteristic melody patterns. Those moving from the dominant to the tonic are very common.

Joseph Haydn, *The Creation,* "The Heavens Are Telling" (1796–98)

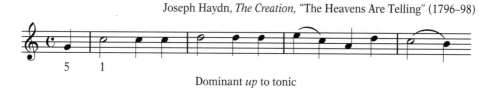

5   1

Dominant *up* to tonic

George Frideric Handel (1683–1759), *Messiah,* "O, Thou That Tellest Good Tidings" (1742)

5   1

Dominant *down* to tonic

The third of the scale may move down to the tonic or the tonic up to the third. The anacrusis with this pattern often fills in the third with stepwise motion, making a two-note anacrusis.

Interval of the third with stepwise motion

Anacrusis

"Wearin' of the Green," Irish folk tune

1   2   3

The broken triad is another common pattern using more than one note in the anacrusis.

John Stafford Smith (1750–1836), "The Star-Spangled Banner"

Though this tune is the American national anthem, the tune itself was by an Englishman!

SIGHT SINGING ASSIGNMENT*

Sing the following melodies in two different ways:

1. Clap the meter and at the same time sing the pitches of the notes in the correct rhythm using scale degree numbers or syllables.
2. Sing the pitches using numbers or syllables without clapping. Learn to maintain a steady tempo without the assistance of clapping.

Johann Sebastian Bach (1685–1750), "Nun ruhen alle Wälder" (Now Are All the Forests Peaceful)

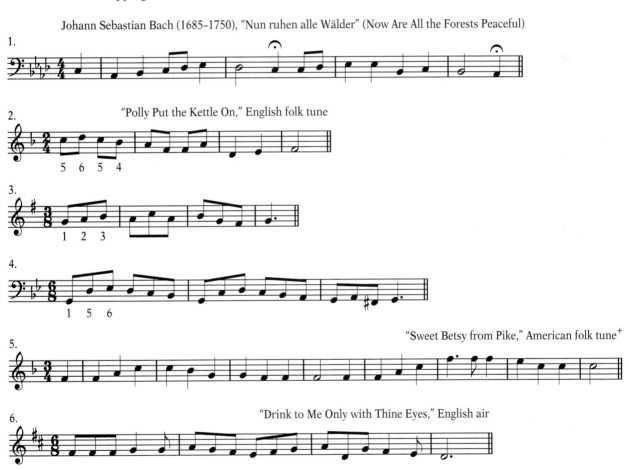

---

* In addition to the melodies given in the sight singing sections of the lessons on melody, sing *all* the melodies in the text of each lesson, using numbers or syllables as in the sight singing assignments. The greatest value will be derived from these exercises if they are sung while you are reading the text.

It will help you to sing this tune if you notice that each skip down from *e'* goes to a note one note lower than did the preceding skip down. So there is a skip down of a third, return to starting point, skip down of a fourth, return, and so forth, until the skip down of an octave.

William Billings (1746–1800), "When Jesus Wept" (1770)[+]

This beautiful melody by the American Revolutionary War composer William Billings can be sung as a round, in four parts. Each new voice begins as the first voice begins a new phrase, at the mark of the asterisk (*).

𝒲RITTEN ASSIGNMENT

A. Below is a group of melodies with more than one phrase in each melody. Mark the end of each phrase with a curved bracket, and under each cadence indicate whether the phrase ends on a strong beat or on a weak beat.

Ludwig van Beethoven (1770–1827), *Sonatina in G Major for Piano,* Op. 49, No. 2, Second Movement (1805)

1. **Tempo di minuetto**

Wolfgang Amadeus Mozart (1756–1791), *Symphony No. 41 in C Major* ("Jupiter"), K. 551, Menuetto (1788)

2. **Allegro**

B. The same concern with anacrusis, cadence, and direction is found in melodies of the twentieth century whether or not they are based on major and minor scales. Identify the kind of phrase beginnings (with or without anacrusis) and cadences (strong or weak) in the following melodies. The phrase endings of Exercise 1 are marked with brackets. Play the melodies.

Paul Hindemith (1895–1963), *Piano Sonata No. 2,* First Movement (1936)
(phrase endings are marked)

1. ♩ = 108

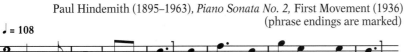

Maurice Ravel (1875–1937), *String Quartet,* First Movement (1910)

2. ♩ = 120

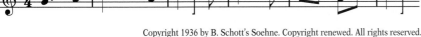

$\mathcal{E}$AR TRAINING ASSIGNMENT

A. *Recognition of the Anacrusis.* In each exercise you will hear a short melody. Some of these melodies begin with an anacrusis, and some begin on the first beat of the measure. Underline the answer that applies in each case.

1. Begins on an anacrusis   Begins on the first beat of a measure

2. Begins on an anacrusis   Begins on the first beat of a measure

3. Begins on an anacrusis   Begins on the first beat of a measure

4. Begins on an anacrusis   Begins on the first beat of a measure

5. Begins on an anacrusis   Begins on the first beat of a measure

6. Begins on an anacrusis   Begins on the first beat of a measure

7. Begins on an anacrusis   Begins on the first beat of a measure

8. Begins on an anacrusis   Begins on the first beat of a measure

B. *Recognition of Active Tones or Tonic at the Phrase End.* In each exercise you will hear a short melody. This melodic phrase will end either on the tonic or an active tone. Underline the proper answer. Each exercise will be played twice.

1. Active tone   Tonic

2. Active tone   Tonic

3. Active tone   Tonic

4. Active tone   Tonic

5. Active tone   Tonic

6. Active tone   Tonic

7. Active tone   Tonic

8. Active tone   Tonic

9. Active tone   Tonic

10. Active tone   Tonic

11. Active tone   Tonic

12. Active tone   Tonic

Chapter 23 ▪ *Conjunct and Disjunct Motion,*
Melodic Direction

Conjunct and Disjunct (Smooth and Jagged)

The melodic contour may be smooth, with most intervals whole steps and half steps (**conjunct motion**), or jagged, with leaps of larger intervals (**disjunct motion**).

Johann Crüger (1598–1662), "Nun danket alle Gott" (Now Thank We All Our God)

Conjunct motion (most motion stepwise—smooth)

Ludwig van Beethoven (1770–1827), *Piano Sonata in C Minor,*
Op. 10, No. 1, First Movement (1798)

Disjunct motion (most motion by skip—jagged)

*M*ovement toward a Melodic Climax

A melody is also described in terms of the direction in which it moves. Some melodies move upward to a high note that is the *climax* of the phrase. The climax may be at the very end of the phrase, coinciding with the cadence.

Ludwig van Beethoven (1770–1827), *String Quartet in C Minor,* Op. 18, No. 4, Fourth Movement (1801)

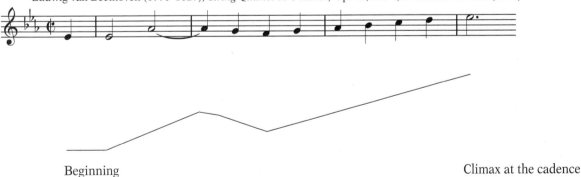

Beginning   Climax at the cadence

Some melodies reach the high point in the middle of the phrase and then fall back to a cadence at a lower pitch.

Robert Schumann (1810–1856), *Album für die Jugend*
(*Album for the Young*), Chorale (1848)

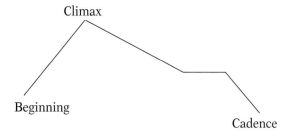

Climax

Beginning

Cadence

The melody may sweep downward toward a low point of arrival.

George Frideric Handel (1685–1759), "Joy to the World"

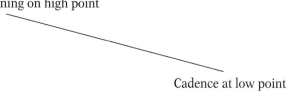

Beginning on high point

Cadence at low point

A melody may even stay on one pitch, building up tension until finally some melodic motion leads to a cadence.

George Frideric Handel (1685–1759), *Messiah*, "And the Glory of the Lord" (1742)

These and other contours are found both in conjunct and disjunct motion. Note in the following melody that the motion is conjunct at first but that the phrase ends with wide-ranging disjunct motion.

Claude Debussy (1862–1918), *Prélude à l'après-midi d'un faune* (Prelude to the Afternoon of a Faun) (1892–94)

Disjunct Motion in Melodies Outlining Chords

When melodies move with many skips, they often form patterns outlining chords, as in the following example:

Ludwig van Beethoven (1770–1827), *Symphony No. 3 in E-Flat Major,* Op. 55, First Movement (1806)

Triad
E♭—G—B♭

Chord outline

Melodies can be written using nothing but the notes of the triad built on the first degree of the scale (the *tonic triad*). Bugle calls are built entirely from the notes of the tonic chord.

"Taps," American military bugle call (1860s)[+]

Triad
F—A—C

Slow

Notice that such a disjunct melody still has a strong sense of direction; it rises to a climax and drops back to a more restful cadence. All the melodic contours used in conjunct melodies are also found in disjunct melodies.

Stepwise movement is often combined with disjunct movement in melodies built on chord patterns. Intervals of the triad may be filled in with stepwise movement passing between the notes of the chord without disturbing the essential triadic outline of the melody.

"Lullaby," German folk song

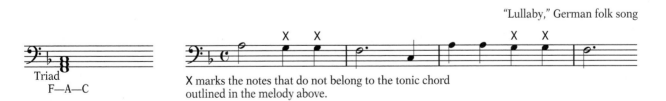

Triad
F—A—C

X marks the notes that do not belong to the tonic chord
outlined in the melody above.

Melodies Constructed of Other Triads

Melodies are often constructed of notes of the dominant triad or subdominant triad. In the following two melodies you can see notes of the dominant and tonic triads used to construct the melody. In the tune "Down in the Valley," only the tonic (I) and dominant (V) triads are used.

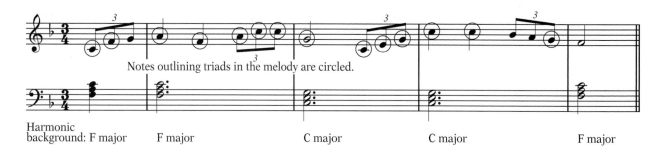

Notes outlining triads in the melody are circled.

Harmonic
background: F major   F major   C major   C major   F major

In a minor key the major form of the dominant triad is usually used.

Giuseppe Verdi (1813–1901), *La Traviata (The Lost One)* (1852), "Addio del passato" (Farewell to the Past)

Fare - well, then, __ to __ the _ past life, ___ to __ the _ past dreams _ of __ sweet _ pleas - ures

a minor   a minor   E major   a minor

As you see in the example, not all the tones of the triad need to be present in the melody to create the feeling of a change in harmony. Notes that do not belong to the chord may be used to decorate the chord outline without changing the harmony that would be used to accompany the melody at that point. Embellishing notes that do not belong to the harmony are called **nonharmonic tones;** they are discussed further in Chapter 27, p. 249.

In the next tune, the subdominant triad is part of the melodic structure.

Wolfgang Amadeus Mozart (1756–1791), *Symphony No. 39 in E-Flat Major,* K. 543, Menuetto (1788)

I   I   IV   I   IV   IV

For further study of putting harmonies to melodies in accordance with the chords that fit them, see Chapter 26, p. 237.

Motion with Two or More Voices

The relation between the direction in which two voices move is called **motion.** If two voices move in the same direction, they are in **similar motion;** if they move in opposite directions, they are in **contrary motion;** and if one voice remains stationary while the other moves, they are in **oblique motion. Parallel motion** is a special type of similar motion in which both voices move the same distance in the same direction at the same time and keep the same interval between them.

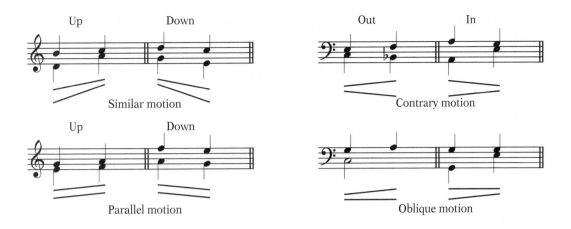

SIGHT SINGING ASSIGNMENT

A. Sing the following melodies in two different ways. Clap the meter and at the same time sing the pitches of the notes using the scale degree numbers or syllables. Then sing the pitches in the correct rhythm using the number or syllables without clapping. Learn to maintain the steady tempo without the assistance of clapping.

B. *Sight Singing Exercises Outlining the Tonic Triad.* Sing the following melodies in one or both of these two different ways. Clap the meter and at the same time sing the pitches of the notes in the correct rhythm using scale degree numbers or syllables. Then sing the pitches using numbers or syllables without clapping. Learn to maintain a steady tempo without the assistance of clapping.

"Clementine," American folk tune[+]

1.

Ludwig van Beethoven (1770–1827), *Symphony No. 3 in E-Flat Major,* Op. 55, First Movement (1806)

2.

George Frideric Handel (1695–1759), *Music for the Royal Fireworks* (1749)

3.
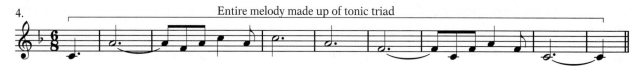

John Philip Sousa (1854–1932), "Semper Fidelis" (1888)[+]

4.

$\mathcal{W}$RITTEN ASSIGNMENT

A. Following is a group of melodies. Find the tonic triads outlined in the melodies and mark the sections of the melody built on the tonic triad with brackets.

B. Try your hand at writing some complete melodies, using arpeggiation of the tonic triad as part of the structure of the melody. Write six phrases, each four measures long, in the spaces provided. You may use upbeats or not as you like. Remember that the true test of a melody is how it sounds. Sing or play your examples. There are two aspects of this assignment on which it will be graded: the correctness with which it is notated *and* the melodic beauty or charm of the melody. In these first melodies, make each phrase end on the tonic note or a member of the tonic chord. Be careful to use clear musical handwriting (*calligraphy*).

𝓔AR TRAINING ASSIGNMENT

A. Each of the melodies you will hear is an example of either conjunct or disjunct motion. Underline the term that best describes the melody. See the example.

You will hear:

EXAMPLE:

1. a. Conjunct motion   b. <u>Disjunct motion</u>

2. a. Conjunct motion   b. Disjunct motion

3. a. Conjunct motion   b. Disjunct motion

4. a. Conjunct motion   b. Disjunct motion

5. a. Conjunct motion   b. Disjunct motion

6. a. Conjunct motion   b. Disjunct motion

7. a. Conjunct motion   b. Disjunct motion

8. a. Conjunct motion   b. Disjunct motion

9. a. Conjunct motion   b. Disjunct motion

10. a. Conjunct motion   b. Disjunct motion

B. *Dictation of Simple Melodies Outlining the Tonic Triad.* In each exercise you will hear a short four-measure melodic phrase. Under the rhythm indicated determine the correct scale degree numbers for each note and write them below the appropriate note. A few scale degree numbers have been written to help you. Each exercise will be played twice.

1.

2.

3.

4.

5.

6.

C. *Recognition of Contrary, Oblique, and Similar Motion.* Each exercise is a two-voice melodic excerpt. Predominating in each exercise is one of the three types of motion. Indicate the type of motion you hear most frequently in the following exercises. Underscore the correct answer. The example is illustrated and is worked correctly for you. Each example will be played twice.

You hear:

EXAMPLE:

1. <u>Contrary</u>   Oblique   Similar   4. Contrary   Oblique   Similar

2. Contrary   Oblique   Similar   5. Contrary   Oblique   Similar

3. Contrary   Oblique   Similar   6. Contrary   Oblique   Similar

Chapter 24 · Rhythmic and Melodic Motives, Melodic Repetition and Sequence

Motives

Phrases are built from smaller groups called **motives.** A **rhythmic motive** is a short, distinctive rhythmic pattern that may be repeated with different pitch patterns.

George Frideric Handel (1685–1759), *Messiah,* "Hallelujah Chorus" (1742)

A **melodic motive** has a distinctive rhythmic pattern *and* a pattern of pitch relationships.

Wolfgang Amadeus Mozart (1756–1791), *Symphony No. 41 in C Major* ("Jupiter"), First Movement (1788)

Motives can be used either without change or with some variation as long as the variation is not so great that their distinctive qualities are lost. A large musical design can be built from a single motive. The first four notes of Beethoven's *Symphony No. 5* form the basis for much of the first movement of the symphony.

Ludwig van Beethoven (1770–1827), *Symphony No. 5 in C Minor,* Op. 67, First Movement (1807–08)

Beginning statement of the rhythmic motive

Melodic variation of the motive, both in its
normal position and inverted (upside down)

Another theme beginning with the opening
rhythmic motive (melodically changed).

Listen to the whole movement of the symphony to hear how many ways Beethoven uses this motive.

Sequence

A common method of constructing a melody out of a motive is to *repeat* it at various pitch levels. This form of repetition is called a **sequence.** Each unit of a sequence is called the *leg of the sequence.*

Felix Mendelssohn (1809–1847), *Concerto in E Minor for Violin and Orchestra,* Op. 64, First Movement (1844)

Sequence of a two-measure motive

When melodic material is repeated with slight changes in some of the intervals or rhythms it is called **modified repetition.** If the pitch level of the restatement is different from that of the first presentation of the motive and changes in intervals or rhythms are used, it is called **modified sequence.**

Antonin Dvořák (1841–1904), *Symphony No. 9 in E Minor,*
Op. 95 (*From the New World*), Second Movement (1893)

Modified repetition (change of rhythm)

Johann Sebastian Bach (1685–1750), *Orchestra Suite No. 2
in B Minor for Flute and Strings,* Badinerie (late 1730s)

Modified sequence (change of interval)

Sight singing assignment

A. *Rhythmic and Melodic Motives, Repetition, and Sequence.* Sing the following melodies using numbers or syllables. Note the instances in which the devices of repetition and sequence have been used.

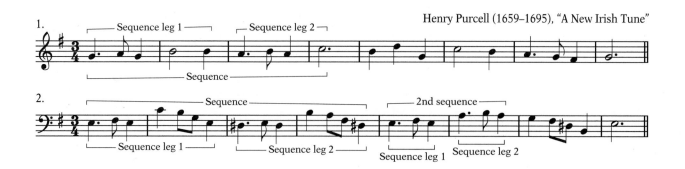

1.
Henry Purcell (1659–1695), "A New Irish Tune"

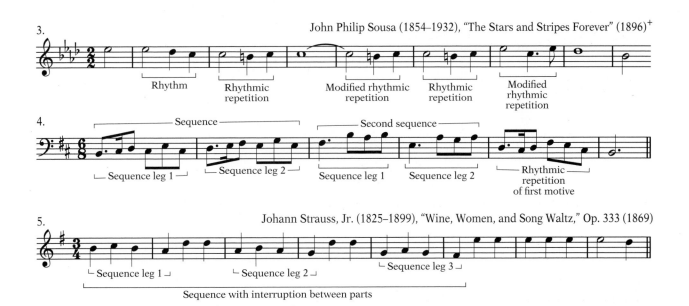

3.
John Philip Sousa (1854–1932), "The Stars and Stripes Forever" (1896)[+]

Rhythm | Rhythmic repetition | Modified rhythmic repetition | Rhythmic repetition | Modified rhythmic repetition

4.
Sequence

Second sequence

Sequence leg 1 | Sequence leg 2 | Sequence leg 1 | Sequence leg 2 | Rhythmic repetition of first motive

5.
Johann Strauss, Jr. (1825–1899), "Wine, Women, and Song Waltz," Op. 333 (1869)

Sequence leg 1 | Sequence leg 2 | Sequence leg 3

Sequence with interruption between parts

$\mathcal{W}$RITTEN ASSIGNMENT

A. Following is a group of three melodies built from *motives*. These motives are used in:

   a. Melodic and rhythmic repetition.
   b. Rhythmic repetition (but *not* melodic repetition).
   c. Sequence.

Mark each motive in brackets. In the blank supplied at the end of the melody, place the letter "a," "b," or "c" describing the way in which the motives were used. Sing all the melodies after you have analyzed them.

Wolfgang Amadeus Mozart (1756–1791), *Sonata for Violin and Piano*, K. 374e, Second Movement (1781)

1.

Georg Philipp Telemann (1683–1767), *Partita a cembalo solo in G Major* (1728)

2.

Joseph Haydn (1732–1809), *String Quartet*, Op. 64, No. 2, Menuetto (1790)

3.

$\mathcal{E}$AR TRAINING ASSIGNMENT

A. *Recognition of Melodic Sequences.* In each exercise you will hear a four-measure melody that uses a sequence. Write the scale numbers in the blanks. Then write the notes on the staff. The example is illustrated and is worked correctly for you. Each exercise will be played twice.

EXAMPLE:

PART V · Harmony

Chapter 25 · Triad Arrangements

One could look through a considerable stack of music and not find a single triad that looks like those illustrated so far. What you have seen so far is a "simple" arrangement of triads for easy identification. However, professional composers prefer to weave (arrange) triads into the fabric of music so that the vertical (harmonic) and the horizontal (melodic) aspects blend to form a more musically satisfying result. Take, for example, the first phrase of "A Mighty Fortress Is Our God" as arranged here. The melody (soprano voice) is a **chorale** or hymn tune by Martin Luther, but many composers, including J. S. Bach, have harmonized and arranged the tune according to their own tastes.

Martin Luther (1453–1546), "Ein' feste Burg," (A Mighty Fortress Is Our God) (1529)

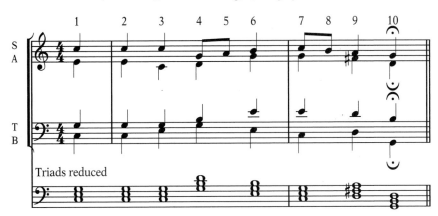

Much can be learned from this short phrase:

1. It is a four-voice (**soprano, alto, tenor, bass**) arrangement intended to be sung, but for the moment you can play it yourself on a piano, or play it together with a friend—one playing the soprano and alto parts and the other playing the tenor and bass parts.
2. If reading all four voices is beyond your capacity, play the soprano (highest) notes together with the block (simple) triads provided on the third staff. You will probably discover also why composers seldom employ triads arranged so simply.
3. For ease in identifying the triads, they are shown in simple arrangement (whole notes) on the bottom staff. This bottom staff is only for convenience and is not a part of the musical composition.
4. Because this arrangement is for four voices and triads contain only three pitches, one must be doubled (appear twice). In all instances the doubled note is the *root* of the triad—a common occurrence in four-voice writing.
5. The bass (lowest voice) contains the root of all triads in the phrase except at number 3. Here the 3rd (E) is the bass note. When the bass note is *not* the root of the triad, it is said to be "inverted." This will be explained later.
6. It is easy to identify and follow the individual voices in this arrangement:
   a. Soprano voice—treble clef—note stems up
   b. Alto voice—treble clef—note stems down
   c. Tenor voice—bass clef—note stems up
   d. Bass voice—bass clef—note stems down

7. The eighth notes at numbers 5 and 8 are not a part of the existing triads. Observe in the soprano voice that note 5 fills in the gap (interval of a third) between notes 4 and 6, whereas note 8 acts in the same capacity between notes 7 and 9. These fall into a large category known as *nonharmonic tones,* and within that category they are known more specifically as **passing tones.** See Chapter 27 for a full discussion of nonharmonic tones.

Musicians add roman numeral **chord symbols** below each triad to show how it relates to the scale, as shown here:

Roman numeral analysis

I   ii   iii   IV   V   vi   vii°

Uppercase means *major triad.*
Lowercase means *minor triad.*
Lowercase and degree sign (°) means *diminished triad.*

Triad Positions—Inversions

In almost all the triads analyzed previously in this chapter, the lowest-sounding tone (usually bass) is also the root (that is, the triad is in root position). Here again it would be rare to find a complete composition in which all the triad roots were also the lowest-sounding tones. For purposes of smooth voice leading, composers found it musically more expressive to exercise freedom of choice in selecting triad positions as well as arrangements.

The **position** of a triad is determined entirely by the lowest note:

Root position—Lowest note is the *root.*
First inversion—Lowest note is the *third.*
Second inversion—Lowest note is the *fifth.*

To arrange (or voice) a triad, C E G for example, you can change the order of the pitches and add voices: C G E C, C E C G, C G C E C, and so on. However, while arranging the triad, if the lowest note remains the same, the position also remains the same. To change the position while arranging, the lowest note must change to another triad tone:

Root position arrangements   First inversion arrangements   Second inversion arrangements

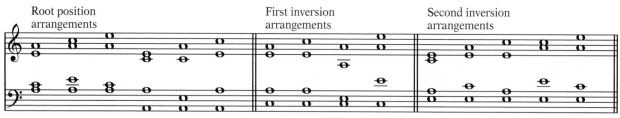

Lowest note is root.   Lowest note is third.   Lowest note is fifth.

WRITTEN ASSIGNMENT

A. The following phrase is similar in type to the illustration on page 229. Play it over several times to get familiar with the sound. If playing all four voices is too much, try playing only the two outer voices (soprano and bass). You'll still get some idea of the composition.

1. On the blank staff reduce the four-voice arrangements to simple triads as shown in the illustration.
2. Circle nonharmonic tones if any.
3. Check to see whether the triad roots are doubled, as they are in the illustration, and place a square around each doubled note.
4. Place an X under any chord where the bass note is *not* the root of the triad (that is, chords in first or second inversion).

"All through the Night," traditional Welsh air

B. This excerpt is similar to the example in Assignment A except that it is written for piano. Observe that all notes in the treble clef are attached to a single stem, meaning that the pianist plays all three notes with the right hand.

Treat Assignment B exactly as you did Assignment A and follow the four assignment steps.

Frédéric Chopin (1810–1849), *Nocturne for Piano*, Op. 37, No. 1 (1839)

C. Three examples are provided to help you determine the correct procedure for this assignment. Complete each of these four steps for each exercise.

1. Using a black notehead, copy the bass note of each arranged triad on the lowest (blank) staff.
2. Using whole notes, copy the remaining two pitches of the triad above or below the black notehead. The *simple* (notes as close together as possible) form of the triad should now be showing on the lowest (third) staff.

3. Determine the *type* (major or minor) of triad and write either "M" or "m" in the blank beneath the lowest staff.
4. Look at the black notehead.
   a. If it is the root of the triad, write "Root" in the blank above the staves.
   b. If it is the third of the triad, write "1st Inv" in the blank above the staves.
   c. If it is the fifth of the triad, write "2nd Inv" in the blank above the staves.

Examples of correct procedure:

*K*EYBOARD ASSIGNMENT

Playing Major Triads in Various Positions.

1. Play the example in A as written.
2. After observing the four-voice pattern played on the C major triad and then for the F major triad, continue the same pattern on B♭, E♭, and A♭ major triads successively.
3. Complete B in the same manner as A. Continue the pattern on with the D, G, and C major triads.

Note in the examples that the soprano and bass both contain the root of the triads. Then the bass moves up from root to third and then to the fifth. Make sure when you continue on (after the written-out patterns) that you maintain the same relationships.

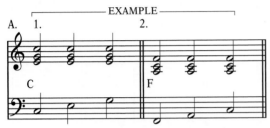

Continue with B♭, E♭, and A♭ major triads

Continue with D, G, and C major triads

SIGHT SINGING ASSIGNMENT

A. *Singing a Bass Line in Four-Part Harmony.* Several short phrases in four-part harmony will be played. The first time each one is played listen to the bass line. Then, when it is played again, sing along with the bass line. Use the letter names of the notes or syllables if you like. If your voice is in a treble range, sing the bass line an octave higher.

$\mathcal{E}$AR TRAINING ASSIGNMENT

A. This assignment examines four-voice major and minor triads in a chorale setting. Each exercise consists of six or seven chords (a phrase), and you are to write "M" (for major) or "m" (for minor) triads in the blanks provided. All are either major or minor except the one noted in No. 5, which is marked as a diminished triad.

1. 1. _____   2. _____   3. _____   4. _____   5. _____   6. _____   7. _____

2. 1. _____   2. _____   3. _____   4. _____   5. _____   6. _____

3. 1. _____   2. _____   3. _____   4. _____   5. _____   6. _____   7. _____

4. 1. _____   2. _____   3. _____   4. _____   5. _____   6. _____   7. _____

5. 1. _____   2. _____   3. _____   4. _____   5. _____   6. _d_   7. _____

6. 1. _____   2. _____   3. _____   4. _____   5. _____   6. _____   7. _____

B. In the following assignment you are to identify four-voice tonic triads in six- or seven-chord phrases.

1. Place an "I" in the blanks under the tonic triads.
2. It is not necessary to write in the other blanks.

Chord numbers:

	1	2	3	4	5	6	7
1.	__	__	__	__	__	__	__
2.	__	__	__	__	__	__	__
3.	__	__	__	__	__	__	__

	1	2	3	4	5	6	7
4.	__	__	__	__	__	__	__
5.	__	__	__	__	__	__	__
6.	__	__	__	__	__	__	

C. In the following assignment you are to identify four-voice tonic triads in seven-chord phrases.
1. Place an "i" (minor tonic) in the blanks representing the tonic triad.
2. It is not necessary to write in the other blanks.

Chord numbers:

	1	2	3	4	5	6	7
1.	__	__	__	__	__	__	__
2.	__	__	__	__	__	__	__
3.	__	__	__	__	__	__	__
4.	__	__	__	__	__	__	__

D. *Bass Line Dictation.* Four short phrases will be played in four-part harmony. All the parts are as you see them, but the bass line is missing. Write the notes on the staff for the bass line. Each exercise will be played twice.

arr. from Louis Bourgeois (1510?–1561?), *Pseaumes octante trois de David,* "Old 100th" (1551)

1.

3.

harm. by Johann Sebastian Bach (1685–1750), "Christ lag in Todesbanden" (Christ Lay in the Bonds of Death), BWV 4 (ca. 1707)

2.

4.

Progressions—The I, IV, and V Triads

Triads, of course, have a nature of their own. They may be major or minor and built on any degree of any scale, but when composers place them one after another in a composition, they create a **chord progression.** A progression may refer to a succession of only two chords or to a series of any length. Some of the most common progressions in music include the tonic, subdominant, and dominant triads—I, IV, and V, respectively.

A very common chord (triad) progression

Primary Triads and the Circle-of-Fifths Progression

The chord progression I, IV, V, I is one of the most common in all of music because it is made up entirely of **primary triads** (I, IV, V) and contains two **circle progressions.** A circle progression occurs when the roots of two adjacent triads lie in a circle-of-fifths relationship:

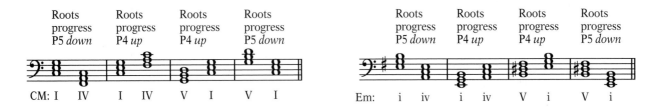

Circle-of-Fifths Progressions

In a circle-of-fifths progression (often shortened simply to *circle progression*), the root of the second triad may lie a perfect fifth *below* or a perfect fourth *above* that of the first. If this seems confusing, remember simply that V to I is a circle progression whether the roots go from V *down* to I or V *up* to I. Likewise, I to IV is a circle progression whether I *down* to IV or I *up* to IV.

The circle progression is the single most important shaping force in all of tonal music, whether it is a folk song, popular song, jazz, rock, or concert music in the European tradition.

Nonharmonic Tones

Almost all melodies are a mixture of notes, some of which duplicate accompanying chord factors and some of which do not. Those melody pitches that also belong to the chord are, of course, **chord tones,** and the others are called *nonharmonic tones.** The nonharmonic tones in the first phrase of "Home on the Range" are circled:

---

* For further study of nonharmonic tones, see Chapter 27, p. 249.

In the above illustration the notes at numbers 1 and 2 are called *passing tones* because they pass from one tone to a different tone. Numbers 3 and 4 are **neighboring tones** because they occur between two tones of the same pitch.

*H*armonic Cadences

Chapter 22 discussed two aspects of musical punctuation (cadences)—melody and rhythm. This chapter adds the third ingredient—harmony.

A *harmonic cadence* consists usually of two chords occurring along with the melodic and rhythmic cadence. The two most common and important harmonic cadences are the **authentic** and the **half.** The authentic cadence ends on a tonic chord, whereas half cadences end on a dominant chord.

Authentic cadence = V to I
Half cadence = I to V or IV to V

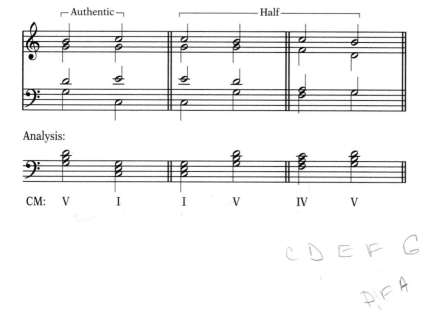

*For further discussion of nonharmonic tones, see Chapter 27.

The following example illustrates both the half and authentic cadences in the context of a composition:

Half and authentic cadences

Robert Schumann (1810–1856), *Album für die Jugend* (*Album for the Young*), "Wild Rider" (1848)

Imperfect and Perfect Authentic Cadences

The authentic cadence is called **perfect** if the melodic phrase ends with the tonic note (root of the tonic triad). When the melody concludes on the third or fifth scale degree (third or fifth of the tonic triad), the cadence is termed **imperfect.**

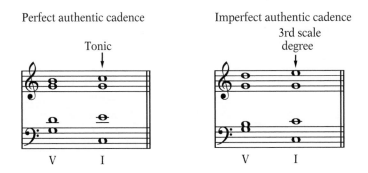

Both perfect and imperfect authentic cadences occur in the folk song "Jimmy Crack Corn."

"Jimmy Crack Corn," American folk song[+]

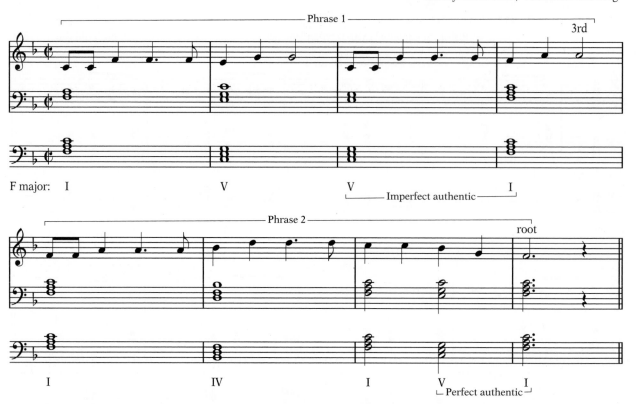

SIGHT SINGING ASSIGNMENT

A. *Sight Singing More Melodies.* Sing the following melodies. Use scale degree numbers, syllables, or the neutral syllable *la*.

WRITTEN ASSIGNMENT

In this assignment, you will be writing the I, IV, and V triads.

A. 1. Write the I, IV, V, I progression in each of the keys indicated. The example indicates correct procedure.
2. Go to a piano and play each progression.
3. Go back to the beginning of the assignment and sing (from lowest to highest note) the triads you have written. This will help in recognizing the same triads in the ear training assignments.

The most efficient way to work out this assignment is to:

1. Write the roots of each triad on the staff first. Be sure your placement of the first root will allow enough lines and spaces for writing the remaining three triads.
2. When all roots have been located and written, fill in the remaining two factors of all triads.

1. EXAMPLE: 2.   3.

B♭M: I   IV   V   I   GM: ___ ___ ___ ___   Em: ___ ___ ___ ___

4.   5.   6.

FM: ___ ___ ___ ___   Dm: ___ ___ ___ ___   Gm: ___ ___ ___ ___

7.   8.   9.

DM: ___ ___ ___ ___   Bm: ___ ___ ___ ___   E♭M: ___ ___ ___ ___

10.   11.   12.

Cm: ___ ___ ___ ___   AM: ___ ___ ___ ___   F♯m: ___ ___ ___ ___

13.   14.   15.

A♭M: ___ ___ ___ ___   Fm: ___ ___ ___ ___   EM: ___ ___ ___ ___

16.   17.   18.

C♯m: ___ ___ ___ ___   BM: ___ ___ ___ ___   G♯m: ___ ___ ___ ___

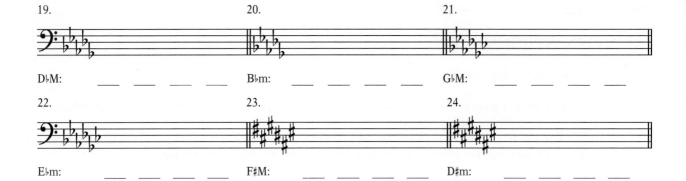

19.

D♭M: ___ ___ ___ ___

20.

B♭m: ___ ___ ___ ___

21.

G♭M: ___ ___ ___ ___

22.

E♭m: ___ ___ ___ ___ ___

23.

F♯M: ___ ___ ___ ___

24.

D♯m: ___ ___ ___ ___ ___

In this assignment, you will be identifying circle progressions.

B. Each exercise consists of roman numeral analysis symbols for a set of progressions. Add slurs (⌣) to connect all circle-of-fifth progressions.

EXAMPLE

1. V ⌣ I ⌣ IV   I   V ⌣ I   6. V   I   IV   V   I   IV

2. I   IV   V   I   V   I   7. V   IV   I   I   V   IV

3. V   V   I   I   IV   I   8. I   IV   V   I   IV   V

4. IV   I   I   IV   IV   V   9. V   V   I   IV   I   IV

5. V   I   V   I   I   IV

C. This is the same as Assignment B except that the triads are written out. The lowest note is always the root.

1. Analyze the triads and write the roman numeral analysis in the blanks.
2. Add the slurs to connect the circle progressions.

The example indicates correct procedure.

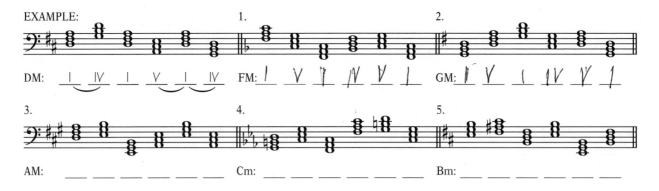

EXAMPLE:

DM: I IV I V I IV

1.

FM: I V I IV V I

2.

GM: I V I IV V I

3.

AM: ___ ___ ___ ___ ___ ___

4.

Cm: ___ ___ ___ ___ ___ ___

5.

Bm: ___ ___ ___ ___ ___ ___

D. This assignment is the same as Assignment C except that the lowest note may be the root, third, or fifth of the triad.

1. Find the root of each triad and blacken the whole note representing it.
2. Write the analysis of each triad in the blank provided. Remember that the root is the filled-in whole note.
3. Add slurs to connect circle-of-fifths progressions.
4. Play each progression on a piano.

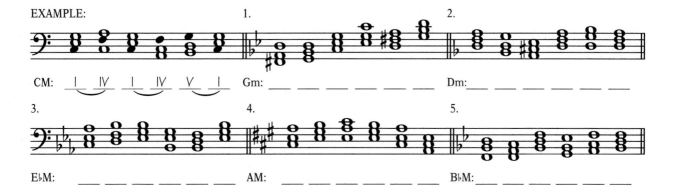

EXAMPLE: 1.   2.

CM: I   IV   I   IV   V   I   Gm: ___ ___ ___ ___ ___ ___   Dm: ___ ___ ___ ___ ___ ___

3.   4.   5.

EbM: ___ ___ ___ ___ ___ ___   AM: ___ ___ ___ ___ ___ ___   BbM: ___ ___ ___ ___ ___ ___

E. In the following exercises identify the nonharmonic tones.

1. Sing each melody and play the triads in simple position (as written).
2. Repeat the procedure in Step 1, but this time restrike the triad each time you sing a new note.
3. Circle each melody pitch you think does not agree (is nonharmonic) with the accompaniment triad.
4. When finished with this procedure, check the answers that you determined by sound alone. If the letter name of a melody note is not one of those found in the accompaniment triad, it is nonharmonic.

Franz Schubert (1797–1828), *Symphony No. 8* ("Unfinished"), First Movement (1822)

G major: I   V   V   I

Patrick Gilmore (1829–1892), "When Johnny Comes Marching Home" (1863)[+]

g minor: i   i   III   VII   i

i   III   V

"Believe Me, If All Those Endearing Young Charms," traditional Irish air

C major: I   IV   I   V   I

Johann Sebastian Bach (1685–1750), *Orchestra Suite No. 1 in C Major,* Bourrée (ca. 1720)

C major: I   I   I   IV   V

F. Each of the following exercises, designed to assist you in identifying cadences, consists of four triads in four-voice harmony. Triads 3 and 4 form a cadence.

1. Write each triad in simple position on the blank staff provided.
2. Place the roman numeral analysis in the blanks provided.
3. In the blank beneath triads 3 and 4 write the type of cadence: (1) perfect authentic, (2) imperfect authentic, (3) half.
4. Play each progression. If you like, one person can play the treble voices while another plays the bass clef voices.

EAR TRAINING ASSIGNMENT

A. In each exercise the teacher will play seven or eight four-voice triads (a chorale phrase). Each triad may be I or i (tonic), V (dominant), or some other triad.

    1.   Write "I" or "i" in the blanks where you hear a tonic triad.
    2.   Write "V" in the blanks where you hear a V (dominant) triad.
    3.   Do not write in the other blanks.

    1. ___ ___ ___ ___ ___ ___ ___   4. ___ ___ ___ ___ ___ ___ ___

    2. ___ ___ ___ ___ ___ ___ ___ ___   5. ___ ___ ___ ___ ___ ___ ___ ___

    3. ___ ___ ___ ___ ___ ___ ___ ___   6. ___ ___ ___ ___ ___ ___ ___

B. In each exercise your teacher will play a phrase of five triads in four-voice harmony. Identify the I, IV, and V triads by writing their roman numeral analysis in the appropriate blanks.

    1. ___ ___ ___ ___ ___   4. ___ ___ ___ ___ ___

    2. ___ ___ ___ ___ ___   5. ___ ___ ___ ___ ___

    3. ___ ___ ___ ___ ___   6. ___ ___ ___ ___ ___

C. The purpose of this assignment is to identify tonic, dominant, and subdominant (i iv V) in seven-chord phrases in minor. Write the appropriate analysis symbols in the blanks provided. The chord (VI) other than i iv V chords used in these exercises is identified for you.

    1. ___ $\underset{\text{VI}}{\_\_\_}$ ___ ___ ___ ___ ___

    2. ___ ___ ___ ___ ___ ___ ___

    3. ___ ___ ___ $\underset{\text{VI}}{\_\_\_}$ ___ ___ ___

    4. ___ ___ ___ ___ ___ ___ ___

Chapter 27 ▪ Nonharmonic Tones

As we saw in "Home on the Range" in the preceding chapter, melodies may contain both chord tones (the notes of the underlying harmony) and **nonharmonic tones,** embellishing notes that do not belong to the chord being sounded. A melody harmonized by chords may have nonharmonic tones that move between or around notes of the chord, make a dissonance that then resolves to a chord tone, or even leap to or from the notes of the chords. Combinations of patterns are also used for more complex decorations, or *ornaments,* added to a melody, as in *trills* (normally a rapid alternation of the chord tone and its upper neighboring tone) or such complicated combinations as a jazz singer's embellishments.

Whether used in groups or as single notes, each type of nonharmonic tone can be described in terms of the *note preceding* the nonharmonic tone (*preparation* note), the *nonharmonic tone itself,* and the *note to which it moves (resolution).* The nonharmonic tone is normally dissonant with the harmony. The pattern can be described as:

preparation note —————— nonharmonic tone —————— resolution

The melody below has several kinds of nonharmonic tones.

"Shenandoah," American folk song[+]

Measure 2 has two *passing tones* (marked PT)—approached and left by step in the same direction. The nonharmonic tone or tones may be accented or unaccented. The pattern may be up or down.

Melodic contour   ← *Passing tone*

Measure 3 has an *appoggiatura* (marked AP)—approached by leap and left by step *downward.*

Melodic contour   ← *Appoggiatura*

Measure 4 has a *neighboring tone* (marked NT)—approached by step and going back to the original pitch for the resolution note. Neighboring tones may be accented or unaccented, and the pattern may go up or down.

Nonharmonic tones may occur anywhere in the texture—in the top voice, in inner parts, or in the bass. Those shown in "Shenandoah" are all notes of a treble melody accompanied by chords. In the next example there are two nonharmonic tones: a *neighboring tone* in measure three of the melody voice (here sung by a bass voice, and so below the accompanying chords in the orchestra). There is also an *escape tone* (ET), which is approached by step and left by skip. It is usually unaccented, and is often approached from below and left by downward leap. It is in measure 2 in the lowest part of the orchestra.

George Frideric Handel (1685–1759), *Messiah*, "But Who May Abide" (1742)

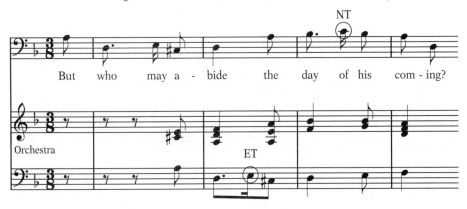

The **suspension** is prepared by a chord tone that is continued into the new chord (either tied or repeated), which then resolves stepwise down into the chord tone of the new chord. The suspension note itself is on an accented part of the beat.

"The Yellow Rose of Texas" (second phrase), American folk song[+]

In this excerpt from "The Yellow Rose of Texas" (a tune that will be discussed further in the next chapter), there is a *suspension* (SUS) without a tie in the melody.

Another nonharmonic tone is the **anticipation** (ANT), which arrives ahead of the beat on which the chord itself changes. This is one of the nonharmonic tones in "A Whole New World."

Melodic contour   *Anticipation*
(may be approached
Chord movement   from above or below)

In the first measure you will find another new pattern, the **changing tones** (CT), in which the melody left the chord tone by step, skipped to another nonharmonic tone, and resolved by step in the next measure at the chord change.

Melodic contour   *Changing tones*

Chord movement   Resolution

In this melody another choice was made for the same melodic pattern when it appeared in the third measure. There, the $b\flat'$ and d'' were set by a $B\flat$ major triad, the IV chord, instead of being treated as nonharmonic tones over the F major I chord.

Tim Rice, lyrics, and Alan Menken (1950–), music, *Aladdin*, "A Whole New World"[+]

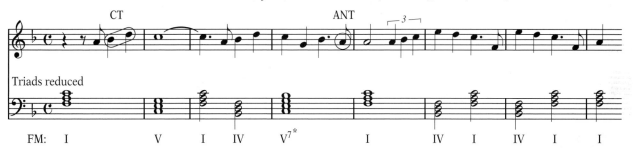

There are other nonharmonic tones in "A Whole New World." Find them and mark them.

The **retardation** (RT) is like a suspension except that the resolution is *up* instead of *down*. The example below also contains a suspension. Find it and mark it.

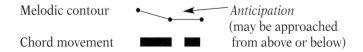

Melodic contour   *Retardation*
(approached from the same
Chord movement   note and resolves up)

Christoph W. Gluck (1714–1787), *Orfeo ed Euridice*, "Che farò senza Euridice?" (What Shall I Do without Euridice?) (1762)

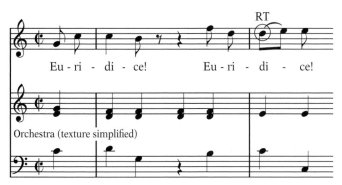

* See Chapter 28 for more discussion of this chord.

When a long note is held in the bass while harmonic or melodic activity in which it does not participate goes on above it, it is called a **pedal tone** because in organ music it is very often found in the pedal part, as in the Bach piece below.

Johann Sebastian Bach (1685–1750), *Organ Fugue in G Minor,* BWV 578 (1703–07)

Pedal tone

Although nonharmonic tones can occur as an essential part of a melody, they can also be added to an existing melody. In the old hymn "Amazing Grace," the original melody may be accompanied by harmony, or decorations may be added to the simple form of the melody. The melody is given below with its basic harmonies; the line above the melody shows some possible embellishments. Some are nonharmonic tones, and some are added notes that are chord tones. Mark the nonharmonic tones with circles, and identify each of them by the abbreviation for the name. Place a square around added notes that use chord tones.

"Amazing Grace," southern hymn tune (originally in *Virginia Harmony,* 1833)[+]

This tune is often played by bagpipes.* Bagpipe tunes are always accompanied by a **drone,** a particular kind of pedal point that lasts for the entire piece without changing. In this piece an octave on A sounds throughout the whole piece. This is not notated in bagpipe music, but you probably have heard the effect! Bagpipes have a special kind of ornamentation. Because a rest or other articulation is impossible since the bagpipe sound is continuous, ornaments are added to articulate between phrases, to separate repeated notes, and to give accents. As you see, they are quite different from the vocal style ornaments on the previous page.

*On this instrument the tune must be played in D Major because a limited number of notes are available on the instrument.

SIGHT SINGING AND WRITTEN ASSIGNMENT

A. In each of the following tunes there are some nonharmonic tones. Sing the tunes alone and also with guitar or keyboard playing the chords, changing chords where indicated. You may sing while a classmate plays the harmonies and then switch roles.

    The examples in the chapter had reduced triads placed under each melody to give you the notes of the chord. However, tunes are often printed with *chord symbols* written above the melody. The uppercase letters refer to the roots of the chords. If only the root name is given, the chord is a major triad (that is, C means a C major triad). If it is a minor triad, the root name is given and followed by a lowercase *m* (that is, Cm means a C minor triad).†

    In the following exercises, see if you can find the notes for each of the symbols given, then play them while you or someone else sings the melody. After singing them with the chords, mark each nonharmonic tone, using the following abbreviations: PT (passing tone), NT (neighboring tone), ANT (anticipation), ET (**escape tone**), and SUS (suspension). There are no changing tones, anticipations, or pedal tones in these exercises.

    The symbol A⁷ calls for the chord A–C♯–E–G, a seventh chord, which will be explained in the following chapter.

†More chord symbols will be discussed in Chapter 28 and are summarized on p. 263.

‡This is a shortened form of the original version of this tune (ca. 1800).

B. *Additional Practice Sight Singing Melodies.*

1.
Robert Schumann (1810–1856), *Album für die Jugend,* "Sicilienne" (1848)

2.
"Hop sa sa!" German folk song

Alexander Muir (1830–1906), "The Maple Leaf Forever" (1867)

3.

$\mathcal{E}$AR TRAINING ASSIGNMENT

A. In each exercise you will hear a short phrase in four-part harmony. The soprano part of each phrase will contain a nonharmonic tone. Write the name or abbreviation of the nonharmonic tone you hear in each phrase in the blank provided.

  The nonharmonic note patterns you will hear will be passing tone (PT), neighboring tone (NT), anticipation (ANT), suspension (SUS), escape tone (ET) or appoggiatura (AP).

1. _____   7. _____

2. _____   8. _____

3. _____   9. _____

4. _____   10. _____

5. _____   11. _____

6. _____   12. _____

B. *Further exercises in hearing tonic and dominant chords in short progressions.* You will hear groups of chords played on keyboard or guitar. Label each I or V in the blanks provided.

1. ____ ____ ____ ____ ____   5. ____ ____ ____ ____ ____

2. ____ ____ ____ ____ ____   6. ____ ____ ____ ____ ____

3. ____ ____ ____ ____ ____   7. ____ ____ ____ ____ ____

4. ____ ____ ____ ____ ____   8. ____ ____ ____ ____ ____

C. A group of melodies accompanied by strummed chords on guitar or block chords on the piano will be played, each melody twice.

  1. The time signature of each melody will be given to you. When it is played the first time, mark bar lines between the appropriate groups of beats. All the melodies begin on the first beat of a measure.
  2. Some beats will have nonharmonic tones in the melody. The second time you hear the tune, write the abbreviation for the nonharmonic tone *on the beat in which the nonharmonic tone is sounded.* Use the abbreviations on the preceding page. If there is no nonharmonic tone on a beat, leave the space blank.

1. $\frac{4}{4}$ ____ ____ ____ ____ ____ ____ ____ ____ ____

2. $\frac{3}{4}$ ____ ____ ____ ____ ____ ____ ____ ____ ____

3. $\frac{4}{4}$ ____ ____ ____ ____ ____ ____ ____ ____ ____

4. $\frac{4}{4}$ ____ ____ ____ ____ ____ ____ ____ ____ ____

5. $\frac{2}{4}$ ____ ____ ____ ____ ____ ____ ____

Chapter 28 ▪ Harmonizing a Melody

Accompanying a Melody

Some melodies, like those often found in the tradition of European concert music, are considered to be an integral part of a composition, are interlaced throughout the work, and are seldom regarded out of context. However, most folk tunes and popular song melodies represent a vast accumulation of melodic wealth that is often given a personal touch by professional composers, arrangers, and, of course, musical amateurs. Most of these melodies will support different chord progressions and interpretations—to suit individual taste. Whether done by professionals or those who simply enjoy music, the process of providing interesting harmony to accompany a melody is known as **harmonizing.**

Harmonizing "The Yellow Rose of Texas"

You may have heard "The Yellow Rose of Texas" harmonized in several ways, but the way shown here is one of the simplest.

"The Yellow Rose of Texas," American folk song[+]

Sing the melody in class without accompaniment. Some observations regarding the melody and its harmonization are:

1. While you sing, some possible accompanying triads might come to mind because a melody will often suggest its own harmony.
2. The notes of the first five measures strongly suggest a tonic (C E G) triad because all, except the nonharmonic tones (circled in the illustration), are notes of that triad.
3. The notes of the last three measures offer a less convincing suggestion of the dominant (G B D) triad. Only the 3rd and 5th (but not the root) of the G B D triad occur in the melody. Furthermore, the increased number of nonharmonic tones weakens the choice.
4. The numbered tones in the example are all nonharmonic tones. 1, 3, 4, 6, and 7 are called passing tones because they pass (either up or down) from one triad note to another.
5. Nonharmonic tones 2 and 8 are known as neighboring tones because after departing from the triad note, they return to the same note.
6. Nonharmonic tone No. 5 is a *suspension* note, which you learned about in Chapter 27.
7. This short excerpt demonstrates a most important point in harmonizing a folk song: *select triads whose notes are also melody notes.* This might be a slight oversimplification, but remembering it as a rule of thumb is quite important.
8. Also, remember that folk songs require simple accompaniments. The three primary triads—I, IV, V—can be used to harmonize about 50 percent of all folk songs.

Harmonize with Mozart

If you now have the impression that only folk songs contain simple harmony, the next illustration, by Mozart, demonstrates that recognized composers of the past also found primary triads (I, IV, and V) of ample expressive quality.

Wolfgang Amadeus Mozart (1756–1791), *Minuet in F Major for Piano*, K. 2 (1762)

Triads reduced:

FM: I   IV   I   V   V   I

Sing the melody and play the simplified accompaniment to this excerpt. Perhaps a class member knows this composition and can play it with its more interesting full accompaniment. When you are well acquainted with the example, observe the following:

1. The first two measures of the melody outline the tonic (I) and subdominant (IV) triads.
2. Measure 3, beats 1 and 2, clearly outlines the tonic triad again.
3. The two melody notes E (fourth bracket) are harmonized by the V triad because the note E is not a part of either I or IV.
4. In measure 1, the melody calls specifically for tonic harmonization because the entire tonic triad is outlined. However, when melody notes are stepwise, as they are near the end of this phrase, the implied harmony is not as clear.
5. Try playing this excerpt again, substituting other triads for those shown. See if you can find a harmonization that you like even better than the chords Mozart selected.

Seventh Chords

Although triads consist of two intervals of a third, one stacked above the other, composers often extend triads to include one further interval of a third. When an additional factor above the fifth is added, the new harmonic unit is called a **seventh chord**—so named because the new interval is a seventh above the root. Thus, a seventh chord has four factors: root, third, fifth, and seventh. Like triads, seventh chords exhibit a variety of sound qualities and are named according to the quality of the triad and the seventh. As an example, a seventh chord containing a major triad and a major seventh is termed a major-major seventh chord (MM 7th). Although theoretically there are twenty possible seventh-chord qualities, only those found within the notes available in the major and minor scales are used often by composers:

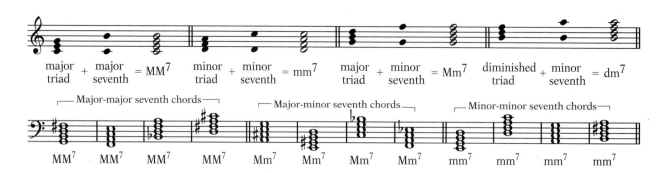

Seventh-Chord Qualities in Major Scales

TRIAD QUALITY	+	SEVENTH QUALITY	=	SEVENTH-CHORD QUALITY	EXAMPLES	ROMAN NUMERALS
M		M		MM	I^7 and IV^7	Uppercase
M		m		Mm	V^7 (only)	Uppercase
m		m		mm	ii^7 iii^7 vi^7	Lowercase
d		m		dm*	$vii^{ø7}$	Lowercase

In this table of seventh-chord qualities, the degree sign (°) alone would mean that both the triad and seventh are diminished, but when the slash is added(ø), only the triad is diminished. Here the triad is diminished, but the seventh is minor.

Summary of seventh chords in the key of C major
Seventh factor is shown in whole notes

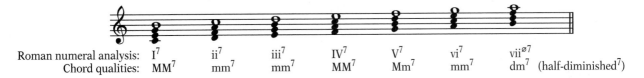

Roman numeral analysis: I^7 ii^7 iii^7 IV^7 V^7 vi^7 $vii^{ø7}$
Chord qualities: MM^7 mm^7 mm^7 MM^7 Mm^7 mm^7 dm^7 (half-diminished^7)

Seventh-Chord Qualities in Minor Scales

The seventh chords of the natural minor scale are exactly the same as the seventh chords of the major scale, although the chords fall on different scale degrees.

Seventh chords in C natural minor

Natural

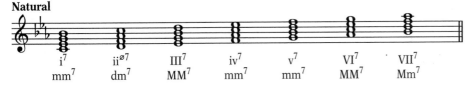

i^7 $ii^{ø7}$ III^7 iv^7 v^7 VI^7 VII^7
mm^7 dm^7 MM^7 mm^7 mm^7 MM^7 Mm^7

The use of the leading tone in the harmonic minor scale creates new seventh-chord qualities that are not found in the major scale.

Seventh chords in C harmonic minor

Harmonic:

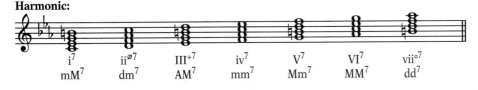

i^7 $ii^{ø7}$ III^{+7} iv^7 V^7 VI^7 $vii^{°7}$
mM^7 dm^7 AM^7 mm^7 Mm^7 MM^7 dd^7

Melodic (ascending): Seventh chords in C melodic minor (ascending)

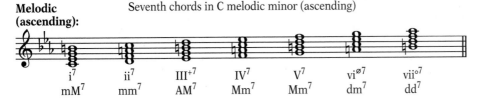

i^7 ii^7 III^{+7} IV^7 V^7 $vi^{ø7}$ $vii^{°7}$
mM^7 mm^7 AM^7 Mm^7 Mm^7 dm^7 dd^7

Summary of the seventh chords in the key of c minor

*The chord with a diminished triad and a minor seventh is known as a *half-diminished seventh chord.*

The chords that include the raised leading tone are the most dissonant chords in the diatonic system.

Dissonant seventh chord qualities in C harmonic minor

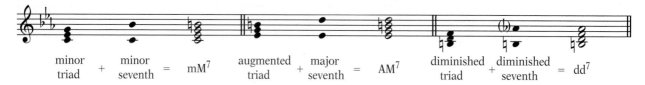

| minor
triad | + | minor
seventh | = | mM⁷ | augmented
triad | + | major
seventh | = | AM⁷ | diminished
triad | + | diminished
seventh | = | dd⁷ |

Seventh-Chord Qualities in Natural and Harmonic Minor Scales

TRIAD QUALITY	+	SEVENTH QUALITY	=	SEVENTH-CHORD QUALITY	EXAMPLES IN HARMONIC (H) AND NATURAL (N) MINOR SCALES	ROMAN NUMERALS
M		m		Mm⁷	N: VII⁷ H: V⁷	Uppercase
m		m		mm⁷	N: i⁷, iv⁷, v⁷ H: iv⁷	Lowercase
m		M		mM⁷	N: none H: i⁷	Lowercase
M		M		MM⁷	N: III⁷, VI⁷ H: VI⁷	Uppercase
d		m		dm⁷	N: ii°⁷ H: ii°⁷	Lowercase
d		d		dd⁷	N: none H: vii°⁷	Lowercase
A		M		AM⁷	H: none H: III⁺⁷	Uppercase

Chord Symbols and Roman Numeral Analysis

Music for jazz and popular songs is generally published in a **fake book.** The fake book is made up of pages of **lead sheets,** or music that contains three primary elements: a single melodic line, chord symbols above the melody that are placed above the measure in rhythmic relation to the moment of harmonic change (thus the use of the word *changes* when referring to chord symbols on a jazz lead sheet), and text (if any) printed below the staff. Some fake books are commonly referred to as *song books* and contain a fully scored piano part and may include guitar tablature. Many song books use the simple guitar chords as found in Appendix 3.

Chord symbols have a very different function from roman numeral harmonic analysis. Roman numeral analysis is designed to show harmonic relationships in any key: major or minor (modal music uses the same analytical system). A review of roman numeral analysis shows that each symbol consists of the following elements:

1. The roman numeral indicates the scale degree of the root of the triad.
2. Uppercase roman numerals indicate major triads; lowercase roman numerals indicate minor triads.
3. Augmented chords use an uppercase roman numeral with an added +, and diminished triads use a lowercase roman numeral with an added °.
4. Numbers are used to indicate notes that are added to the triad.

5. The number indicates the interval of the note above the root of the triad.
6. Numbers indicating the harmonic extension above the triad, such as 7ths and other dissonances, always assume the diatonic interval above the root of the chord. Although major and minor sevenths do not use special notations to indicate the quality of the interval, diminished sevenths that are found in fully diminished seventh chords use °, whereas ø indicates a minor seventh added to a diminished triad (the half-diminished seventh chord).

Chord symbols give information about the notes of the chord and imply additional notes that may be used in improvisation. A chord symbol has these elements:

1. The uppercase letter always indicates the root of the triad.
2. The accidental (if any) of the note follows the uppercase letter.
3. The major triad uses the uppercase letter only.
4. Minor triads include an "m" or "mi" after the chord.
5. Diminished triads are usually indicated with °.
6. Augmented triads are indicated with +.
7. Extensions of the chord beyond the triad are indicated by numbers that represent the interval above the root.

Following are some frequently used chord symbols:

CHORD SYMBOL	MEANS	SPELLED			
G	Major triad whose root is G	G	B	D	
Gm	Minor triad whose root is G	G	B♭	D	
G♯m	Minor triad whose root is G sharp	G♯	B	D♯	
G^7	Mm7th chord whose root is G (triad is major, 7th is minor)	G	B	D	F
Gm^7	mm7th chord whose root is G (triad is minor, 7th is minor)	G	B♭	D	F
Gmaj^7	MM7th chord whose root is G (triad is major, 7th is major)	G	B	D	F♯
G^{ø7}	dm7th chord whose root is G (triad is diminished, 7th is minor)	G	B♭	D♭	F
G$^{°7}$	dd7th chord whose root is G (triad is diminished, 7th is diminished)	G	B♭	D♭	F♭

Observe the use of chord symbols in the following song. In this example the actual chords (in simple position) have been added (bass clef) below the melody so that you can see how the melody would be harmonized. A pianist familiar with chord symbols would fashion an interesting accompaniment from these block chords.

First, sing the melody enough times to become familiar with it. Try playing the melody on the piano as well. When you have a good grasp of the melody, accompany it with the printed harmony—there are only three different chords: (1) G major triad, (2) A minor-minor seventh chord, and (3) D major-minor seventh chord.

The chord symbols are shown above the melody and the roman numeral analysis is shown below it.

Illustration of Chord Symbols and Roman Numerals

"The Man on the Flying Trapeze," American song[+]

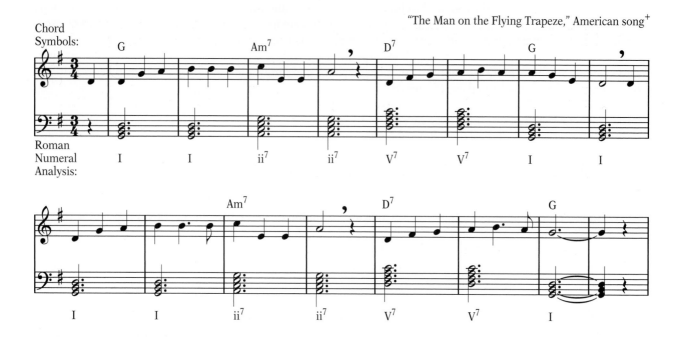

The breath mark (𝄒) indicates the end of a phrase. When a chord symbol is printed, it is continued in force until the next symbol appears.

KEYBOARD AND SIGHT SINGING ASSIGNMENT

A. In the following assignment you will be singing melodies and reading chord symbols.
The suggested procedure for each melody is:

1. Play, then sing the melody until you learn it thoroughly.
2. On the piano, play the chord represented by each chord symbol.
3. Option: If you have difficulty playing the chords, write them out (simple position) on the blank staff below the melody.
4. After you have rehearsed the melody and chords separately, sing the melody and accompany it with the block chords, played on the piano.
5. If you have had sufficient piano study, play the chords in an accompaniment pattern like one of the following:

Jacques Offenbach (1819–1880), *La Périchole*, "My Sweetheart" (1868)

1.

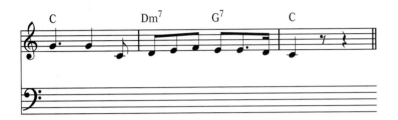

"My One Mistake," American folk song[+]

2.

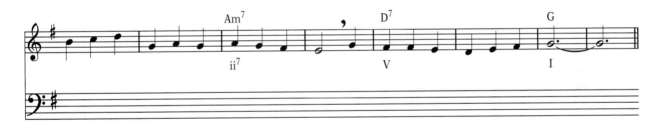

"Wabash Cannon Ball," American folk song[+]

3.

4.

5.

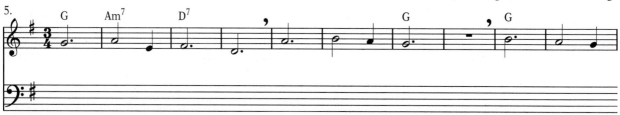

𝒲RITTEN ASSIGNMENT

A.   In the following exercises you will be harmonizing melodies.

1.   Sing each of the four melodies until they are thoroughly familiar to you.
2.   On the staves, write the triad you think best harmonizes the melody.
3.   Circle nonharmonic tones—melody notes that do not match triad notes.
4.   In the blanks under the score, write the roman numeral triad analysis.
5.   Use only the primary triads (I, IV, or V).

Use first the strategy suggested in this chapter for harmonizing each melody. Analyze the melodic segments under each bracket. As an example, in the first piece, "Home on the Range," the first bracket contains seven notes, five of which are also notes of the tonic (I) triad. The logical choice is obviously the I triad. The remaining notes (A and F♯) are passing tones and are thus circled.

When finished with this approach, cover up your answers and go to a piano, guitar, keyboard synthesizer, or some other harmonic instrument. Without any system whatsoever, and remembering that your are restricted to I, IV, and V, pick out the triad harmonization you think *sounds* best. Do the results of both approaches agree? They should! But at least you know what you are doing when you apply the first (strategic) method.

To give expression to your creative urge, try a third approach. Avoid entirely the I, IV, and V triads and see if you can come up with another harmonization that you think is exciting—but perhaps unorthodox!

"Home on the Range," American cowboy song[+]

Wolfgang Amadeus Mozart (1756–1791), *Le Nozze di Figaro*, (The Marriage of Figaro), K. 492, Overture (1786)

Johann Sebastian Bach (1685–1750), *French Suite No. 5 in G Major,* Gigue (1722)

3.

GM: |

"Little Brown Jug," American popular tune[+]

4.

|

B. Each of the following notes is the root of a seventh chord. Write the whole seventh chord on the staff.

Remember: 1. Uppercase *M* means major
                2. Lowercase *m* means minor
                3. First letter indicates the type of *triad.*
                4. Second letter indicates the type of *7th interval.*
                5. MM = Major triad and major 7th
                6. Mm = Major triad and minor 7th
                7. mm = Minor triad and minor 7th

EXAMPLE: 1.   2.   3.   4.   5.   6.   7.   8.   9.   10.

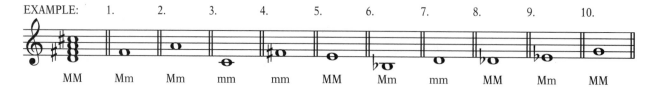

      MM   Mm   Mm   mm   mm   MM   Mm   mm   MM   Mm   MM

C. This assignment will assist you in identifying seventh chord types. The possibilities are: MM (major-major), Mm (major-minor), and mm (minor-minor).

1. Rewrite each 7th chord in simple position (root first, then the 3rd above it, then the 5th, and finally the 7th) on the blank staff provided.
2. Write MM, Mm, or mm in the blanks under the staves.

EXAMPLE: 1.   2.   3.   4.   5.   6.   7.   8.   9.   10.

Mm ___ ___ ___ ___ ___ ___ ___ ___ ___ ___

$\mathcal{E}$AR TRAINING ASSIGNMENT

A. In this assignment you are to identify (using roman numeral analysis) all chords including the V^7. Each exercise consists of five chords (listed below as 1 through 5). Write your analysis in the blanks provided.

Chord no. 1	2	3	4	5		1	2	3	4	5
1. ___	___	___	___	___	4.	___	___	___	___	___
2. ___	___	___	___	___	5.	___	___	___	___	___
3. ___	___	___	___	___	6.	___	___	___	___	___

B. Each exercise is a short set of chord progressions ending in either an authentic or half cadence. In the blanks provided, write the cadence type (*authentic* or *half*). After the first note write the other bass notes on the staff. The example illustrates correct procedure.

You hear:

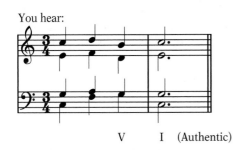

         V   I   (Authentic)

1. EXAMPLE: 2.   3.   4.

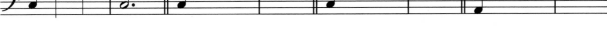

      Authentic   _____   _____   _____

5.   6.   7.   8.

    _____   _____   _____   _____

C. Each exercise consists of five triads. Only tonic (I), subdominant (IV), and dominant (V) triads are used. Write the roman numeral analysis in the blanks provided.

Chord no. 1	2	3	4	5		1	2	3	4	5
1. ___	___	___	___	___	4.	___	___	___	___	___
2. ___	___	___	___	___	5.	___	___	___	___	___
3. ___	___	___	___	___	6.	___	___	___	___	___

D. Each exercise consists of five triads played in four-part harmony. Four are correct as played, but one differs from that played. Circle the "wrong" chord and analyze all printed chords (roman numeral analysis).

1. EXAMPLE (The teacher plays this):

actual
chords
played: i   iv   V   i   V

1. EXAMPLE (You see this):

printed
chords
analyzed: i   V   V   i   V

E. In this assignment you are asked to identify *major, minor, diminished,* and *augmented* triads. Each exercise consists of four triads (three-voice, root position). Using the abbreviations (M m d A), label all triads.

1. ___ ___ ___ ___   3. ___ ___ ___ ___   5. ___ ___ ___ ___

2. ___ ___ ___ ___   4. ___ ___ ___ ___   6. ___ ___ ___ ___

Chapter 29 · Further Harmonizations Using I, ii, ii⁷, IV, V, and V⁷

In Chapter 28 you were introduced to the basic steps in harmonizing a melody. Expansion of this process, including some added harmonic possibilities and a few shortcuts, will facilitate and refine the undertaking.

Melody with Chord Symbols

Assuming that only the I, IV, and V^7 chords are available, examine the following short melody and chord symbols:

Regarding "The Lorelei":

Friedrich Silcher (1789–1860), "The Lorelei" (legendary nymphs of the Rhine River)

Bracket 1   Choices: C or G^7. C was chosen because most conventional melodies such as this often begin on the I (tonic) chord. CEG = I (tonic).

Bracket 2   Choice: F (only). F (FAC) is the only chord that contains both a C and an A.

Bracket 3   Choices: C or G^7. Either could have been used here, but the composer probably chose C (I or tonic) to avoid using the same chord for brackets 3 and 4.

Bracket 4   Choices: F or G^7. Because C is selected for bracket 3, either F or G^7 would be quite musical. Free choice here.

Bracket 5   Choice: C (only). E is the third scale degree, and it can be harmonized only with C (I or tonic). E is not a note of either FAC or GBDF.

Bracket 6   Choice: G^7 (only). The G^7 chord is the only one that contains all three notes, G, F, and D.

Bracket 7   Choices: C or F. Because composers customarily harmonize the final tonic note with a tonic chord, there is little choice here. You will understand this better by playing the melody and harmonizing bracket 7 with an FAC (IV) triad.

Some General Suggestions for Harmonizing Melodies

1. For each melodic segment, choose the chord whose notes match the largest number of melody notes. Example: For a melodic segment, G F E D C, select a C major triad (C E G) in preference to an E minor triad (E G B) because the C major triad contains three melodic notes (G E C), whereas the E minor triad contains only two (G and E).

2. At the end of each phrase be sure to select chords that form a cadence (authentic, half, or plagal). As an example, don't end a phrase with a ii chord because it does not form an authentic, half, or plagal cadence. A **plagal cadence** is the progression IV to I.

3. Chord tones should match those in the melody that are either preceded or followed by a skip (more than a whole step).

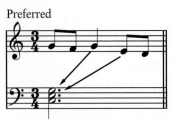

Preferred

G is followed by a skip.
E is preceded by a skip.
Both are found in the chord.

Avoid

E is preceded by a skip
but is *not* a note of the chord.

4. A V or V⁷ chord followed by a IV triad is seldom found in the harmonization of most melodies, except in many twentieth-century popular styles.*

Chord	Proceeds Usually to	Sometimes to
I	any other chord	
ii	V	I
ii⁷	V	
IV	V	I
V	I	
V⁷	I	

The ii, ii⁷, and IV chords are considered **pre-dominant** (progressing to the dominant), whereas the V and V⁷ chords are said to be **pre-tonic** (most often progressing to the I—tonic).

SIGHT SINGING AND KEYBOARD ASSIGNMENT

A. Harmonize each melody with only the chord symbol choices listed above it. Circled notes are nonharmonic.

1. First, reread the beginning of Chapter 29 and the harmonization of "The Lorelei." Without playing or singing the melody, apply the information gained from the analysis of the seven brackets in "The Lorelei" to each melody in the assignment.
2. Write down your choices in the first (highest) set of blanks provided.
3. Play and sing each melody until you can perform it from memory.
4. Also play the chords to be used for each harmonization until they are also familiar.
5. Play both the melody and chords you selected (from Step 1), being critical of any chord progression that sounds unmusical. If you find some you do not like, experiment with other chord combinations.
6. When you are satisfied with any chord changes you have made, write down the new chord symbol choices in the second (lower) set of blanks provided.
7. Bring to class your two sets of harmonizations (1) selected according to calculated choice and (2) chosen through decisions made after playing and hearing your original preference.

    Circled tones are nonharmonic tones.

* See Chapter 30, p. 279.

Chord choices: C Dm Dm^7 G^7
                 (I) (ii) (ii^7) (V^7)

"Holland," folk song

Chord choices: C Dm Dm^7 F G G^7
                 (I) (ii) (ii^7) (IV) (V) (V^7)

Giovanni Paisiello (1740–1816), "The Miller"

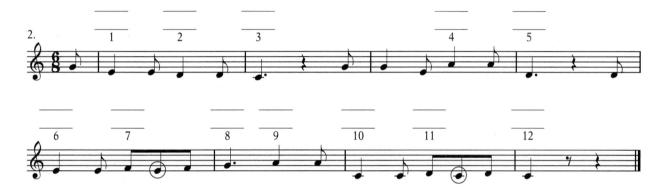

Chord choices: C Dm Dm^7 F G G^7
                 (I) (ii) (ii^7) (IV) (V) (V^7)

"O Tannenbaum" (Oh, Christmas Tree), German Christmas carol

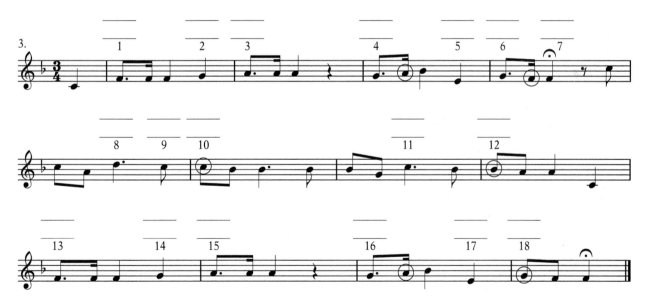

Chapter 29 Further Harmonizations Using I, ii, ii^7, IV, V, and V^7   **275**

Chord choices: Dm Gm A A⁷   Johannes Brahms (1833–1897), *Hungarian Dance No. 5* (in the 1850s)
(i) (iv) (V) (V⁷)

Chord choices: D G A A⁷   Johannes Brahms (1833–1897), "Wiegenlied" (Lullaby), Op. 49, No. 4 (1868)
(I) (IV) (V) (V⁷)

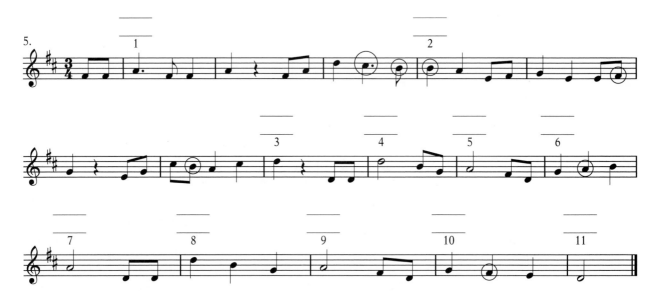

B. Select one of your favorite popular or folk songs and sing it while playing the accompanying chord symbols on a piano or guitar. Perform it in class or for your teacher.

C. Select one of your favorite popular or folk songs and provide a harmonization for it. If chord symbols are already provided, erase them and write your own.

D. Compose a melody of your own in a popular or folk style. Provide a chord symbol harmonization and perform the composition in class.

$\mathcal{E}$AR TRAINING ASSIGNMENT

A. Each exercise consists of five triads. Harmony in this assignment is limited to the following:

I   ii   IV   V

In the blanks provided, write the roman numeral analysis of all chords.

EXAMPLE:

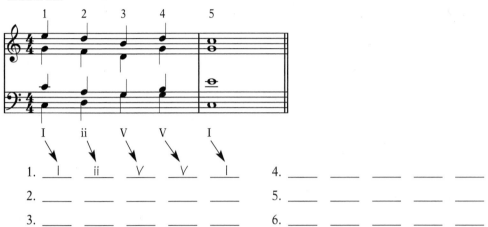

1. __I__ __ii__ __V__ __V__ __I__   4. ____ ____ ____ ____ ____

2. ____ ____ ____ ____ ____   5. ____ ____ ____ ____ ____

3. ____ ____ ____ ____ ____   6. ____ ____ ____ ____ ____

B. Each exercise consists of five triads. The harmony in this assignment is limited to the following:

i   i⁶   ii°⁶   iv   V   vii°⁶

The ^{6} following some roman numerals means first inversion chord (that is, the third is in the bass).

First, write the bass notes on the music staff. Then, in the blanks provided, include a harmonic analysis of all triads. The example illustrates correct procedure.

1. EXAMPLE:

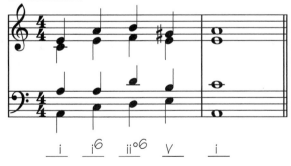

__i__ __i⁶__ __ii°⁶__ __V__ __i__

3.

____ ____ ____ ____ ____

2.

____ ____ ____ ____ ____

4.

____ ____ ____ ____ ____

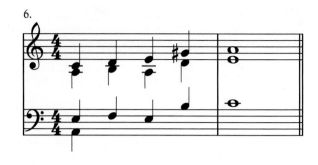

Chapter 30 ▪ Chord Symbols and Their Application in Jazz, Blues, and Popular Music

Jazz is a truly American art. In the nineteenth century, work songs, ragtime, blues and gospel music of African-Americans, and jazz emerged from New Orleans, St. Louis, Kansas City, Chicago, and many other American towns and cities. It became established as a major musical form during the Harlem Renaissance (ca. 1920–32). Throughout this prolific period of musical development, many of the greatest musicians and composers of the twentieth century performed in New York City. The names of these musicians are now legendary: W. C. Handy, Duke Ellington, Count Bassie, Louis Armstrong, Bessie Smith, Billie Holiday, and Sarah Vaughn, to name only a few of a long, distinguished list. From the classroom to the ballroom, from the orchestra hall to the town square, and from the church to the honky-tonk, jazz, with its deep roots in the blues, has influenced the music of this century like no other art form.

Jazz thus became the dominant popular musical form, establishing a worldwide audience through music publication, recording, radio, and the movies. With the emergence of many new mid–twentieth century popular music styles, including rock and roll, soul, and rhythm and blues, music publishers turned to jazz in developing an appropriate format for written music. Although musicians learned this music through recordings and live performance, much of it has been transmitted around the world through the publication of **lead sheets** in **fake books.** By listening to recordings, viewing video and listening to performances, and many hours of perfecting technical skills in the practice room, jazz and popular musicians are able to read a lead sheet and develop their own musical interpretation and style of **jazz standards** (jazz tunes that have become a standard part of the repertoire).

The Lead Sheet: The Musical Score of Jazz, Blues, and Popular Music

The lead sheet contains mainly a melody, chord symbols, and sometimes text. Alternate versions of rhythm, tune, or chords might be shown at the bottom of the page. Good-quality fake books include publication and copyright histories. The following lead sheet contains all these elements, including suggested **chord substitutions,** which are enclosed in parentheses, as in mm. 7 to 8 of the example. "Med. Swing" indicates the tempo and style, a moderate tempo in a swing style. This example is taken from *The New Real Book,* a multivolume set of fake books that have become classics because of their high quality. Only the B (second) section is included here. It is the practice in lead sheets to use the clef sign only for the first line of music.

All of Me

Seymour Simons
Gerald Marks
"All of Me"

This chapter will examine **chord symbols,** which constitute the primary harmonic notation for publications of jazz, blues, and popular music and give the basic harmonic information of the lead sheet. Chord symbols have been modified many times through the years, and to this day popular and jazz musicians must be able to recognize a variety of symbols that refer to the same chord. In this chapter we will examine some additional chord symbols, study 7th chords in greater detail and learn about 9th and *sus4* chords. It is important to have a thorough understanding of the sus4, 7th and 9th chords because they appear in nearly every published fake book.

Finally, we will conclude with a brief introduction to the musical form that pre-dates jazz and modern popular music: the *blues.* The blues is considered the foundation of twentieth-century jazz and is the basis for early developments in most forms of popular music. Although jazz and most popular music contain elements of the blues, the blues has emerged throughout the twentieth century as an American art form that is unique in its own right.

7th Chords in Chord Symbols*

In addition to 7th chords, numbers in chord symbols also include 2nd, sus4, 6th, 9th, 11th, and 13th chords. While 2nd, 6th, 11th and 13th chords are beyond the scope of this text, they follow basically the same principles that apply to 7th and 9th chords.

It is important to remember that there are a number of different ways to indicate triads. For example, a minor triad might be indicated with an "m," a "mi," or a "-". For example, C-, Cmi, and Cm are all symbols for the same minor triad: c–eb–g. Many fake books use all three chord symbols.

---

* In jazz and pop chord symbols and in discussions of jazz and pop harmony, it is customary to use the forms 7th, 9th, 11th, and 13th rather than spelling out the names seventh, thirteenth and so forth, as has been done for the earlier chapters in the book and which conform to traditional theory usage.

The actual interval of the number that is used in chord symbols has been established through tradition and common usage. Chord symbol notation is based mainly on the dominant 7th chord, not the tonic major-seventh chord. In the roman numeral system of traditional harmonic analysis, the 7th represents the diatonic interval above the root of the chord and could be either a major or a minor seventh. The diminished 7th is indicated by an additional symbol. In jazz, blues, and pop, 7th chord symbols always indicate a *minor seventh* above the root, unless otherwise specified.

There are four types of 7th chord symbols in jazz, blues, and pop:

1. A number alone always indicates the minor seventh above the root of the chord. For example, C7 is spelled c–e–g–b♭.
2. The major seventh is preceded by "maj," an uppercase *M,* or a triangle and is a major seventh above the root of the chord. For example, a Cmaj7 (also CM7 or C△7) is spelled c–e–g–b. It is important to note that the "maj" refers to the quality of the *seventh,* not the triad. For example, a Cmimaj7 is spelled c–e♭–g–b and is the tonic seventh chord of the c harmonic minor scale. Cmi refers to the quality of the triad, whereas the maj7 describes the 7th.
3. As we indicated in earlier chapters, the diminished triad is indicated by ° alone. If the seventh above the root of a diminished triad is a minor seventh, this chord is noted as a half-diminished 7th chord using the ø or, more commonly, is indicated as a minor 7th flat 5 (♭5) chord. For example, a chord spelled c–e♭–g♭–b♭ is a Cø or a Cmi7(♭5).
4. As we indicated earlier, the fully diminished 7th chord is indicated by a °7 alone. In this case, the ° indicates both the diminished triad and the diminished seventh above the root of the chord. For example, C°7 is spelled c–e♭–g♭–b♭♭.

The Ninth Chord

Adding a third above the seventh creates the *ninth of a chord.* Whereas roman numerals indicate the diatonic interval of the 9th above the root of the chord, chord symbols use three different-sized intervals of 9ths. In chord symbol notation 9th chords always assume the interval of a major 9th unless a ♭ or ♯ is added. ♭9 indicates the interval of a minor ninth above the root. ♯9 indicates the interval of an augmented 9th above the root.

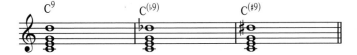

It is important to note that the ♯ in a ♯9 chord does not indicate the accidental being used in the chord itself. The ♯9 indicates the note that is raised by a half step above the major 9th of the chord. Similarly, the ♭9th indicates the interval of one half step below the major 9th of the chord. Some fake books use –9th for ♭9 and +9 for ♯9.

When using chord symbols, *harmonic extensions* above the triad are usually added to the symbol in ascending order. Musicians have learned that this system can quickly become cumbersome when there are too many numbers indicating nondiatonic color tones. Therefore, most jazz musicians abbreviate a chord symbol by omitting some of the numbers. This is especially true of the 9th chord. For example, C9 usually includes the minor 7th even though it is not in the chord symbol. Therefore, C9 is the same as C79. 9th chords are typically found in the following contexts:

1. The 9th: The 9th chord is by far the most common and is used on virtually every scale degree in popular music. Remember, the 9th is a major ninth in the chord.
2. The ♭9th: Although less common, this chord is based on the V in the harmonic minor scale. The ♭9th usually leads to a minor tonic or a minor 7th chord. Some jazz musicians use the ♭9th.
3. The ♯9th: The least common of the 9th chords is the ♯9th chord. It is considered a nondiatonic *color chord* and is the most dissonant of the 9th chords.

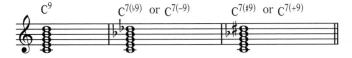

You might have noticed that parentheses have been placed around the Cmi$^{7(\flat5)}$, C$^{(\flat9)}$, and C$^{(\sharp9)}$ chords. Lead sheets using chord symbols are often published in handwritten manuscripts where the intent of the composer could be unclear. In chord symbol notation parentheses are used on nondiatonic 7ths, 9ths and other harmonic extensions which require an accidental $\flat$ or $\sharp$. The parentheses are used to clarify confusion in reading a chord symbol. For example, in manuscript copy a C$^{\sharp9}$ could be confusing because it could be read as a C major triad with a $\sharp$9th or a C$\sharp$ major triad with a 9th. The parentheses make it clear that C$^{(\sharp9)}$ is a C major triad with an added extension of the $\sharp$9th.

It is imperative that musicians learn to spell 9th chords quickly and accurately if they are to be able to improvise using chord symbols. Many jazz and popular musicians will assume that a chord symbol indicates a diatonic 9th even though the symbol might be only a 7th. For hundreds of years musicians have used the human hand as an important learning tool. One way to develop improvisational skill is to use the hand to learn to spell ninth chords based on any note and to practice singing them.

The ninth-chord hand

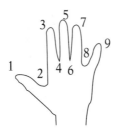

With thumb as 1, each finger represents chord tones 3, 5, 7, and 9. The spaces between the fingers are the scale tones between the chord tones. As you sing each note of the ninth chord, bend the finger that represents that chord tone.

$\mathcal{S}$us4 Chords

In chord symbols, "sus4" means that the perfect fourth above the root of the chord is *substituted* for the third of the chord and that the third is omitted altogether. The sus4 chord is considered to be a separate chord, not an embellishment of a triad. The substitution of the 4th is very common in jazz and popular music and is notated as follows:

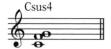

Most sus4 chords also add a seventh and/or ninth. For example:

There are many jazz and popular music tunes that make use of the sound of the sus4 chord. An example of a slow tune using these chords follows. Class members can perform this short tune with one performer on the melody, one playing the chords on a keyboard, and a third player on the bass line.

Bruce R. Jackson (1951–   ), "Suspend it!" (1998)[+]

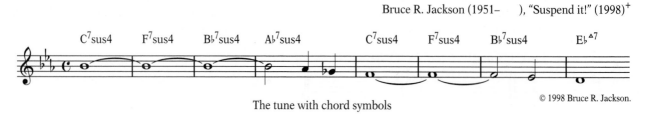

The tune with chord symbols

The tune with root position chords notated on the lower staff

The tune with chords on the staff in an easy keyboard arrangement and a bass line for another performer to play

*N*ondiatonic or Altered Notes in Chord Symbols

Chord symbols in jazz and popular music also use many *nondiatonic* chord tones. Nondiatonic or *altered notes* are tones outside the notes commonly suggested by the chord symbol. Improvising musicians use nontraditional harmonic structures to add color and interest to the music. Chord symbols often indicate these nondiatonic harmonic structures with parentheses around the altered chord tones. For example, jazz musicians can alter the fifth of a chord using the following notation:

1. The diminished fifth is notated ($\flat$5). For example, a $C^{(\flat 5)}$ is a C major chord with a lowered fifth spelled c–e–g$\flat$.
2. Additional harmonic extensions are usually listed in ascending order. For example, $C^{(\flat 5)7}$ is spelled c–e–g$\flat$–b$\flat$.
3. A dominant with an augmented 5th is common and is notated $C^{(\sharp 5)7}$. There are a number of additional spellings of this chord, including C^{+7}, $C^{(+5)7}$, and $C^{7(\sharp 5)}$ (not all fake books are consistent in the order of numbers). This chord would be spelled c–e–g$\sharp$–b$\flat$.
4. Often a lead sheet uses parentheses around the sus4 and places the harmonic extensions last, for example, $C(sus4)^7$ or $C(sus4)^9$.
5. Many fake books will use parentheses around the $\flat$9 or $\sharp$9. For example, a $C^{7(\flat 9)}$ is spelled c–e–g–b$\flat$–d$\flat$.
6. Again, if only the 9 is used, the 7th is generally implied. A $C^{(\flat 9)}$ is the same as a $C^{7(\flat 9)}$ and is spelled c–e–g–b$\flat$–d$\flat$.

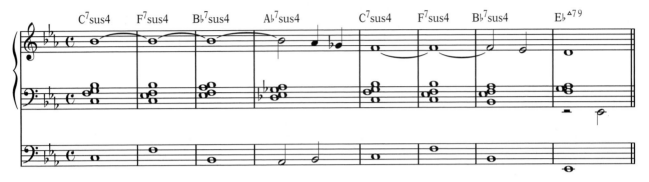

Parentheses are used to reduce confusion, as the $\flat$ or $\sharp$ relates to the number, not to the root of the chord. For example, a $C^{\sharp 9}$ could be misinterpreted as a C$\sharp$ triad in the handwritten manuscripts that are still common in jazz and popular music. $C^{(\sharp 9)}$ is much easier to read. You will notice that parentheses were used in several examples earlier in this chapter.

The Dominant 7th Chord

Major/minor seventh chords (the dominant 7th sound in traditional harmony) pervade jazz, blues, and popular music even though that particular seventh chord might or might not function as a dominant chord in those styles. For example, although C7 could be a dominant chord of F, it can also be the tonic chord of a blues in C. These chords will function as a dominant only when their roots progress downward by a fifth. Seventh chords that resolve by a fifth serve the same function as the dominant in traditional harmony even though the chord might relate to the following chord only rather than to the diatonic key of the composition. Chord symbols need not relate to the key signature and often use notes outside the diatonic scale.

Seventh chords often use notes that are outside the diatonic scale indicated by the dominant. These notes are referred to as altered tones or *color tones*. Color tones are notes that are foreign either to the key of the composition or to the key of the particular moment in the music. They are especially common at cadences and in the dominant chord.

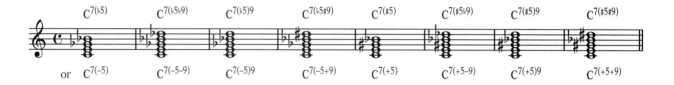

Analysis of Jazz Diatonic Progressions Using Roman Numerals

There is a type of analysis of jazz, blues, and popular music that uses the uppercase roman numerals plus chord symbols for chord quality immediately following the roman numeral. Harmonic extensions and altered tones follow. All roman numerals are uppercase in this system of analysis.

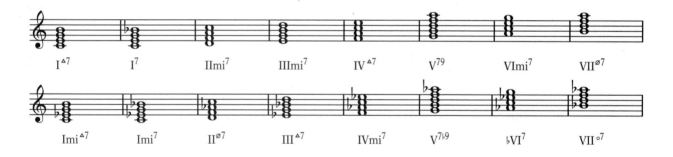

Many popular music performers will communicate on stage using the roman numerals. It is essential that a musician wishing to improvise at a professional level develop skill in using diatonic numbers in all keys. Jazz, blues, and popular musicians often perform where no music is used and all chords are indicated by hand using chord numbers. This is especially true in blues and country music bands.

The Blues

The **blues** can be traced back to the work songs of the nineteenth century. By the early twentieth century, the blues had emerged as a significant African-American art form. By 1905, Jelly Roll Morton had popularized the blues with his "Jelly Roll Blues," and W. C. Handy's "St. Louis Blues" was one of the earliest recording hits. Many of the earliest gramophone recordings were blues compositions, and the influence of the blues can be found in virtually every popular music form around the world today.

The harmonic structure of the blues is based on three chords: I, IV, and V. The most common length of a blues **chorus** is 12 measures. The most important harmonic event that characterizes the blues progression is the IV in the fifth measure.

The melodic content of the blues is not the traditional diatonic scale that we have studied in earlier chapters. The unique sound of the blues is found through the incorporation of the **blues scale.** Although the blues is harmonically based on a I–IV–V progression, all these harmonic structures are based on the dominant seventh chord and use the blues scale, which contains color tones called **blue notes** (the ♭3, ♭5, and ♭7):

Because the chord progression of blues is harmonically simple, many jazz and popular musicians create interest and variety through *chord substitution*. Although many tunes use the same basic blues structure, in chord substitution the blues and jazz performer replaces the original chord with another chord either to add color or to make a more elaborate progression. The addition of V^7 in the final measure is especially common, so that the dominant returns to the I of the next 12-bar strain and establishes a cycle of many choruses over which musicians can improvise.

Measure	1	2	3	4	5	6	7	8	9	10	11	12
	I^7	I^7	I^7	I^7	IV^7	IV^7	I^7	I^7	V^7	IV^7	I^7	I^7
Gmaj	G^7	G^7	G^7	G^7	C^7	C^7	G^7	G^7	D^7	C^7	G^7	G^7

Thousands of variations are possible through chord substitution in improvisation. The following chart contains some of the most important examples:

CHORD SUBSTITUTIONS IN A BLUES PROGRESSION												
Measure	1	2	3	4	5	6	7	8	9	10	11	12
Progression 1	G^7	G^7	G^7	G^7	C^7	C^7	G^7	G^7	D^7	C^7	G^7	D^7
Progression 2	G^7	C^7	G^7	G^7	C^7	C^7	G^7	E^7	Ami^7	D^7	G^7	D^7
Progression 3	G^7	C^7	G^7	Dmi^7/G^7	C^7	$C\sharp^\circ$	G^7	E^7	Ami^7	D^7	G^7/E^7	Ami^7/D^7

$\mathcal{W}$hat's Next?

This text has only introduced the study of chord symbols; there is much more to be learned. Music theorists working with jazz contend that a chord symbol represents far more than just a triad with harmonic extensions; it also represents a *scale*, which is the basic note inventory for **improvisation** on that particular chord. Refer to the ninth-chord hand on page 282 to see how this would work.

One of the most important jazz pedagogues, Jamey Abersold, publishes many play-along CDs with his books. The CD includes a basic rhythm section of piano, bass, and drums. The books are in lead sheet format and include chord changes in a solo section and scales for improvisation over each chord symbol as well as other teaching materials.*

It is beyond the scope of this text to cover much of that material, which is so important for the development of improvisation and so distinctive a part of the creative performance of jazz, blues, and popular music. However, once the student has a good understanding of chord symbols, can spell the triads, and can find the harmonic extensions and color tones above them, he or she has the tools to learn to use the lead sheet effectively and creatively.

*Jamey Abersold, New Albany, Indiana.

DATE _____ NAME _____

$\mathcal{W}$RITTEN ASSIGNMENT

Below are two different blues progressions. Transpose each progression into the indicated key. The key of G major is given as an example for each progression. Professional musicians do this type of transposition continually and must become proficient at this skill. The experienced musician learns to do this at sight, but writing out the same progression in many keys is a useful way to prepare to transpose it directly on a keyboard or guitar.

Measure	1	2	3	4	5	6	7	8	9	10	11	12
	I^7	I^7	I^7	I^7	IV^7	IV^7	I^7	I^7	V^7	IV^7	I^7	I^7
G major	G^7	G^7	G^7	G^7	C^7	C^7	G^7	G^7	D^7	C^7	G^7	G^7
C major												
F major												
B♭ major												

Measure	1	2	3	4	5	6	7	8	9	10	11	12
	I^7	IV^7	I^7	I^7	IV^7	IV^7	I^7	VI^7	II^7	V^7	I^7	V^7
G major	G^7	C^7	G^7	G^7	C^7	C^7	G^7	Em^7	Am^7	D^7	G^7	D^7
C major												
F major												
B♭ major												

$\mathcal{K}$EYBOARD ASSIGNMENT

The II–V–I progression is common in jazz. This three-chord progression, with 7th and 9th included, is given below followed by a transposition of a whole step down (C major to B♭ major or C minor to B♭ minor). Once you have learned to play the pattern of the three-chord progression, you can continue to transpose it down by step until you run out of notes!

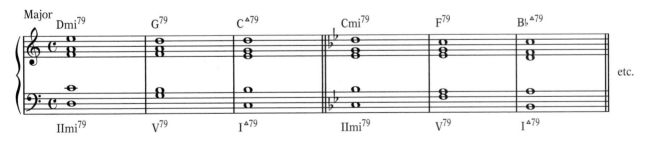

SIGHT SINGING ASSIGNMENT

1. Sing the following chords and test your intonation with the piano. Transpose these chords up by a half step as many times as is comfortable in your voice range.

2. Using a similar approach, arpeggiate each chord indicated by a chord symbol. Check your intonation at the piano. Be sure that the chord is spelled properly.

    1. E♭ maj7

    2. B♭mi⁷

    3. C♯mi⁷

    4. Bmi⁷♭⁵

    5. Dmaj7

    6. Fmaj7

3. Find a lead sheet and arpeggiate each chord in order. This is a very important skill in learning to hear chords. Aural images of actual chord symbols are necessary to the development of improvisational skill.

EAR TRAINING ASSIGNMENT

You will hear a series of chords. Indicate the chord that you hear.

EXAMPLE:

1. <u>7th chord</u> Major 7th chord Minor 7th chord mi⁷♭⁵ chord

2. 7th chord Major 7th chord Minor 7th chord mi⁷♭⁵ chord

3. 7th chord Major 7th chord Minor 7th chord mi⁷♭⁵ chord

4. 7th chord Major 7th chord Minor 7th chord mi⁷♭⁵ chord

5. 7th chord Major 7th chord Minor 7th chord mi⁷♭⁵ chord

6. 7th chord Major 7th chord Minor 7th chord mi⁷♭⁵ chord

7. 7th chord Major 7th chord Minor 7th chord mi⁷♭⁵ chord

8. 7th chord Major 7th chord Minor 7th chord mi⁷♭⁵ chord

9. 7th chord Major 7th chord Minor 7th chord mi⁷♭⁵ chord

10. 7th chord Major 7th chord Minor 7th chord mi⁷♭⁵ chord

Appendix 1 ▪ Introduction to Musical Forms

The materials and patterns studied in the preceding chapters are formed into larger structures that also show coherent patterns. Although the study of these forms in depth is beyond the scope of this book, a brief description of some forms from which examples have been drawn for this book would be handy for you to have. Our description starts with the ways in which phrases are combined to form larger units.

Combination of Phrases: The Period

Phrases can be combined to form a larger structure called the **period.** Most periods contain two phrases that are sometimes called *question* and *answer* phrases. The formal name for the first phrase of a period (the question) is the **antecedent** (that which goes before); for the second phrase (the answer), the **consequent** (that which follows).

Johannes Brahms (1833–1897), *Symphony No. 1 in C Minor,* Fourth Movement (1876)

If the two phrases of a period begin alike, the structure is called a *parallel period.*

Wolfgang Amadeus Mozart (1756–1791), *Piano Sonata in A Major,* K. 330i, First Movement (1781–83)

Parallel period (first two measures alike)

The two phrases of a period may be related in such a way that melodic motion in one direction is answered by motion in the opposite direction. Sometimes tonic harmonies in the first phrase are answered by dominant harmonies in the second phrase and vice versa. Either of these types of period construction is called an *opposite construction of a period.*

Ludwig van Beethoven (1770–1827), *Sonata in D Major for Piano,* Op. 28, First Movement (1801)

Opposite melodic motion in a period

Ludwig van Beethoven (1770–1827), *Sonata in C Minor for Piano*, Op. 10, No. 1, First Movement (1797)

Opposite harmonic construction in a period

When the two phrases of a period begin in different ways and use contrasting materials, the period is called a *contrasting period*.

Carl Maria von Weber (1786–1826), *Der Freischütz* (The Freeshooter), Overture (1817–1821)

Contrasting period (phrases use different materials)

The cadence of the first phrase of a period usually has less a feeling of finality than that of the second phrase. Often the cadence of the first phrase uses a note of the dominant triad for the final note of the cadence. This means that the first phrase will be harmonized with a dominant chord on the final note (a *half cadence*). The consequent phrase then answers this with a cadence ending on the tonic chord (*authentic cadence*).

"On the Bridge at Avignon," French folk song

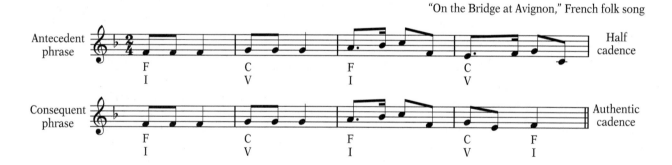

*L*arger Complete Forms

Because musical forms are intimately connected with the style periods in which they originate, these descriptions will be grouped according to historical periods. Forms first used in one period usually continue to affect music of succeeding eras and often are used in new ways by composers of a later age. It also often happens that a form name will refer to one kind of piece when it is first used and will later come to have a very different meaning.

Form names tell us something about the way a piece of music is organized or structured. They may tell us what to expect as one section follows another, or they may indicate the musical procedures or devices by which it is put together. Some form names also indicate the character or spirit of the piece. Sometimes the name shows the way the music would be used, as in dance music or music for religious services. Another type of form name may tell us that the music is organized as part of a dramatic stage presentation, that it takes its shape from the text, or that some other relationship to another art has helped shape the musical plan. And, of course, many musical structures are a mixture of several of these aspects.

Medieval Period (Ending about A.D. 1400)

Carol. Although we now use **carol** to mean a Christmas song, in the Middle Ages it referred to songs with refrains (sections of recurring text and music) that were frequently religious seasonal songs. They were festive in spirit and originally were also *dance songs.*

Mass. The service of the Catholic Church that celebrates the Last Supper is the **Mass.** In the Middle Ages the whole service could be sung; the music for service use, which was sung in unison, was called *Gregorian chant.* The melodies of Gregorian chant have been in use for over a thousand years. A *Requiem* is a special mass for the dead.

Round. A composition in which one voice has a melody that is exactly imitated by each succeeding voice that begins the melody at a different time. "Row, Row, Row Your Boat" is a familiar modern example. The oldest known round, "Sumer Is Icumen in" (p. 151), dates from about A.D. 1240. A *round* can also be called a **canon.**

Renaissance Period (Ending about 1600)

Chorale. The hymns sung by the congregation in the Lutheran service from the sixteenth century on (p. 49) are called *chorales.* "Sleepers, Awake" is an example of a *chorale* tune. The first section of the music is usually repeated (with new words) and is followed by a section that is not the same as the first part. These three parts of the tune can be represented by the letters AAB. "A Mighty Fortress Is Our God," by Martin Luther, is another well-known example of a chorale (p. 229).

Madrigal. A term commonly used for sixteenth-century polyphonic compositions setting Italian or English poetry, *madrigal* does not imply a specific or predictable formal plan; the pieces are often planned to reflect the meaning of the text. Some of you may have sung in a *madrigal group,* which sings music such as "The Silver Swan," by the English composer Gibbons.

Mass. Fifteenth-century composers began to set portions of the text of the Catholic Mass, in which the words were always the same, as a multisectional musical whole. The practice has continued since that time. Typically five sections of the Mass were set with polyphonic music, and in the service the other portions of the ritual might still be sung with the old melodies of Gregorian chant. Listen to a mass by Palestrina (a sixteenth-century Italian composer of church music).

Pavan. By the Renaissance many kinds of dance music were being written down. One of the important dances of the time was the *pavan,* a slow, stately processional dance in duple time. There is an example for you to sing on page 99.

Baroque Period (Ending about 1750)

Dance Forms. New kinds of dances arise with every new style period reflecting changes in taste and fashion. Dance music was used to dance to, but eighteenth-century listeners also enjoyed hearing the music by itself. Even when these pieces were not danced to, the distinctive rhythms that accompanied the dance remained the basis of the music. Dances of this period usually have a two-part form (also called **binary form**), and each part is repeated. Some of the dances in the musical excerpts in this book include the **sarabande, minuet** (*menuet*), and **gavotte.** You may know others from music you have heard or played—**allemande, courante,** and **gigue** are also dances from this period. Listen to J. S. Bach's *French Suite in E Major* for some wonderfully characteristic baroque dances.

Fugue. A **fugue** is an imitative contrapuntal piece in which each line enters with a distinctive melodic idea (called a *subject*) that is imitated by each other entering voice and that appears again and again in the course of the piece. Unlike the round, the strict imitation does not continue throughout. J. S. Bach wrote many fugues. Listen to the first fugue of the *Well-Tempered Clavier* (a collection of preludes and fugues in all keys).

Prelude. **Preludes,** as the name suggests, are intended to precede something. A special type of prelude often preceded the singing of Lutheran chorales; preludes may also be the first movement of a *suite* or other group of movements. In the *Well-Tempered Clavier* by Bach, each fugue is preceded by a prelude; listen to the first prelude. The form name does not indicate a predictable formal pattern but instead refers to the function as an opening musical event.

Opera and Oratorio. These large scale dramatic-musical forms were born in the baroque period and have been important in all subsequent periods. **Opera** is performed with stage action, and many types of opera are sung throughout. **Oratorio** is usually a dramatic choral work that is performed without stage action. A **cantata** is a smaller, similar work. Extended musical pieces for a soloist in an opera, oratorio, or cantata are called *arias.* Baroque arias are usually in a **three-part musical form,** with the last part a repeat (**da capo**) of the first part, making a form that can be represented by the letters ABA. The best-known baroque oratorio is probably Handel's *Messiah.* The aria "The Trumpet Shall Sound" in *Messiah* is an *ABA form.*

Suite. Dances and other short instrumental pieces were grouped together to form **suites.** Another term that usually means the same thing is **partita.** Listen to J. S. Bach's *Orchestra Suite No. 2 in B Minor.*

Concerto. In the early eighteenth century, **concerto** meant an orchestral piece in several movements that was sometimes for the orchestra as a whole but usually for one or more soloists and orchestra. Commonly there were three movements of contrasting tempo: fast-slow-fast. You will enjoy hearing Vivaldi's "Primavera" (Spring) *Concerto,* which is the first of a group of concertos depicting the four seasons.

*C*lassic Period (Ending in the Early Nineteenth Century)

Classic Concerto. Classic concertos are usually for one soloist and orchestra, and frequently the solo instrument is the piano. There are three movements, fast-slow-fast, but the formal patterns found within each movement are new in the late eighteenth century. The first movement is related to the **sonata,** and an outline of its formal plan will be found with the discussion of **sonata form.** Many different patterns might be chosen for the slow movement, and the last movement is usually a **rondo,** discussed below. Mozart loved the new woodwind instrument of the period, the clarinet, and wrote a wonderful concerto for it that you should hear.

Rondo. The last movement of many classic sonatas, concertos, and symphonies is a rondo, a form in which the opening theme returns again and again after contrasting sections called *episodes.* A common rondo plan, in which the *rondo theme* is A, would be A B A C A. Its character is usually lively, like the last movement of Haydn's *Trio for Violin, Cello and Piano in C Major.*

Sonata. In the classic era, this is a multimovement instrumental form. It may be for piano or for piano with another instrument. If more than two instruments are involved, the name given the piece will indicate how many. Therefore, we speak of *trios, quartets, quintets, octets,* and so on. Such combinations frequently do not use piano. Commonly there are three or four movements using various classic forms. The opening movement (and sometimes other movements as well) uses a form called *sonata form,* in which the order of events is as shown in the following diagram. The concerto modification of this plan is also shown in the diagram in simplified form. You may listen to the first movement of Beethoven's *Sonata in F Major for Violin and Piano, Op. 24* (known as the "Spring" sonata) for an example of sonata form.

Symphony. A work using classic forms in a multimovement piece for orchestra is called a **symphony.** Commonly symphonies have four movements. The first movement is usually in *sonata form,* the second movement is usually a slow movement, and the third movement is a dance movement, usually a *minuet.* The minuet in a classic symphony is actually a large *ABA form,* in which each part of the form is a complete *binary form.* This dance is in triple time. The last movement may be a sonata form, a theme and variations, a rondo, or some other form.

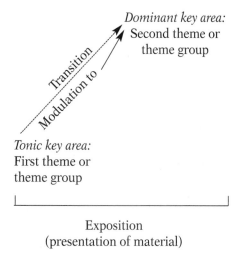

Dominant key area:
Second theme or
theme group

Transition
Modulation to

Tonic key area:
First theme or
theme group

Exposition
(presentation of material)

Development
(manipulation of
material and
modulations)

All in tonic key

First theme   Second theme
or   Transition   or
group   group

Recapitulation
(return of material)

Classic sonata form

Dominant

Orchestra
Exposition
(tonic)

Tonic
Soloist's
Exposition

Development

(tonic)
Recapitulation

Cadenza

Coda

Classic concerto first movement form

Romantic Period (Nineteenth Century)

The romantic period continued to use most of the classic forms. Some new dances appeared, especially the **waltz,** a dizzying dance in triple time that became almost a symbol for Vienna. National dances from other parts of Europe often were used as instrumental pieces, especially for the piano. The Polish composer Chopin uses **mazurkas** and **polonaises** for wonderful piano pieces. He also wrote evocative pieces called **nocturnes,** a word that originally meant "night music." Romantic music often emphasizes representation of extramusical ideas, something that was *not* new to the nineteenth century but that acquired the name **program music.**

In the United States, religious songs of African-Americans called **spirituals** became widely known, especially after the Civil War.

The Twentieth Century

Musicians of the twentieth century have been free to experiment with all sorts of new designs or to use new materials with any of the formal plans or procedures of the past. Often they use old terms, as in Bartók's *Concerto for Orchestra,* which uses the *concerto* form, as some baroque composers did, for a piece exploiting the orchestra as a whole rather than as a work for soloist and orchestra.

Some important new elements have come from the music of the United States, especially through African-American influences. *Ragtime* was a syncopated style of the early twentieth century employed especially in piano *rags* with very regular formal plans based on the 16-bar period (or **strain**), similar to marches and dances of the end of the nineteenth century. Scott Joplin's "Maple Leaf Rag" is in the form AABBACCDD. *Blues* is a term that describes the spirit and expressive devices used to perform music as well as its special forms of harmonic progression and scale. *Jazz* has been a major American contribution to the world's music.

Appendix 2 · Keyboard Harmony Supplement

In Parts IV and V of this text, suggestions have been made for playing common progressions on the keyboard and for using model progressions to transpose to all keys. A group of common progressions is given here in one place for convenience. Each progression is given in both C major and c minor and can be played in all major and minor keys.

It is quite helpful to practice keyboard harmony progressions as rhythmically as possible, so these examples are metrically notated. You may practice them with other rhythmic patterns of your own invention once you have learned the progression. They can be practiced all in one mode or as given here, with the minor immediately following the form of the progression in the same meter and tempo.

Remember that ^{6} after a roman numeral means a first inversion chord, and $^6_4$ after a roman numeral means a second inversion chord.

Play the following progressions as notated and then play them substituting the V^7 for the V chord in each progression.

Notice that this progression is like no. 2, with ii⁶ (ii°⁶) substituted for IV (iv).

Appendix 3 ▪ *Fingerboard Harmony for Guitar*

The guitar is tuned as follows:

When guitar music is written on a staff, it is notated an octave higher and is read in treble clef.

When guitar music is notated to show fingering and finger patterns instead of pitches, the notation is called *tablature.* Each vertical line corresponds to a string with the lowest string at the left. Each horizontal line represents a *fret,* with the top line representing the end of the string.

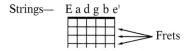

An X above a string means that the string is not to be sounded; the black dots show the placement of each finger (just behind the fret). Arabic numbers show a common way of fingering each chord (index finger, 1; middle finger, 2; ring finger, 3; and little finger, 4), and o means an *open string* (with no fingers stopping the string).

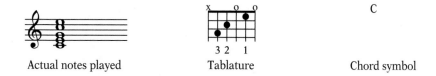

| Actual notes played | Tablature | Chord symbol |

Therefore, a C major chord could be notated in the three ways shown above.

When chords are strummed on the guitar, they do not necessarily follow the same principles of doubling or voice leading as in keyboard harmony. The chords given in this supplement are arranged (voiced) so that they sound good strummed on the guitar and are easy to reach with the hand.

When letter notation is used, an uppercase letter stands for a major triad; an uppercase letter followed by "m" stands for a minor triad, and an uppercase letter with "7" stands for a major-minor (dominant type) seventh chord. Common major keys used in popular music on the guitar are F, C, G, D, A, and E. The common minor keys used in popular music are d, a, and e. Because jazz often features horns, most jazz tunes are in flat keys.

The Commonly Used Triads

First, learn to strum these common triads, starting with the bottom string to be played and brushing across the strings with the right thumb. For some chords, alternate fingerings are given. Use the one you find easiest and most comfortable.

Here are the most commonly used major triads.

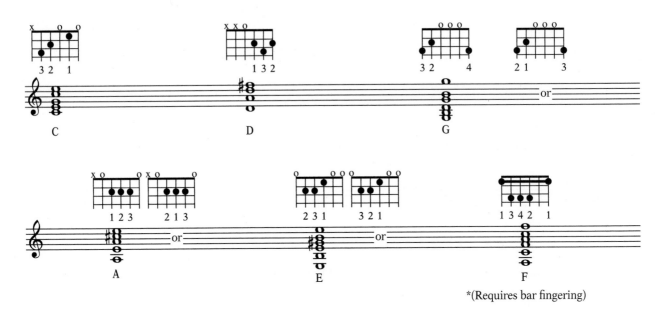

*(Requires bar fingering)

Here are the most commonly used minor triads.

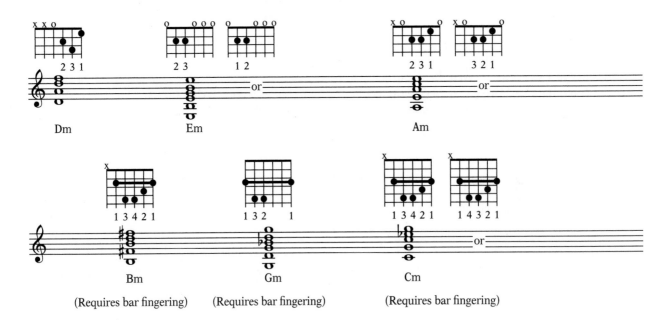

(Requires bar fingering)   (Requires bar fingering)   (Requires bar fingering)

*For bar fingering lay the finger across the strings so that it forms the note shown by dots.

The Dominant Seventh Chord

The V^7 in the commonly used keys for the guitar is notated as follows:

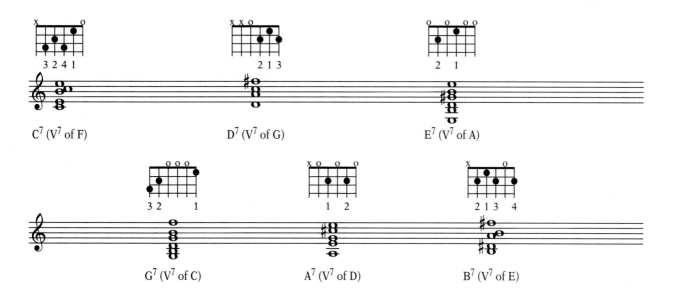

C^7 (V^7 of F) D^7 (V^7 of G) E^7 (V^7 of A)

G^7 (V^7 of C) A^7 (V^7 of D) B^7 (V^7 of E)

 *Glossary*

Words in *italics* in a definition are found elsewhere in the glossary with their own entries. Chapter numbers at the end of entries indicate where the term is introduced in the text.

Accelerando (accel.)—Increasing the tempo gradually, to accelerate. Chapter 5.

Accent—To place emphasis on a note or chord, usually by making it louder than the surrounding notes. Often notated $<$. Chapter 5.

Accidental—A sharp, flat, or natural, not in the key signature, which is added to a note or notes. An accidental affects all notes of that pitch within a measure after it occurs, but is canceled by the next bar line. Chapter 10.

Acoustics—The branch of physics that deals with sound and sound waves. Introduction.

Alla breve—$\frac{2}{2}$ or $\mathbb{C}$ meter. Also referred to as "cut time." The beat is in half-note values. Chapter 18.

Allegro—A quick tempo. The word is the Italian word for "happy" and in music has come to mean a sprightly tempo. Chapter 4.

Allemande—A dance from the sixteenth through the eighteenth centuries in moderate quadruple time. In Bach's time it was often the first movement of a *suite*. Appendix 1.

Alto—1. The voice range below the highest range (*soprano*); the lower range of female or children's voices. 2. In four-part music, the second part is the alto part. Chapter 25.

Anacrusis—Upbeat or pickup note or notes. If a beat or parts of beats occur before the first bar line they form the *upbeat, pickup,* or anacrusis. Chapters 4, 22.

Andante—A slow, walking tempo. Chapter 4.

Antecedent—The first of two phrases in a *period*. The two phrases form an *antecedent* (question) and a *consequent* (answer) relationship. Appendix 1.

Anticipation—A nonharmonic tone that anticipates a note of the chord to follow. The anticipation occurs before the beat, and the chord to which it leads is on the beat, usually the first beat of a measure. Chapter 27.

Appoggiatura—1. A type of ornament that falls on the beat and resolves stepwise downward, usually taking half the value of the principal note. Notation: ♪. Chapter 5. 2. A nonharmonic tone that is approached by a leap and resolves stepwise downward. The nonharmonic tone is normally dissonant. Chapter 27.

Articulation signs—Markings used to indicate degrees of separation or connection between notes. Chapter 5.

Atonal—Without a tonal center. Atonality has been used in some twentieth-century music. Chapter 6.

Augmented interval—An interval equal to a perfect or major interval plus one half step. For example, P4th = C to F, but an augmented 4th = C to F♯. Chapter 12.

Authentic cadence—A closing harmonic formula (*cadence*) consisting of V to I or, occasionally, vii°⁶ to I. Chapter 26.

Bar—Same as *measure*. Chapter 4.

Bar line—A vertical line drawn through a staff (or staves) to indicate the end of one measure and the beginning of the next. Chapter 4.

Bass—1. The lowest voice range and the lowest range of men's voices. 2. In four-part music, the bottom part is the bass part. Chapter 25.

Bass clef—The sign that indicates that the fourth line (up) of the staff is the F below middle C. It is also known as the F clef. Notation: 𝄢. Chapter 2.

Beam—A thick, straight line connecting two notes at the end of the stems. Beams are used for note values smaller than the quarter note. These small note values may either have a *flag* or *flags* at the end of the stem for each individual note or be beamed together. Notation: ♩ or ♪♪. Chapter 4.

Beat—A regularly recurring pulse in music. Chapter 4.

Beat unit—The note value that receives a single beat in a meter. For example, in $\frac{4}{4}$ time the beat unit is the quarter note. Chapter 4.

Binary form—A two-part form. In the classic period, each part was repeated. Appendix 1.

Blue note, blues scale—Color tones that characterize the *blues scale,* usually the flat third, flat fifth, and flat seventh. Chapter 30.

Blues—A style of music and a form developed by African-Americans in the early twentieth century. It often features a major scale with flatted third, fifth, and seventh (*blue notes*). The form is a 12-measure form, harmonically based on a I–IV–V progression. It served as the earliest form of jazz and later became the foundation of rock and roll and most other popular music. Chapter 30.

Breve—A long note found mostly in older music. The breve equals two whole notes in value. Notation: ⊨. Chapter 4.

Cadence—A melodic-harmonic formula that occurs at the end of a composition, section, or phrase and gives it closure. Melodic cadence, Chapter 22. Harmonic cadence, Chapters 22, 26.

Canon—A contrapuntal device that features strict melodic imitation. The leading part is imitated exactly in its entirety by the next entering voice. *Rounds* are special types of canons. Chapter 17, Appendix 1.

Cantata—A vocal form that originated in the seventeenth century. It uses a sectional text of a sacred or secular nature. The sections are frequently arias, recitatives, duets, and choruses and may include some purely instrumental parts. The accompaniment for a cantata is usually organ or orchestra. Appendix 1.

Carol—In modern usage, a traditional song celebrating Christmas or some other sacred or secular holiday or event. The term originated in medieval times, when it also implied a type of dance. Appendix 1.

C clef—The sign that indicates that middle C is located wherever the clef is placed. It is also known as the "movable clef" because it has several possible positions. Viola players use a C clef on the middle line of the staff (in this position also called the *alto clef*); trombone players and cellists use a C clef on the fourth line (up) of the staff for high passages (in this position also called the *tenor clef*). Notation: 𝄡 𝄡 . Chapter 2.

Changes—The harmonic progression of the *main tune, chorus,* and improvised sections in jazz and popular music compositions; often called the "chord changes." Chapter 30.

Changing meters—Meter signatures that change during the course of a composition. For example, the piece might begin with $\frac{4}{4}$ meter, change to $\frac{3}{4}$, eventually become $\frac{5}{4}$, and so on. Chapter 4.

Changing tones—A pattern of two nonharmonic tones, the first of which leaves the chord tone stepwise and then skips to another nonharmonic tone, which resolves stepwise in the opposite direction to the next chord tone. Chapter 27.

Chorale—A Lutheran hymn tune, often the basis in German music of the seventeenth and eighteenth centuries for more elaborate compositions. Chorale tunes were often harmonized and arranged by many different composers, such as J.S. Bach, and have often become models for writing four-part harmony. Chapter 25.

Chord—Although in some harmonic systems a chord can be any three or more pitches sounding simultaneously, this text deals only with chords built by stacking thirds on top of each other to form *triads* and *seventh chords.* Harmony based on chords formed in this way is called *tertian harmony.* Chapter 9.

Chord progression—A succession of chords, which may be as few as two chords or a series of any length. Chapter 26.

Chord substitution—In blues, jazz, and pop music the replacement of the original chord of a progression with another chord to add color or to make a more elaborate progression. Chapter 30.

Chord symbols—Symbols usually placed above the staff to indicate the use of particular chords. Capital letters stand for major triads, capital letters with a lowercase m following stand for minor triads, and seventh chords are indicated by the numeral 7 following the chord root name. For example, A⁷ D Bm Em A D G. Chapters 25, 28, 30.

Chord tones—Notes or pitches that are part of the harmony. Chapter 25. *Nonharmonic tones* are notes that are not part of the harmony being sounded with them. Chapter 27.

Chorus—1. A group of singers (a choir). 2. In popular music and jazz forms, the chorus is the repeating melody and *changes* of the compositions. In a vocal piece the same text is used with each repetition. Chapter 30.

Chromatic—1. Half-step melodic movement in which the letter name does not change but the accidental does, for example, C to C♯ or D♭ to D. Chapter 3. 2. A style of music in which there are many chromatic notes outside the normal scale of the piece or passage.

Chromatic scale—The scale made up of all the half steps within an octave. Chapter 3.

Circle of fifths—Two circular patterns showing the order of all the sharp and flat keys. Each circle is created by moving up in perfect fifths, that is, from C to G to D and so on. After the twelfth fifth, the first key is reached again. One can display all the major keys with this diagram (see p. 86), and a second diagram will display the minor keys (see p. 95). Chapters 10, 11.

Circle progression—A harmonic progression or progressions whose roots proceed by descending perfect fifths. For example, the chords A D G C form a circle progression. Chapter 26.

Clef—A symbol placed on a line (or occasionally a space) of a staff to indicate the name and pitch of a note. The pitches of all the other lines and spaces of the staff will be determined by their relation to this note. See also *bass clef, C clef,* and *treble clef.* Chapter 2.

Coda—The closing section of a composition. Chapter 30, Appendix 1.

Color tones—Notes outside the diatonic scale used to create dissonance. Jazz musicians use color tones as the foundation for creating an improvised melody. Chapter 30.

Common time—$\frac{4}{4}$ or **C** meter. Chapter 18.

Comp (or **comping**)—The basic outline of the harmonic progression (*changes*) used by the rhythm section as the foundation on which a jazz soloist improvises. Although individual chords may change (called *chord substitution*), the basic harmonic structure remains the same throughout the improvisation section. Chapter 30.

Compound intervals—Intervals larger than an octave. For example, the major tenth is equivalent to a major third plus a perfect octave. Chapter 17.

Compound meter—Meters with a background of three sub-beats per beat unit instead of two; for example, $\frac{6}{8}$ meter, with two main beats (1 and 4) divided into three sub-beats each: 1 2 3 and 4 5 6. In contrast, a *simple meter,* such as $\frac{2}{4}$, also has two main beats (1 and 2) divided into two sub-beats each. Some other compound meters are $\frac{9}{8}$, $\frac{12}{8}$, $\frac{6}{4}$, and $\frac{9}{4}$. Chapter 21.

Concerto—A composition for a soloist (such as piano, violin, trumpet, or clarinet) or group of soloists and orchestra. In a concerto the orchestra has a major role and is not merely accompaniment. Appendix 1.

Conjunct motion—Notes in a melodic line in which adjacent notes are no further apart than a major second. The opposite kind of melodic motion is *disjunct,* in which there are intervals greater than a major second between adjacent pitches. Chapter 23.

Consequent—The second phrase of a *period* in an *antecedent-consequent* (question-answer) relationship. Appendix 1.

Consonance—A smooth or agreeable sounding interval. The consonances are perfect unisons, major and minor thirds, perfect fourths, perfect fifths, major and minor sixths, and perfect octaves, in contrast to the dissonant intervals (see *dissonance*). Chapter 8.

Contrary motion—The relationship between two simultaneously moving parts in which one voice moves up and the other down. This can be diagrammed as ⬦. Chapter 23.

Counterpoint—A compositional technique in which two or more melodic lines sound simultaneously. Contrapuntal style emphasizes the melodic aspects of each line and usually involves imitation. Appendix 1.

Courante—A seventeenth- and eighteenth-century dance in $\frac{3}{4}$, $\frac{3}{8}$, or $\frac{3}{2}$ meter. It is often part of a *suite* from the time J.S. Bach lived. Appendix 1.

Crescendo (**cresc.**)—Gradually getting louder, also notated ⸺. Chapter 5.

Da capo—Return to the beginning and stop at a point marked by the word "Fine" (the end). Appendix 1.

Decrescendo (**decr.** or **decresc.**)—Gradually getting softer. Same as *diminuendo,* also notated ⸺. Chapter 5.

Diminished interval—An interval created by reducing a perfect or minor interval by one half step while maintaining the same letter names. For example, P5 (C up to G) minus a half step = diminished fifth (C♯–G); m7 (D up to C) minus a half step = diminished seventh (D♯ up to C). Chapters 9, 12.

Diminuendo—Gradually getting softer. Same as *decrescendo.* Chapter 5.

Discography—A listing of musical recordings. Discographies may include such additional information as copyright date, date of recording, artists performing, composer(s), titles of recordings, publisher, and ISBN number. Chapter 30.

Disjunct motion—Notes in a melodic line in which adjacent notes are farther apart than a major second. The opposite kind of melodic motion is *conjunct,* in which there are no intervals greater than a major second between adjacent pitches. Chapter 23.

Dissonance—A harsh or restless sounding interval. The dissonances are major and minor seconds, major and minor sevenths, and the *tritone* (augmented fourth and diminished fifth). Chapters 8, 12.

Dominant—The fifth scale degree. In the key of C major, G is the dominant. The term may also be used to refer to the *dominant chord.* Scale degree, Chapter 22; Chord, Chapter 26.

Dominant chord—Most commonly, the triad or seventh chord built on the fifth degree of a scale. In C major the dominant triad is G B D, and the dominant seventh chord is G B D F. In a minor key the dominant triad usually uses a raised leading tone, so in the key of a minor the triad would be E G♯ B and the seventh chord E G♯ B D. The roman numeral analysis symbols would be V and V⁷. Chapter 26.

Dot—1. A rhythmic notational symbol added after a note to add half again as much durational value. For example, ♩. = ♩ + ♪ (or ♩‿♪). Chapter 4. 2. A marking placed above or below a notehead that means that the note is played detached, or *staccato,* that is, as a short note with a silence filling the rest of the note value. Notated: ♩. Chapter 5.

Double bar—Two vertical lines drawn through a staff or staves to show the end of a composition or section. Two light lines in a double bar normally mean a section end. Notation: ‖ . A light line followed by a heavy line indicates a final close. Notation: ‖ . Chapter 5.

Double flat—Two flat signs before a note that lowers its pitch by two half steps. For example, for B♭♭, the pitch is lowered two half steps from B (to sound the same pitch as A). Chapter 3.

Double sharp—A decorated sign, like an X, before a note that raises the original note pitch by two half steps. For example, for C𝄪 the pitch is raised two half steps from C (to sound the same pitch as D). Chapter 3.

Downbeat—The first beat of a measure. The conductor shows a downbeat by moving his baton downward on the first beat and in other directions for other beats of the measure. Chapter 18.

Drone—A pitch that sounds continuously throughout a piece of music. Bagpipes are built in such a way that they always produce a drone (actually, two drones forming an octave) while the melody is played on another pipe (called the chanter) of the same instrument. Some other instruments or groups of instruments can also produce this effect. Chapter 27.

Drum set—The core of the percussion of the rhythm section in a jazz ensemble. The drums usually include snare drum, mounted tom(s), floor tom(s), and bass drum. Cymbals include high hat, ride, crash, splash, and specialty cymbals such as china and sizzle. Ancillary percussion may include cowbell, bells, shakers, and so on. Chapter 30.

Duple meter—Two beats per measure, such as $\frac{2}{2}$, $\frac{2}{4}$, and $\frac{2}{8}$. Chapter 18.

Duration—The length of time a musical sound lasts. Chapter 1.

Dynamic—The intensity of loudness or softness. Dynamics are indicated by signs such as *f* (forte) for loud and *p* (piano) for soft. Chapter 5.

Eighth note—The note with a filled notehead, a stem, and a flag at the end of the stem, which is equal to *half* the value of a quarter note. Two or more eighth notes may be connected by a beam instead of using flags. Notation: ♪ or in a group ♫ . Chapter 4.

Embellishments—Ornamental notes that are often written in small notation or indicated by special signs, such as *trills* or *turns.* Chapter 5. Embellishments can also be improvised by the performer in some styles of music. Chapters 27, 30.

Enharmonic—Pitches that sound the same but are spelled differently; for example, the note B is enharmonic with C flat. Chapter 3.

Escape tone—A nonharmonic tone approached by step and left by skip. Chapter 27.

Fake book—A collection of *lead sheets* bound into a publication of jazz and popular music. Most fake books include chord changes, melody (the tune), and text (if applicable). Good fake books will include style, tempo, authors of texts, composers, copyright information, and sometimes discography. Chapters 28, 30.

Fermata—Literally, "a held" note. The sign ⌒ lengthens a note for an unspecified amount of time, often making the note about twice its normal length. Chapter 5.

Fifth—An interval embracing five scale degrees. If it has seven half steps, it is called a *perfect* fifth. If there are only six half steps, the interval is a *diminished* fifth. For example, C up to G is a perfect fifth, and B up to F is a diminished fifth. Chapter 9.

Fifth of the triad—The note a fifth above the root of a triad; the fifth factor of a triad. Chapter 9.

First inversion—The position of a triad in which the third of the chord is the lowest-sounding pitch. For example, E G C is the first inversion of the C major triad. The symbol to show a first inversion chord is a ^{6} or $^6_3$ below the bass note. Chapter 25.

Flag—A part of a notational sign that affects the value of the note to which it is attached by reducing it by a half. If a flag is attached to a quarter note ♩ to become ♪, the note is an eighth note. If two flags are attached ♫, the note is a sixteenth note, and so on. Chapter 4.

Flat—1. A symbol that, when placed before a note on the staff, lowers the pitch by one half step. Notation: ♭. Chapter 3. 2. Sometimes used in tuning to mean a note is lower than it should be. For example, "The C you are playing is too flat (i.e., too low)."

Forte—A dynamic indication that means loud. Notation: $\boldsymbol{f}$. Chapter 5.

Forte piano—A dynamic indication that means loud, then suddenly soft. Notation: $\boldsymbol{fp}$. Chapter 5.

Fortissimo—The dynamic indication for very loud. Notation: $\boldsymbol{ff}$. Chapter 5.

Fourth—An interval embracing four scale degrees. If it has five half steps, it is called a *perfect* fourth. If there are six half steps, the interval is an *augmented* fourth. For example, C up to F is a perfect fourth, and F up to B is an augmented fourth. Chapter 12.

Fret—A small metal strip or gut placed across the fingerboard of stringed instruments, such as the mandolin, guitar, or lute. Frets mark off the fingerboard in half steps, guiding the player in placing his or her fingers on the desired pitches. By contrast the violin, viola, cello, and string bass are nonfretted instruments. Chapter 1.

Fugue—A contrapuntal form based on a short melodic idea (the subject) that is introduced one voice at a time and reappears throughout the composition. Fugues are frequently written for keyboard instruments and were especially cultivated during the eighteenth century, although they have been written by many composers in later times. Fugal style may be used for sections within larger compositions that are not fugal throughout. Appendix 1.

Gavotte—An accented old French dance in $\frac{4}{4}$ meter. Gavottes begin with a strong upbeat. During Bach's time, a gavotte was often one of the movements of a *suite*. Appendix 1.

Gigue—A fast dance, usually in $\frac{6}{8}$ meter, that was often one of the movements of a suite in Bach's time. The French gigue was a descendant of the English jig. Appendix 1.

Glissando—A musical effect caused by "sliding" rapidly between two pitches on an instrument. On the piano, this is done by sliding the thumb quickly over the white keys of the instrument. Harps also use the effect by pulling the hands rapidly across the strings. On instruments such as the trombone or violin, and even on the clarinet, a continuous pitch slide can be performed. The most famous clarinet glissando is the opening of George Gershwin's orchestral piece *Rhapsody in Blue*. Chapter 3.

Grace note—An ornament in which a small note with a slash through it precedes the principal note to which the ornament is attached. It is performed rapidly just before the beat on which the principal note occurs. Notation: ♪ ♩. Chapter 5.

Grand staff—The two staves with the treble clef on the top staff and bass on the bottom. Piano music is customarily written on a grand staff. Chapter 2.

Half cadence—A closing harmonic formula that ends with a dominant chord, for example, I to V or IV to V. Chapter 26.

Half note—The note value that is one half the value of a whole note and twice the value of a quarter note. Notation: ♩. Chapter 4.

Half step—The smallest interval on the piano keyboard or the interval between two adjacent frets on the guitar. C to C♯ is a half step. The only half steps between adjacent white keys on the piano are E to F and B to C. Chapter 3.

Harmonic—1. Relating to harmony or simultaneous sounds. 2. Sometimes used as a synonym for *upper partials* or *overtones*. Chapter 1. 3. A special effect on stringed instruments created by lightly touching the string exactly at points that produce the high upper partial note only, giving a flutelike sound. 4. One of the forms of the minor scale. Chapter 15.

Harmonic interval—The interval between two pitches that sound at the same time. Chapter 7.

Harmonic minor scale—A form of the minor scale that uses an accidental to raise the seventh degree of the scale by one half step. This produces a *leading tone* (a raised note tending to move upward by a half step) between the seventh and eighth notes of the scale. For example, in a minor, the harmonic form of the scale is A B C D E F G♯ A. Chapter 15.

Harmonizing—The process of selecting chords to accompany and support a melody. Chapter 28.

Harmony—In general, any combination of simultaneously sounding tones; the vertical aspect of music that forms *chords*. In this text, the harmonic patterns used are chords built by stacking up thirds to form *triads* and *seventh chords* (*tertian harmony*). Introduction.

Hemiola—A special accent shift within a bar. In $\frac{6}{8}$ meter rhythmic accents can shift from the first and fourth eighth notes to the first, third, and fifth eighth notes, giving the effect of $\frac{3}{4}$ meter to the passage. This device is frequently found in the compositions of Brahms. Chapter 21.

Imitation—The reappearance in close succession of a melodic motive or theme in different voices of a contrapuntal composition. Appendix 1.

Imperfect cadence—An *authentic cadence,* which differs from the *perfect authentic cadence* in that the final tonic chord does not contain the tonic note in its highest-sounding voice. Chapter 26.

Improvisation—1. The spontaneous creation of a musical line, harmonic progression, and/or rhythmic elements during live performance. This may involve embellishment of preexisting material. The art of improvisation is found in virtually every musical culture around the world. 2. Jazz musicians employ improvisation in creating a solo line, changing and evolving the bass line or percussion rhythms, or *comping* a variety of chord *changes* during the solo section of a jazz composition. Improvisation is the essence of the jazz art. Chapter 30.

Intensity—The loudness or softness of a musical sound. Chapter 1.

Interval—The difference in pitch between two tones. The interval between C and D is two half steps (one whole step) and is called a "major second." Chapter 7.

Intro—A shortened term for introduction, the opening section of a composition. Chapter 30.

Inversion of an interval—An interval is inverted by placing the lowest of the two pitches above the upper pitch or placing the upper of the two pitches below the lower one. For example, the P5, C up to G, inverts to form the P4, G up to C. Chapter 17.

Inversion of a triad—A triad placed in any arrangement where the root is not the lowest-sounding pitch. See also *first inversion* and *second inversion.* Chapter 25.

Jam session—An improvised, usually unrehearsed and often spontaneous performance of music. Playing in such a session is called "jamming." Chapter 30.

Jazz standard—A jazz tune that has been recorded by numerous artists and has become a standard part of the jazz musicians' repertoire. Chapter 30.

Jazz styles—Jazz musicians communicate with one another through an understanding of a wide variety of jazz styles. Each style dictates (to some degree) how a soloist improvises and what is played by members of the rhythm section. Some examples of jazz styles are ballad, blues, boogie, bop, bounce, funk, fusion, shuffle, swing, rock, waltz, and a wide variety of Latin musical style from Latin America and the Caribbean, including bossa nova, samba, and tango. Chapter 30.

Key signature—The flats or sharps that are arranged in a particular order at the beginning of each staff to indicate the key of a composition. Chapters 10, 12.

Lead sheet—The individual tune in a fake book, which includes the primary elements of a popular or jazz music composition, including chord changes, melody, text (if any), and occasionally keyboard realizations and/or guitar tablature. Chapter 30.

Leading tone—The seventh scale degree in the major, harmonic minor, and ascending melodic minor scales. It is one half step below the tonic note. In contrast, the seventh scale degree in natural minor is called the *subtonic* because it is a whole step from the adjacent tonic note. Chapter 15.

Ledger lines—Short horizontal lines above or below a staff on which can be written notes not within the normal range of the staff. Chapter 3.

Legato—a term indicating phrasing, derived from an Italian word meaning "bound together." The notes are to be played smoothly, with no interruption between the notes. Chapter 5.

Major scale—A *scale* with half-step intervals between scale degrees 3 and 4 and 7 and 8. The other intervals are all whole steps. There are seven different notes in a major scale, with the *tonic* note repeated at the end. Chapter 7.

Mass—The highest ceremony of the Catholic Church. It may be performed with the text spoken or set to music. The Ordinary (the parts for which the text is always the same) includes the Kyrie, Gloria, Credo, Sanctus, and Agnus Dei, the parts usually set to music. The texts of other parts of the mass (known as the Proper) vary. Chapter 8, Appendix 1.

Mazurka—A dance originating in Poland, usually in $\frac{3}{4}$ meter with a characteristic accent on the third beat of the measure. Appendix 1.

Measure—A group of meter beats separated by *bar lines* (vertical lines also known as measure bars, drawn through the staff or staves). For example, in $\frac{3}{4}$ meter, a measure consists of three beats. Chapter 4.

Mediant—The third scale degree. The term may also be used for the chord on that degree. Chapter 22.

Melodic contour—The shape formed by the ascending and descending pitches of a melody. Chapter 22.

Melodic interval—The difference in pitch between two notes that are sounded melodically, that is, one after the other. Chapter 7.

Melodic minor scale—A minor scale in which accidentals raise the sixth and seventh degrees in the ascending form of the scale so that there are half-step intervals between scale degrees 2 and 3 and 7 and 8. These accidentals are not used in the descending form of the scale, so it is the same as the *natural minor scale.* Chapter 15.

Melodic motive—A short but identifiable fragment of melody that is often repeated exactly or with modification in the course of a composition. A motive consists of as few as two notes and generally does not exceed eight or ten. Chapter 24.

Melody—A horizontal succession of musical tones that possess shape or pattern. Introduction.

Meter—The basic system of a musical pulse with regularly recurring strong and weak beats. The meter is indicated by a *meter signature.* Chapter 4.

Meter signature (or time signature)—The numbers at the beginning of a piece of music that show the grouping of the beats and the value of the basic beat unit. In *simple meter* the upper number shows the number of beats per measure, and the lower indicates the note value of the beat. For example, in $\frac{3}{4}$ meter, the 3 indicates that there are three pulses with a strong beat on the first pulse of each group. The 4 indicates that the beat unit is a quarter note. Chapter 18. In *compound meter,* such as $\frac{6}{8}$, where there are three sub-beats per beat, the upper number, 6, indicates the number of sub-beat units in the measure, and the lower number, 8, indicates that the sub-beats are eighth notes. In compound meter the beat units are dotted notes. For example, in $\frac{6}{8}$, the beat unit is a dotted quarter note. Chapter 21.

Metric—Having to do with musical *meter.* Chapter 4.

Metronome—A device that can set a regular pulse at any tempo desired and is calibrated with numbers indicating the number of beats per minute. Modern metronomes are electric and give the pulse with a clicking sound or by a flashing light. Earlier metronomes used a pendulum with a weight that could be moved to the desired number to produce clicks at the exact tempo desired. Chapter 4.

Mezzo forte—Moderately loud. Notation: *mf*. Chapter 5.

Mezzo piano—Moderately soft. Notation: *mp*. Chapter 5.

Middle C—The note C nearest the middle of the keyboard. In musical notation it is the C written on the ledger line between the bass and treble clefs. When referring to this note in its exact octave without using staff notation, it is *c'*. Chapter 2.

Minor key—A key in which the interval between 1 and 3 is a minor third, and the normal notes of the key are summarized by the three forms of the minor scale: *natural minor, melodic minor,* and *harmonic minor.* For example, F minor means a key using the minor scales beginning on the pitch F. Chapters 11, 15.

Minor scale—A generic term for a scale that may refer to any of the three: *natural minor, harmonic minor,* or *melodic minor.* Chapters 11, 15.

Minor triad—A triad made up of a minor third from root to third and a perfect fifth from root to fifth. For example, D F A is a minor triad. Chapter 13.

Minuet—A French court dance of the eighteenth century. It was of moderate tempo and $\frac{3}{4}$ meter. The name indicates that small steps were used in the dance. Appendix 1.

Mode—One of several scales used in old church music and also found in folk music, popular music, and jazz. The modes differ from major and minor scales in their placement of half steps and whole steps. Chapter 6.

Moderato—Moderate tempo. Chapter 4.

Modified repetition—Repetition of units such as *phrases* in which the second is similar to the first but including changes such as melodic decorations or slight harmonic modifications. Chapter 24.

Modified sequence—A *sequence* in which subsequent segments are altered slightly without destroying the basic sequential nature of the passage. Chapter 24.

Motion—1. The relation between the directions in which two voices move is called motion. See *contrary motion, oblique motion, similar motion,* and *parallel motion.* Chapter 23. 2. Motion is also used to describe the way a single voice moves in a melody. In a melody, motion is *conjunct* if the pitches move smoothly to adjacent pitches. If the melody has skips of larger intervals, the motion is *disjunct.* Chapter 23.

Motive—A distinctive melodic or rhythmic figure. See also *melodic motive* and *rhythmic motive.* Chapter 24.

Music—The art of sound moving in time that expresses ideas and emotions in significant forms through the elements of harmony, melody, rhythm, and tonal color. Introduction.

Music appreciation—The term used for studies intended to increase the love and understanding of music, especially for listeners. Introduction.

Music history—Studies of the general history of music, musical styles, musicians, notation, musical instruments, and so on. Introduction.

Music literature—The vast repertory of musical compositions. It is often studied in separate courses that treat the literature of a particular medium of performance. Introduction.

Music theory—The study of patterns (melodic, harmonic, rhythmic, and formal) and their use in music. Introduction.

Natural—A symbol used to cancel a sharp or flat. It is placed just before the affected note. Notated: ♮. Chapter 3.

Natural minor scale—A scale with half steps between scale degrees 2 and 3 and 5 and 6 and with whole steps between the other scale degrees. It uses only the notes of its key signature, whereas the other two forms of the minor scale add accidentals. It is also known as "pure minor." Chapter 11.

Neighboring tone—One of the nonharmonic patterns that can be used between two chord tones of the same pitch. In the melodic pattern D C D, C is a neighboring tone if it is nonharmonic and the two D's are chord tones. Chapter 27.

Nocturne—A piece often evoking the expressive qualities of night (hence the name) and usually written for piano in the romantic era. It was characteristically an expressive melody accompanied by broken chords. Many nocturnes were written by Chopin. Appendix 1.

Nonharmonic tone—A tone or tones that are not part of the accompanying or prevailing triad or chord. *Passing tones, neighboring tones, suspensions, anticipations,* and so on, are types of nonharmonic patterns. Chapters 23, 27.

Nonmetric—Music that has no defined steady meter (regularly recurring pattern of strong and weak beats, as in some types of church chant) or pulse (as in some electronic music). Chapter 4.

Note—1. A written symbol that can be put on a *staff* to indicate the pitch and duration of a music sound. Chapter 2. 2. Can be used to mean a specific musical sound, as in the sentence "You just played a wrong note!"

Notehead—The oval portion of a written note. Notation: ♩ . A *stem* is added to most noteheads. One note, however, is made up entirely of a notehead: the whole note. Notation: 𝅝 . Chapter 4.

Oblique motion—The relationship between two simultaneously sounding parts in which one voice moves and the other stays on the same pitch. This may be diagrammed as ⟋ or ⟍ . Chapter 23.

Octave—The interval of eight notes. It is a *perfect* interval and is so smooth sounding that the harmonic interval almost sounds as one. The number of vibrations in a note is doubled when the next octave is reached. The letter name of the two notes of an octave is the same. From *c'* up to *c''* is an octave. Chapter 8.

Opera—A staged musical drama that is usually sung throughout. Appendix 1.

Opus—Literally, a work or composition. Composers often number their works in order of publication with an opus number. For example, Opus 1 is followed by Opus 2. It is abbreviated op. or Op. Chapter 4.

Oratorio—A dramatic literary text, often of sacred or heroic content, that is set musically for chorus, soloists, and orchestra. *Messiah,* an eighteenth-century work by G. F. Handel, is probably the best-known oratorio. Appendix 1.

Organum—A very early (about A.D. 900) way of "harmonizing" a melody by accompanying it with parallel perfect fourths or perfect fifths. Later organum developed more complex patterns. Chapter 9.

Ornament—A pattern of notes decorating the principal notes of a melody, often shown by special signs, such as the *trill* or the *turn*. Ornaments that cannot be designated by special signs can be shown in print smaller than the principal notes. Notation: *tr* (trill) or ∿ (turn). Ornaments can be improvised by the performer in some styles of music. Chapter 5.

Parallel intervals—The interval or intervals does not change between parts when they are moving in *parallel motion*. For example, D E F♯ G are parallel perfect fifths. Chapter 23.
         G A B C

Parallel motion—A special case of *similar motion* in which the same interval distance is maintained between the moving voices. This may be diagrammed as ⟋ or ⟍ . Chapter 23.

Parallel scales—The major and minor scales that begin on the same tonic note. Parallel keys do not have the same key signature. For example, C major is the parallel major of C minor, and conversely the C minor scale is the parallel minor of C major. Chapter 11.

Partita—A term originating in the seventeenth century for a group of dances or other movements. Appendix 1.

Passing tone—A nonharmonic tone that passes stepwise between two chord tones. For example, in the pattern C D E, D is a passing tone if C and E are chord tones. Chapters 25, 27.

Pavan—A stately Renaissance processional dance in moderate to slow duple meter. Chapter 11.

Pedal tone—A note of extended length, usually in the bass voice, over which are sounded various harmonic progressions, both dissonant and consonant with the pedal tone. Chapter 27.

Perfect cadence—Perfect *authentic cadence* (V to I), in which the tonic note is both the highest and the lowest sounding tone in the final chord. Chapter 26.

Perfect consonances (perfect intervals)—Very smooth and acoustically closely related intervals, of which there are only four: the perfect *octave*, the perfect *fifth*, the perfect *fourth*, and the perfect *unison*. Chapter 8.

Period—A combination of two or more related phrases culminating in a strong cadence, usually a perfect authentic cadence. Appendix 1.

Phrase—The "sentence" of musical speech. Phrases are often about four measures long and end with some kind of cadence. Chapter 22.

Phrase marking—A curved line sometimes used to connect a whole phrase in piano music. Chapter 5.

Pianissimo—Very soft dynamic. Notation: *pp*. Chapter 5.

Piano—Soft dynamic. Notation: *p*. Chapter 5.

Pickup—Synonym for *anacrusis* or *upbeat*.

Pitch—The sound property that the ear perceives as high or low. What the ear hears is created by regular number of vibrations per second of the sounding body. For example, the note *a'* (the middle A on the piano) has a rate of 440 vibrations per second. Chapter 1.

Plagal cadence—The cadence formula sub-dominant to tonic (IV–I). This is often called an amen cadence since it is the formula often used for the word "amen" following a hymn. Chapter 29.

Polonaise—A processional dance in $\frac{3}{4}$ meter of Polish origin. Appendix 1.

Position—The arrangement of a triad with regard to which member of the triad is in the bass. *Root position* means that the root is in the bass, *first inversion* that the third is in the bass, and *second inversion* that the fifth is in the bass. Chapter 25.

Pre-dominant harmonies—Chords which lead to the dominant chord, such as the supertonic (ii) or subdominant (IV). Chapter 29.

Pre-tonic harmonies—Chords which most often lead to the tonic chord, such as the dominant (V) or leading tone (vii°). Chapter 29.

Prelude—An introductory movement or section, sometimes a short separate piece. Appendix 1.

Preparation—The consonant pitch (a chord tone) that prepares the nonharmonic device called the *suspension*. Chapter 27.

Primary triads—The most important triads in a key: *tonic* (I), *subdominant* (IV), and *dominant* (V). Chapter 26.

Program music—Music written to conform to or express an extramusical idea, program, poetic idea, or other imaginative scheme. Appendix 1.

Progression—The succession of one chord to the next, sometimes referring to an entire series of chord movements. Chapter 26.

Quadruple meter—Meters containing four beats. The *simple* quadruple *meters* include $\frac{4}{2}$, $\frac{4}{4}$, $\frac{4}{8}$, and $\mathbf{C}$. The *compound* quadruple *meters* include $\frac{12}{8}$, $\frac{12}{16}$, and so on. Chapter 18.

Quality—1. Used with respect to that property of sound that distinguishes the sound of different instruments. Tonal quality is a synonym for *timbre*. Chapter 1. 2. When used in connection with harmony, it refers to the type of chord, as in the phrase "the chord quality is major." Chapters 9, 13, 28. 3. It may also be used to describe intervals, as in the phrase "the interval qualities are dissonant." Chapter 8.

Quarter note—The note with a filled notehead and a stem that is the equivalent of one pulse in $\frac{4}{4}$ meter. Notation: ♩. Chapter 4.

Rags—Ragtime compositions, often written for the piano, for example, Scott Joplin's "Maple Leaf Rag." Chapter 19.

Ragtime—Originally a type of highly syncopated music that later became associated with jazz. Chapters 19, 30.

Relative scales—The major and minor scales that share the same key signature. For example, C major is the relative major of a minor, and conversely a minor is the relative minor of C major. Chapter 11.

Repeat sign—A double bar with two dots beside it; the symbol means that a section should be repeated. Notation. ▤ . Chapter 5.

Resolution—To relieve dissonance by following it with an appropriate consonance. Chapters 27, 29.

Rest—A silence indicated by a musical symbol; also the sign indicating this measured silence. Chapter 4.

Retardation—A nonharmonic tone that is similar to a *suspension* except that the retardation resolves upward by step, whereas suspensions resolves downward by step. Chapter 27.

Rhythm—The time relationships in music. Introduction.

Rhythm section—The core group of a jazz ensemble that usually includes three components: harmony (piano or guitar), bass (double bass or bass guitar), and rhythm (drum set and ancillary percussion). Chapter 30.

Rhythmic motive—A *motive* whose distinguishing features are primarily rhythmic rather than pitch relationships. Chapter 24.

Ritardando (or **Rallentando**)—Slow the tempo gradually. It is abbreviated rit. (or rall.). Chapter 5.

Roman numeral analysis (**Roman numeral symbols**)—A system of analytical symbols that are placed beneath a staff to show the functions in the key of the chords above. For example, a dominant chord is symbolized by the roman numeral V. Chapter 25.

Rondo—A large musical form with a recurring main theme alternating with one or more contrasting elements. For example, if the main theme is labeled A, and B and C are contrasting material, a rondo might be diagramed as A B A C A B A. Appendix 1.

Root—The generating pitch on which a triad is based. For example, in the triad C E G, C is the root. Chapter 9.

Root position—An arrangement of a triad (chord position) in which the root is the lowest sounding pitch. Chapter 25.

Round—A type of *canon* in which voices entering at regular time intervals imitate each other exactly. "Row, Row, Row Your Boat" is an example of a round. Chapter 17, Appendix 1.

Sarabande—A dance of Spanish origin, usually with a slow tempo, in triple meter. Appendix 1.

Scale—The notes of a particular tonality arranged stepwise. Chapter 6.

Scale degree—The particular note of a scale. For example, in C major the third scale degree, or mediant, is the note E. Chapter 7.

Scherzo—An Italian term which literally means "joke." The scherzo was often used as a movement of a sonata or a symphony in place of the *minuet*. It is in $\frac{3}{4}$ time and is faster than a minuet with more vigorous rhythms and accents. Chapter 19, Appendix 1.

Second—The interval formed by adjacent notes of a major or minor scale. Seconds may be major (two half steps), minor (one half step), or augmented (three half steps, as in the interval between the sixth and seventh degrees of the *harmonic minor scale*). Seconds are *dissonant* intervals. A diminished second would sound like a unison and does not occur in major or minor scales. Chapter 7.

Second inversion—The position of a triad in which the lowest-sounding tone is the fifth of the triad. For example, G C E is the second inversion of the C major triad. The symbol for a second inversion chord is ⁶₄, placed under the bass note. Chapter 25.

Sequence—A musical device in which a short section of music (usually a melodic pattern) is repeated on different scale degrees, for example, C D E, D E F, E F G. Each part of a sequence is called a leg of the sequence. Chapter 24.

Seventh—The interval formed by a note that is seven letter names above or below a given pitch. Sevenths may be major (eleven half steps), minor (ten half steps), or diminished (nine half steps). Sevenths are *dissonant* intervals. An augmented seventh would sound like an octave and does not occur in the major or minor scales. Chapter 14.

Seventh chord—The chord formed by adding an additional third (above the fifth) to a triad. For example, G B D is a triad, and G B D F is a seventh chord. Chapters 28, 29.

Sforzando (or sforzato)—Sudden accent. Notation: *sf* or *sfz*. Chapter 5.

Sharp—1. The symbol meaning to raise the pitch of a note by one half step. Notation: ♯. Chapter 3. 2. Sometimes used in tuning to mean the note is higher than it should be. For example, "The C you are playing is too sharp (i.e., too high)."

Similar motion—The relationship between two (or more) simultaneously moving parts in which the voices move in the same direction. This may be diagrammed as ⟋. Chapter 23.

Simple intervals—Intervals no larger than an octave. Chapter 17.

Simple meter or **simple time**—Meter in which there are two subdivisions of the beat. Chapter 18.

Simple position—The closest possible arrangement of the notes of a triad or chord in root position. For triads and seventh chords all the notes fit within an octave. For example, if all the notes are in the same octave, C E G is the simple position of the C major triad. Chapter 25.

Sixteenth note—The note that is half the rhythmic value of an eighth note. Four sixteenth notes equal one quarter note. Notation: ♪. A group of sixteenth notes can be beamed together as ♬♬. Chapter 4.

Sixth—The interval formed by a note that is six letter names above or below a given pitch. Sixths may be major (nine half steps) or minor (eight half steps). Sixths are *imperfect consonances*. For example, C up to A is a major sixth, and E up to C is a minor sixth. Chapter 14.

Sixty-fourth note—The note that is half the rhythmic value of a thirty-second note. Sixteen sixty-fourth notes equal one quarter note. Notation: ♪. A group of sixty-fourth notes can be beamed together as ♬♬♬♬. Chapter 4.

Slur—A curved line above or below a series of notes indicating that the notes are to be played without articulation between notes (*legato*). For string players the notes are to be played on one bow stroke, for singers sung on one syllable, and for wind players without interruption of the windstream. Notation: ♩‿♩. Chapter 5.

Sonata—An instrumental composition (often for solo piano or for piano and a melodic instrument such as violin or flute) that usually has three or four movements. Appendix 1.

Sonata form—A particular form used for one or more movements of a sonata, symphony, string quartet, or a variety of individual compositions. The three main sections of a sonata are the exposition, in which the main thematic material is presented; a development, in which this material is manipulated in various ways; and the recapitulation, which brings back the original material. Appendix 1.

Soprano—1. The highest voice range; the higher range for voices of women and children. 2. The top part in four-part music. Chapter 25.

Spiritual—A religious folk song or composed song that is an important part of the cultural heritage of African-Americans. More recent spirituals are often called "gospel songs." Appendix 1.

Staccato—An articulation in which the notes are distinctly separated, sometimes by as much as half their notated value, with silence during the remainder of the note's value; detached style. Notation: A dot placed directly above or below a note. Chapter 5.

Staff (pl. **staves**)—The group of five parallel lines forming the lines and spaces on which the notes are placed. The higher lines and spaces are higher in pitch than the lower ones. Chapter 2.

Stem—The straight line up or down from the notehead. The symbols for all note values smaller than the whole note include stems. Chapter 4.

Stepwise motion—Melodic movement to an adjacent note. Chapter 3.

Strain—A musical unit, possibly a phrase or period; a term used especially in popular music forms. For example, in *ragtime* a piece usually has four strains of which each is 16 measures long, and each is repeated. Appendix 1.

Subdominant—The fourth scale degree (or step) of major and minor scales or the chord on that degree. For example, F is the subdominant of C major. Chapter 22.

Submediant—The sixth scale degree (or step) of major and minor scales or the chord on that degree. For example, A is the submediant of C major. Chapter 22.

Subtonic—The seventh scale degree (or step) of the natural minor scale. It is a whole tone below the tonic, in contrast to the leading tone, which is a half step below the tonic. For example, G is the subtonic of a minor, but G♯ is the leading tone of A major, a harmonic minor, or the ascending form of the a melodic minor scale. Chapter 22.

Suite—From the seventeenth through the nineteenth century, a suite was usually a group of dances. In the twentieth century the term was broadened to include a set of shorter compositions of any type. Appendix 1.

Supertonic—The second scale degree (or step) of major and minor scales or the chord on that degree. For example, D is the supertonic of C major. Chapter 22.

Sus4 chord—A type of chord used in jazz and pop harmony in which the fourth above the root is *substituted* for the normal third of the chord. The fourth does not resolve and is not treated as an embellishment of a triad. Chapter 30.

Suspension—An accented nonharmonic tone that is prepared by the same note and resolved by a tone one step lower. For example, in the pattern C C B, if the first C is a chord tone and the second C a nonchord tone on an accented beat or part of a beat, the second C is the suspension, which then should move downward stepwise to the B, the new chord tone. Chapters 27, 28.

Symphony—1. A large composition, usually with several movements, written for orchestra (or sometimes for band). 2. An orchestra usually having string, woodwind, brass, and percussion sections. Appendix 1.

Syncopation—A shift from the normal metric accent to a beat or part of a beat not usually accented. Chapter 19.

Tablature—A system of notation in which notes are not placed on a staff but are indicated by letters, special symbols (such as drawings of a segment of a fingerboard), or other symbols. For example, guitar tablature shows parts of the fingerboard of the instrument and places dots where the fingers are to be placed. Appendix 3.

Tempo—The speed at which the beat moves. Tempo is usually indicated by special Italian words or may be shown exactly by using a *metronome* marking. *Allegro* is a fast tempo; *adagio* is a slow tempo. Chapter 4.

Tenor—1. The upper voice range of adult male voices. 2. In four-part writing, the third voice down is the tenor voice. Chapter 25.

Tertian harmony—A system of harmony in which the chords are constructed by piling thirds on top of each other. Triads and seventh chords are the most important chords in this system. Although chords can be constructed of other intervals, only tertian harmony is covered in this text. Chapter 9.

Third—The interval formed by a note that is three letter names above or below a given pitch. Thirds may be major (four half steps) or minor (three half steps). Thirds are *imperfect consonances.* For example, C up to E is a major third, and E up to G is a minor third. Under special circumstances thirds, like other intervals, can be made smaller (*diminished*) or larger (*augmented*) than the normal sizes. Chapter 8.

Third of the triad—The note a major or minor third above the root of the triad. Chapter 9.

Thirty-second note—The note that has half the value of a sixteenth note. Eight thirty-second notes equal a quarter note. Notation: ♪. A group of thirty-second notes can be beamed together as ♫♫♫♫. Chapter 4.

Three-part musical form—Made up of three sections, each with a strong cadence. The third section is a repeat or modified repeat of the first section, forming the pattern A B A, for example, the minuet-trio-minuet movement of classic symphonies. Appendix 1.

Tie—A curved line connecting the noteheads of two notes of the same pitch, indicating that the note values are to be added together. Notation: ♩‿♩. Chapter 4.

Timbre—The tone color or quality of a sound. The difference between the sound of a violin and the sound of a clarinet is the difference in timbre. Chapter 1.

Time signature—Same as *meter signature.*

Tonal center—The note around which the pitch organization of a piece is centered. Chapter 6.

Tonality—A musical system in which one note (the *tonic* or *tonal center*) is the center (point of maximum repose) of the system and all other notes gravitate around it and eventually lead toward it. Chapter 6.

Tonic—1. The first step of a major or minor scale that is also the *tonal center.* Chapters 6, 15. 2. The chord on the first scale degree.

Transpose—To move a note to another pitch. This may be done with a whole piece of music by rewriting it (or playing it) at a specified interval above or below the original. For example, a piece in C major may be transposed to the key of G major by writing or playing all the notes a perfect fifth above their original pitch. The process of doing this is called *transposition.* Chapter 9.

Treble clef—The sign that indicates that the second line (up) of the staff is the G above middle C. It is also known as the G clef. Notation: 𝄞. Chapter 2.

Triad—A chord formed by arranging three pitches one above the other in thirds. There are four common types: major (with a major third and perfect fifth above the *root*), minor (with a minor third and perfect fifth), diminished (minor third and diminished fifth), and augmented (major third and augmented fifth). Chapter 9.

Trill—An ornament in which the principal note and its upper neighbor are performed in rapid alternation. Notation: *tr*. Chapter 5.

Triple meter—Any meter with three beats per measure. *Simple triple meters* include $\frac{3}{2}$, $\frac{3}{4}$, and $\frac{3}{8}$. *Compound triple meters* include $\frac{9}{16}$, $\frac{9}{8}$, and $\frac{9}{4}$. Chapters 18, 21.

Triplet—A group of three equal notes in the time normally allotted to two. It is indicated by a 3 above or below the group of notes. It will also have a bracket to show the grouping if the notes are not beamed. Notation: ♫♪ or ♩♩♩ . Chapter 20.

Tritone—An interval of three whole steps. Both the diminished fifth (such as B up to F) and the augmented fourth (such as D up to G♯) are tritones. The only tritones between white keys of the piano are B up or down to F. The tritone is the only interval that is the same size after it has been inverted. Chapter 12.

Turn—An ornament of four or five notes that turn around the principal note. Notation: ∞. Chapter 5.

Twelve-tone row—An early twentieth-century method of composing with all twelve notes of the octave arranged in such a way that no pitch is duplicated until all have been sounded. It is a technique used in *atonal* compositions. Chapter 6.

Unison—1. The interval formed by two notes of the same pitch. Chapter 8. 2. The performance of the same notes by several players or singers at once. If several people sing or play something at the same pitch, they are said to be "in unison."

Upbeat—The note or group of notes that immediately precede an accented beat, especially at the beginning of a composition or phrase. It received its name because a conductor's baton is raised for an upbeat in preparation for the downbeat (accented beat) to follow. At the beginning of a phrase or composition it can also be called the *pickup* or *anacrusis*. Chapters 4, 8.

Voicing of chords—The arrangement of the notes of a chord in a harmonic texture of four or more voices, with one or more notes of the chord doubled. Examples of chords voiced in four parts (hymn style) are found in Chapter 25. In jazz and popular music, chord voicing also plays a very important role in defining the harmonic sound of the art. Popular music voices chords in relation to simple guitar harmonies, whereas jazz chord voicings generally relate to chords used by a pianist. Chapter 30. Appendix 3.

Waltz—A dance that originated in the nineteenth century and is in moderate triple meter, usually $\frac{3}{4}$. Appendix 1.

Whole note—A rhythmic symbol that has the value of four quarter notes or two half notes. It is the only note in common use at present that does not have a stem. Notation: **o**. Chapter 4.

Whole step—The interval equal to two half steps. On the piano keyboard there is a whole step between each pair of adjacent white keys, except for E to F and B to C. Chapter 3.

Whole-tone scale—A scale made up entirely of whole steps, used especially during the early twentieth century by some composers. The scale has one less note (six) than the major and minor scales, each of which has seven different notes. An example of a whole-tone scale is C D E F♯ G♯ A♯ C. Chapter 16.

Index to Musical Examples

+ by a composer's name indicates American

A

"All through the Night" (Welsh traditional song), 321

+"Amazing Grace: (American hymn), 252

anonymous, folk and traditional songs and carols,

"All through the Night" (Welsh), 231

+"Amazing Grace" (American), 252

"Auld Lang Syne" (Scottish), 162

"Believe Me, If All Those Endearing Young Charms" (Irish), 243

"The Birch Tree" (Russian), 98

"The Boar's Head" (English), 40

+"Clementine" (American), 216

+"Down in the Valley" (American), 191

"Drink to Me Only with Thine Eyes" (English), 205

"Early One Morning" (English), 63

"Farmer in the Dell," 201

"The Foggy, Foggy Dew" (English), 109

"Frère Jacques" (French), 203

+"Go Down, Moses" (American spiritual), 124

"God Rest Ye Merry Gentlemen" (English), 143

"Greensleeves" (English), 134

+"Hello, Girls!" (American), 163

"Holland," 275

+"Home on the Range" (American cowboy song), 238, 267

"Hop sa sa!" (German), 256

+"Irene, Goodnight" (American), 266

"Is That So?" (Polish), 143

+"Jimmy Crack Corn" (American), 240

+"Joshua Fit de Battle of Jericho" (spiritual), 175

+"The Land of Arizona" (American), 266

+"Little Brown Jug" (American), 268

"Lullaby" (German), 213

+"The Man on the Flying Trapeze" (American), 264

+"Michael, Row de Boat Ashore" (American spiritual), 90

+"My One Mistake" (American), 265

"O Come, O Come, Emmanuel" (from Gregorian chant), 98, 199

"O Tannenbaum" (Oh, Christmas Tree) (German), 275

"Oh, How Lovely Is the Evening," 76

"On the Bridge at Avignon" (French), 290

"Polly Put the Kettle On" (English), 205

"Row, Row, Row Your Boat," 151

"St. Patrick" (Irish), 98

"Santa Lucia" (Italian), 255

"Scotland's Burning" (Scottish), 204

+"Shenandoah" (American), 249

+"Simple Gifts" (American Shaker hymn), 63

"Song of the Volga Boatmen" (Russian), 161

+"The Streets of Laredo" (American cowboy song), 255

+"Sweet Betsy from Pike" (American), 205

+"Taps" (bugle call), 213

+"Wabash Cannon Ball" (American), 265

"We Gather Together" (Dutch), 99

"Wearin' of the Green" (Irish), 204

+"When the Saints Go Marching In" (American spiritual), 63

+"The Yellow Rose of Texas" (American), 250, 259

anonymous, formerly attributed to Henry Carey.

"My Country 'Tis of Thee" (God Save the King, America), 87

anonymous, medieval. *See also* Gregorian chant.

"Rex caeli" (King of Heaven, 9th century), 106

"Sumer Is Icumen In," 151

Arbeau, Thoinot.

Pavan from *Orchesographie*, 99

"Auld Lang Syne" (Scottish traditional song), 162

B

Bach, Johann Sebastian.

"Christ lag in Todesbanden" (Christ Lay in the Bonds of Death), BWV 4, 236

French Suite No. 5 in G Major, Gigue, 268

"Herr, straf mich nicht" (Lord, Punish Me Not), 203

Notenbüchlein für Anna Magdalena Bach (Little Notebook for Anna Magdalena Bach), Menuetto, 215

"Nun ruhen alle Wälder" (Now Are All the Forests Peaceful), 205

Orchestra Suite No. 1 in C Major

Bourée, 244

Forlane, 192

Orchestra Suite No. 2 in B Minor for Flute and Strings, Badinerie, 222

Organ Fugue in G Minor, BWV 578, 252

"Schwing' dich zu deinen Gott" (Soar Upwards to Thy God), 133

Sonata for Violin and Continuo, BWV 1021, third movement, 112

Bartók, Béla.

Concerto for Orchestra

"Giuoco delle Coppie" (Game of Pairs), 52, 61, 73, 122

"Intermezzo Interotto," 30

Introduzione, 107

"New Hungarian Folk Song" from *Mikrokosmos (Little Universe)*, Vol. V, 98

"Ostinato" from *Mikrokosmos (Little Universe)*, Vol. VI, 125

"Believe Me, If All Those Endearing Young Charms" (Irish traditional song), 243

Beethoven, Ludwig van.

Leonore Overture No. 3, 173

Piano Sonata in C Minor, Op. 10, No. 1, first movement, 211

Sonata No. 3 in E-Flat Major for Violin and Piano, Op. 12, Rondo, 217

Sonata No. 5 ("Spring") for Violin and Piano, Op. 24, Scherzo, 173

Sonata No. 10 in F Major for Violin and Piano, Op. 96, Scherzo, 174

Sonata in C Minor for Piano, Op. 10, No. 1, first movement, 290

Sonata in D Major for Piano, Op. 28, first movement, 289

Sonatina in G Major for Piano, Op. 49, No. 2, second movement, 207
String Quartet in C Minor, Op. 8, No. 4, fourth movement, 211
Symphony No. 3 in E-Flat Major, Op. 55, first movement, 213, 216
Symphony No. 5 in C Minor, Op. 67
  first movement, 221
  fourth movement, 40
  third movement, 107
Symphony No. 7 in A Major, Op. 42
  first movement, 193
  second movement, 161
+Billings, William.
  "When Jesus Wept," 206
Binchois, Gilles.
  De plus en plus (More and More), 193
"The Birch Tree" (Russian folksong), 98
Bizet, Georges.
  "Fate Motive" from *Carmen*, 162
"The Boar's Head" (English folksong), 40
Bourgeois, Louis.
  "Old 100th" from *Pseaumes octante trois de David* (arr. from), 236
Brahms, Johannes.
  Hungarian Dance No. 5, 276
  Liebeslieder Waltzer (Love-Song Waltzes), Op. 52
    No. 6, 193
    No. 13, 206
  Piano Concerto No. 1 in D Minor, Op. 15, first movement, 192
  Sonata in E Minor for Cello and Piano, Op. 38, third movement, 29
  Sonata in G Major for Violin and Piano, Op. 78, first movement, 192
  Symphony No. 1 in C Minor, fourth movement, 289
  Symphony No. 2, third movement, 173
  Symphony No. 4, Op. 98, second movement, 192
  Trio for Violin, Cello, and Piano in B Major, Op. 8, first movement, 161
  "Vergebliches Ständchen" (False Serenade), 99
  "Wiegenlied" (Lullaby), Op. 49, No. 4, 276
Byrd, William.
  "Hugh Ashton's Ground" (adapted from), 134

C

Carey, Henry (attributed to).
  "My Country 'Tis of Thee" (God Save the King, America), 87

Chaminade, Cécile.
  Concertino for Flute and Orchestra, Op. 107, first movement, 183
Chopin, Frédéric.
  Nocturne, Op. 9, No. 1, 192
  Nocturne for Piano, Op. 37, No. 1, 231
  Prelude No. 7 (for piano), Op. 28, 39
+Clayton, William.
  "Come, Come, Ye Saints," 150
+"Clementine" (American folksong), 216
Cohen, Sam, arr.
  "Hatikvah," 133
+Copland, Aaron.
  Billy the Kid, 200
Crüger, Johann.
  "Jesu, meine Freude" (Jesus, My Joy), 199
  "Nun danket alle Gott" (Now Thank We All Our God), 211

D

Dare, Elkanah.
  "Morning Song," 255
Debussy, Claude.
  Prélude à l'après-midi d'un faune (Prelude to the Afternoon of a Faun), 213
  Préludes pour Piano, Book I
    "La Cathédrale engloutie" (The Engulfed Cathedral), 72
    "La fille aux cheveux de lin" (The Girl with the Flaxen Hair), 107
    "Voiles" (Sails), 142
+Douglas, Winfred
  "Sohren," 134
+"Down in the Valley" (American folksong), 191
"Drink to Me Only with Thine Eyes" (English folksong), 205
Dvořák, Antonin.
  Dmitri, Op. 64 (theme from), 143
  Symphony No. 9 in E Minor ("From the New World")
    first movement, 98
    fourth movement, 60
    second movement, 215, 222

E

"Early One Morning" (English folksong), 63

F

"Farmer in the Dell" (traditional song), 201

Faure, Gabriel.
  Requiem (Mass for the Dead), "Libera me" (Set Me Free), 98
"The Foggy, Foggy Dew" (English folksong), 109
Fuller, H. J. (pseud.). *See* Pratt.

G

Gautier, Denis.
  "Le secret," 240
+Gilmore, Patrick S. (pseud. Louis Lambert).
  "When Johnny Comes Marching Home," 240, 243
Gluck, Christoph W.
  Orfeo ed Euridice, "Che farò senza Euridice?" (What Shall I Do without Euridice?), 251
  "Frère Jacques" (French folksong), 203
+"Go Down, Moses: (American spiritual), 124
Gregorian chant.
  "Aeterna Christi Munera" (Mass on this melody by Palestrina), 64
  "Dies Irae" (Day of Wrath) from the *Requiem* service, 46
  "O Come, O Come, Emmanuel" (carol based on Gregorian chant), 98, 199
Grieg, Edward.
  Peer Gynt, 133

H

Handel, George Frideric.
  "Cappricio" (adapted from), 134
  "Joy to the World," 212
  Messiah
    "And the Glory of the Lord," 212
    "But Who May Abide," 250
    "Hallelujah Chorus," 221
    "He Shall Feed His Flock," 201
    "I Know That My Redeemer Liveth," 200
    "O, Thou That Tellest Good Tidings," 204
    Overture, 204
  Music for the Royal Fireworks, 216
Haydn, Joseph.
  The Creation
    "The Heavens Are Telling," 204
    "With Verdure Clad," 29
  "Gott, erhalte Franz den Kaiser!" (Austrian), 200
  String Quartet, Op. 64, No. 2, Menuetto, 225

Haydn, Joseph.—*(Cont.)*
  String Quartet in G Minor, Op. 74,
    No. 3, fourth movement, 174
  Symphony No. 94 in G Major ("Sur-
    prise"), first movement, 191
Haydn, Michael.
  "Salzburg," hymn tune, 76
  "Greensleeves" (English folksong),
    124
Hensel, Fanny Mendelssohn.
  Trio in D Minor, Op. 11, Finale, 133
Hindemith, Paul.
  Piano Sonata No. 2, first movement,
    207
+"Hello Girls" (American traditional
    song), 163
"Holland" (traditional song), 275
+"Home on the Range" (American
    cowboy song), 238, 267
"Hop sa sa!" (German folksong), 256
Hopkins, John H., Jr.
  "We Three Kings of Orient Are," 98
Humperdinck, Engelbert.
  "Children's Prayer" from *Hansel and
    Gretel,* 108
Hymn tunes and spirituals.
  +"Amazing Grace" (American), 252
  Bach, Johann Sebastian, "Christ lag
    in Todesbanden" (Christ Lay in
    the Bonds of Death), BWV 4, 236
  "Herr, straf mich nicht" (Lord,
    Punish Me Not), 203
  "Nun ruhen alle Wälder" (Now Are
    All the Forests Peaceful), 205
  "Schwing' dich zu deinen Gott"
    (Soar Upwards to Thy God),
    133
  Bourgeois, Louis, "Old 100th" from
    Pseaumes octante trois de David
    (arr. from), 236
  Crüger, Johann
    "Jesu, meine Freude" (Jesus, My
    Joy), 199
    "Nun danket alle Gott" (Now
    Thank We All Our God), 211
  +Douglas, Winfred, "Sohren," 134
  +"Go Down, Moses," 124
  "God Rest Ye Merry Gentlemen"
    (English), 143
  Handel, George Frideric, "Joy to the
    World," 212
  Haydn, Joseph, "Gott, erhalte Franz
    den Kaiser!" (Austrian), 200
  Haydn, Michael, "Salzburg," 76
  Hopkins, John H., Jr., "We Three
    Kings of Orient Are," 98
  +"Joshua Fit de Battle of Jericho", 175
  Luther, Martin, "Ein' feste Burg" (A
    Mighty Fortress Is Our God),
    229
  +"Michael, Row de Boat Ashore," 90

"O Come, O Come, Emmanuel"
    (from Gregorian chant), 199
"O Tannenbaum" (Oh, Christmas
    Tree) (German), 275
+"Simple Gifts," 63
+Steffe, William, "Battle Hymn of
    the Republic," 203
Sullivan, Arthur, "St. Kevin," 76
"We Gather Together," 99
+"When the Saints Go Marching In," 63

I

+"Irene, Goodnight" (American tradi-
    tional song), 266
"Is That So?" (Polish folksong), 143

J

+Jackson, Bruce R.
  Augmentoz, 142
  Dimentoz, 141
  "Suspend it!," 282
+"Jimmy Crack Corn" (American folk-
    song), 240
+Joplin, Scott.
  "Maple Leaf Rag," 175
Jordan, Mrs. Dorothea.
  "The Blue Bell of Scotland," 200, 255
+"Joshua Fit de Battle of Jerico"
    (American spiritual), 175

L

Lalo, Eduard.
  *Symphonie Espagnole for Violin and
    Orchestra,* Op. 21.
    Allegro non troppo, 29
    first movement, 184
+Lambert, Louis (pseud.). *See* Gilmore.
+"The Land of Arizona" (American tra-
    ditional song), 266
Lantins, Arnold de.
  "Puisque je voy" (Since I Saw Her), 63
Liebmann, Hélène Riese.
  "Kennst du das Land?," Op. 4, 125
+"Little Brown Jug" (American folk-
    song), 286
"Lullaby" (German folksong), 213
Luther, Martin
  "Ein' feste Burg" (A Mighty Fortress
    Is Our God), 229

M

+"The Man on the Flying Trapeze"
    (American traditional song), 264

Marks, Gerald. *See* Simons.
Mendelssohn, Felix.
  *Concerto in E Minor for Violin and
    Orchestra,* Op. 64
    first movement, 222
    third movement, 133
  Midsummer Night's Dream, Op. 21,
    Scherzo, 161, 215
  Symphony No. 4 in A Major (Italian),
    Op. 90
    fourth movement, 184
    second movement, 112
Mencken, Alan.
  Aladdin, "A Whole New World," 251
Merbecke, John.
  "Agnus Dei" (Lamb of God), from
    *The Book of Common Prayer
    Noted,* 98
+"Michael, Row de Boat Ashore"
    (American traditional song), 90
+Miller, Anne L.
  "Give Peace, O God, the Nations
    Cry," 99
Mozart, Wolfgang Amadeus.
  Minuet in F Major for Piano, K. 2,
    260
  Le Nozze di Figaro, K. 492
    Overture, 267
    "Se vuol ballare" (If You Want to
    Dance), 76
  Piano Concerto No. 20 in D Minor, K.
    466, first movement, 174
  Piano Sonata in A Major for Piano,
    K. 300i
    first movement, 192
    fourth movement, 289
  Symphony No. 39 in E-flat Major, K.
    543
    first movement, 112
    Menuetto, 214
  Symphony No. 40 in G Minor, K. 550
    first movement, 125
    Menuetto, 217
    third movement, 134
  Symphony No. 41 in C Major
    ("Jupiter"), K. 551
    first movement, 221
    Menuetto, 207
Muir, Alexander.
  "The Maple Leaf Forever," 256
Musorgsky, Modest.
  Pictures at an Exhibition, Prome-
    nade Theme, 46, 112
+"My One Mistake (American), 265

N

Nicolai, Philipp
  "Wachet auf!" (Sleepers, Awake!),
    49

O

"O Come, O Come Emmanuel" (from Gregorian chant) 98, 199
"O Tannenbaum" (Oh Christmas Tree) (German traditional song), 275
"Oh How Lovely Is the Evening" (traditional song), 76
"On the Bridge at Avignon" (French traditional song), 290

P

Paisiello, Giovanni.
"The Miller," 275
Palestrina, Giovanni Pierluigi da.
Mass on the Gregorian chant "Aeterna Christi Munera," 64
Pope Marcellus Mass, "Kyrie eleison" (Lord, Have Mercy), 184
Pepusch, Johann Christoph.
"Can Love Be Controlled by Advice?" from The Beggar's Opera, 150
+Persichetti, Vincent.
Divertimento for Band, 91
+Peter, John Frederick.
"Glory Be to Him," 91
"Polly Put the Kettle On" (English folksong), 205
Pratt, Charles (pseud. H. J. Fuller).
"My Bonnie Lies over the Ocean," 124
+Price, Florence B.
First Sonata for Organ, first movement, 150
"Offertory," 109
Purcell, Henry.
"A New Irish Tune," 222

R

Ravel, Maurice.
String Quartet, first movement, 207
Reuenthal, Neidhart.
"Sinc an, Guldin Huon!" (Sing on, Golden Cockerel!), 28
Rossini, Gioachino.
Overture from William Tell, 183
"Row, Row, Row Your Boat, (traditional song)" 151

S

"St. Patrick" (Irish folksong), 98
Sanderson, James.
"Hail to the Chief," 99
"Santa Lucia" (Italian traditional song), 255
Schoenberg, Arnold.
String Quartet No. 4, first movement, 46
Schubert, Franz.
"Frülingsglaube" (Spring Joy), 175
"Heiden-Röslein" (Hedge Rose), 28
Octet, 144
Sonata in A Minor for Arpeggione and Piano, first movement, 125
Symphony No. 8 ("Unfinished"), first movement, 243
Schumann, Clara.
Trio in G Minor, Op. 17
Allegretto, 28
first movement, 134
Scherzo, 40
Schumann, Robert.
Album für die Jugend (Album for the Young)
Chorale, 212
"Sicilienne," 256
"Wild Rider," 239
"Scotland's Burning" (Scottish traditional song), 204
Scott, Lady John.
"Annie Laurie," 199
+"Shenandoah" (American folksong), 249
Shostakovich, Dimitry.
Symphony No. 5 in D Minor, second movement, 215
Silcher, Friedrich.
"The Lorelei," 273
"Simple Gifts" (American Shaker hymn), 63
Simons, Seymour, and Gerald Marks.
"All of Me," 280
Smith, John Stafford.
"The Star-Spangled Banner," 205
"Song of the Volga Boatmen" (Russian traditional song), 161
+Sousa, John Philip.
"Semper Fidelis March," 112, 216
"The Stars and Stripes Forever," 162, 223

+Steffe, William.
"Battle Hymn of the Republic," 203
Strauss, Johann, Jr.
"Emperor Waltz," 215
"Wine, Women, and Song Waltz," Op. 333, 223
+"The Streets of Laredo" (American cowboy song), 255
Sullivan, Arthur.
Princess Ida, "If You Give Me Your Attention," 76
"St. Kevin" (hymn tune), 76
+"Sweet Betsy from Pike" (American cowboy song), 255

T

"Taps" (bugle call), 213
Telemann, Georg Philipp.
Partita a cembalo solo in G Major, 225
Tschaikovsky, Piotr Ilyitch.
Symphony No. 6 in B Minor ("Pathétique"), second movement, 30

W

"Wabash Cannonball" (American traditional song), 265
Wagner, Richard.
Die Meistersinger, 240
Die Walküre.
"Ride of the Valkyries," 29
"We Gather Together" (Dutch hymn), 99
"Wearin' of the Green" (Irish traditional song), 204
Weber, Carl Maria von.
Der Freischütz (The Freeshooter), Overture, 290
+"When the Saints Go Marching In" (American spiritual), 63

Y

+"The Yellow Rose of Texas" (American traditional song), 250, 259

General Index

A

accelerando, 40
accent
   (defined), 25
   mark, 39
   metric, 25
accidentals, 88
accompanying a melody, 259
acoustics, vii
active tones, 202–03
allegro, 31
altered notes, 283
alto clef, 5
anacrusis, 28, 200–01, 204
andante, 31
anticipation, 251
appoggiatura, 41, 249
atonal, 46
augmented fourth, 105–06. *See also* tritone.
augmented third, 123
augmented triad, 139–43
authentic cadences, 238–40

B

bar, 26
bar line, 26
bass clef, 5
beam, 30
beat. *See also* meter *and* tempo.
   (defined), 25
   divisions in compound meters, 29,
      191–92
   divisions in simple meters, 28,
      161–63
beat unit(s)
   (defined), 28
   dotted notes as, 29, 191
   eighth [and smaller] note groups
      with beams, 30
   notation of, 25–30
   subdivisions of, 28–29, 161–63, 192
   and time signature, 28
   with triplets, 29, 183–84
blues, 284–85
breve, 26

C

C clef, 5
cadence
   authentic, 238–39
   (defined), 199
   half, 238–39
   harmonic, 238–39
   imperfect authentic, 239–40
   melodic patterns in, 203–04
   perfect authentic, 239–40
   strong, 200
   weak, 200
canon, 291
carol, 291
changing meter, 30
changing tones, 251
chorale, 291
chord(s). *See also* triads *and* seventh
     chords.
   built of thirds, 69
   circle of fifths progression, 237
   (defined), vii, 45, 69
   inversion, 230
   substitution, 285
   symbols (guitar), 73, 116, 143,
      279–85
   symbols (Roman numeral), 262–64,
      284
   triads, 69–71
   voicing, 8
chromatic
   (defined), 17
   scale, 17
   tones, 46
circle of fifths
   for major scales, 86
   for minor scales, 95
   progressions, 237
clefs, 5
climax of phrase, 211–02
color tones, 8
compound intervals, 149
compound meter, 29, 191–93
concerto, 292,293
conjunct motion, 211
consonance, 60, 123
crescendo, 39

D

decrescendo, 39
diatonic progressions, 284
diminished fifth, 71. *See also* tritone.
diminished third, 123
diminished triad, 139–43
diminuendo, 39
disjunct motion, 211, 213
dissonance, 60, 123
dominant, 201
dominant seventh chord, 284, 299
dotted notes, 27, 162, 191
double flat, 16
double sharp, 16
drone, 253
duple meter, 26, 159
duration (defined), 1

E

eighth note, 26
electronic music, 2
enharmonic spellings, 17
escape tone, 250

F

fake book, 32, 262
fermata, 40
fifth(s)
   circle of, 86, 95, 237
   diminished, 71, 106
   how to write, 72
   melodies set with, 72
   parallel, 73
   perfect, 70
   in triads, 71
first inversion of triad, 230
flag, 26
flat
   (defined), 16
   notation of, 16
   placement of accidental sign, 88
forms, musical, 289–93
   grouped by historical period, 291–93
forte, 39
forte piano, 39

fortissimo, 30
fourths
    augmented, 105–06
    (defined), 105
    harmonies based on, in medieval
        music, 106
    perfect, 105
    in twentieth-century music, 107
fugue, 291
fundamental tone, 1

G

gavotte, 291
gigue, 291
glissandi, 15
grand staff, 7
guitar
    chords, 73, 116, 143
    fingerboard harmony for, 297–99
    tablature, 8, 143, 262, 297–99

H

half cadences, 238–39
half note, 26
half step, 15, 51
harmonic cadences, 238–39
harmonic minor scale, 131
harmonization of melodies, 259–64,
        273–74
harmony. See also triads and seventh
        chords.
    (defined), vii
    fingerboard, for guitar, 297–99
    keyboard, 74, 295–96
hemiola, 193

I

imperfect cadences, 239–40
instruments
    brass, 1, 2
    fretted, 2, 8
    keyboard, 2
    percussion, 2
    plucked, 2
    string, 1, 2
    synthesizer, 2
    wind, 1
    woodwind, 1–2
intensity (defined), 1
interval(s). See also names of specific
        intervals.
    augmented, 105–06, 123
    compound, 149
    consonant, 123
    diminished, 71, 123

dissonant, 123
fifth, 70–73, 104
fourth, 105–07
harmonic, 6, 52
inversion of, 149
major and minor, 51
melodic, 6, 52
names of, 59
interval(s)—Cont.
    octave, 6, 59
    second, 51
    seventh, 121–22
    simple, 149
    sixth, 121–22
    third, 60–61
    tritone, 105–06
    unison, 59
inversion
    (defined), 149
    of intervals, 149
    of triads, 230

J

jazz, 279–85, 293

K

key signatures
    (defined), 45, 87
    of flat keys, 85–86
    of major scales, 83–86
    of minor scales, 95–96
    of sharp keys, 83–84
keyboard
    arrangement of notes on, 6
    harmony, 74, 295–96
    pitch and, 15–18

L

lead sheet, 32, 279–80
leading tone, 202, 203
ledger lines, 6
legato, 40

M

madrigal, 291
major scale(s), 45, 49–50, 83–86
    circle of fifths for, 86
major triad. See also triad.
    construction of, 73
    (defined), 70
    in major scale, 73
mass, 291
mazurka, 293

measure, 26
mediant, 201
melodic minor scale, 131–32
melody
    accompanying, 259
    conjunct motion of, 211–12
    constructed with triads, 213–14
    (defined), vii, 199
    disjunct motion of, 211, 213
    harmonizing, 259–64
    movement and rest in, 199–05
    sequence in, 222–23
meter
    alla breve, 160
    changing, 30
    common time, 160
    compound, 29, 191–93
    (defined), 26
    duple, 25, 26, 30, 159
    quadruple, 30, 160
    quintuple, 30
    septuple, 30
    simple, 28, 161
    triple, 25, 26, 30, 159
metric, 26
metronome, 31
mezzo forte, 39
mezzo piano, 39
middle C, 6, 7, 15
minor key, 132
minor scale(s), 45, 49, 95–96
    circle of fifths for, 95
    harmonic, 131
    melodic, 131–32
    natural (pure), 95
    parallel, 96
    relative, 96
minor triad. See also triad.
    (defined), 115
    in the major scale, 115
    in the natural minor scale, 115
    on the white keys, 115
minuet, 291
moderato, 31
modes, 46
music
    appreciation, vii
    history, vii
    literature, vii
    (defined), vii
    theory, vii
motives, 221–22

N

natural(s),
    (defined), 16
    notation of, 16
    placement of accidental sign, 88
natural (pure) minor scale, 95

neighboring tone, 250
ninth chords, 281–82
nondiatonic notes, 283
nonharmonic tones, 237–38, 249–53
    anticipation, 251
    appoggiatura, 249
    changing tones, 251
    escape tone, 250
    neighboring tone, 250
    passing tone, 249
    pedal tone, 252–53
    retardation, 251
    suspension, 250
nonmetric, 26
notation of musical sounds
    accidentals, 88
    beam, 30
    breve, 26
    clef signs, 5
    dotted notes, 27
    double bar, 39
    double flat, 16
    double sharp, 16
    dynamics, 39
    eighth note, 26
    eighth rest, 27, 35
    fermata, 40
    flat, 16
    for guitar and similar instruments,
        8, 73, 116, 143
    half note, 26
    half rest, 27, 34
    natural, 16
    pitch, 5–8
    quarter note, 26
    quarter rest, 27, 35
    repeat sign, 40
    rests, 27, 34–35
    rhythm, 25–31
    sharp, 16
    sixteenth note, 26
    sixteenth rest, 27, 35
    sixty-fourth note, 26, 35
    slur, 40
    staff, 5–8
    thirty-second note, 26
    thirty-second rest, 27, 35
    tie, 27
    triplets, 29, 183–84
    whole note, 26
    whole rest, 27, 34
note(s)
    pitch names of, 6
    values for duration of, 26
notehead, 26

O

octave. *See also* interval.
    abbreviation for, 7

interval of, 6, 59
    layout of piano keyboard, 6
opera, 291–92
opus number, 28
oratorio, 291–92
organum, 72
ornament signs, 40–41
overtone series, 1

P

passing tone, 249
pavan, 291
perfect cadences, 239–40
perfect consonances, 60
perfect interval(s)
    (defined), 59
    fifth, 70
    octave, 59
    unison, 59
period
    cadences in, 290
    contrasting, 290
    opposite, 289–90
    parallel, 289
phrase
    antecedent, 289
    beginning, 200–01
    consequent, 289
    cadence of, 199
    (defined), 39, 199
phrase marking, 39
piano
    dynamic, 39
    the keyboard instrument, 2, 6
    pitch and the keyboard, 15–17
pianissimo, 39
pickup, 28
pitch
    (defined), 1
    and keyboard, 15–17
    notation of, 5–8
    system for naming, 7–8
polonaise, 291
prelude, 291
preparation note, 249
principal notes, 40
progressions of chords, 237–40

Q

quadruple meter, 160
quarter note, 26

R

ragtime, 175, 293
repeat sign, 40

requiem, 291
resolution, 249
rest(s), 27
    notation of, 34–35
rest tones, 202
retardation, 251
rhythm. *See also* accent, beat, *and*
        tempo.
    (defined), vii
    notation of, 25–31
ritardando, 40
ritenuto, 40
Roman numeral analysis, 262–64, 284
rondo, 292
root
    position of triad, 230
    of triad, 71
round, 291

S

sarabande, 291
scale(s)
    chromatic, 17
    degree, 50
    (defined), 17, 45
    major, 45, 49, 83–86
    minor, 45, 49, 95–96
Scotch snap, 162
second(s), 59
    (defined), 51
    major, 51
    minor, 51
second inversion of triad, 230
semitone, 15
seventh(s)
    (defined), 121
    major, 121
    minor, 121
    in major key, 122
    parallel, 122
seventh chords
    chord symbols, 262–64, 280–81
    dominant, 299
    (defined), 260
    in major scales, 261
    in minor scales, 261–62
sforzando, 39
sharp
    (defined), 16
    notation of, 16
    placement of accidental sign, 88
simple intervals, 149
simple meter, 28, 161–63
simple position of triads, 69
sixteenth note, 26
sixth(s)
    (defined), 121
    major, 121
    minor, 121

sixth(s)—*(Cont.)*
    in major key, 122
    parallel, 122
sixty-fourth note, 26
slur, 40
sonata, 292
spiritual, 293
staccato, 40
staff, 5–8
    grand, 7
stem, 26
stepwise motion, 15
subdominant, 201
submediant, 201
subtonic, 202
suite, 292
supertonic, 202
sus4 chords, 282–83
suspension, 250
syllable systems,
    for pitch, 52
symphony, 292
syncopation, 173–75

T

tablature, 8
tempo, 31
tenor clef, 5
third(s), 59

(defined), 60
major and minor, 60
melodies set with, 60–61
of triad, 71
thirty-second note, 26
thirty-second rest, 27
tie, 27, 162
timbre (defined), 1
time signature, 28
tonal center
    avoidance of, 46
    (defined), 45–46
    in major and minor scales, 45–46
tonality, 45. *See also* tonal center.
tone color, 1
tone quality, 1
tonic, 49, 201
transposition, 8
treble clef, 5
triad(s)
    arrangements, 229–30
    augmented, 139–43
    commonly used, 298
    construction of, 69, 73
    (defined) 8, 45
    diminished, 139–43
    in four voices, 229
    inversions of, 230
    major, 70, 73
    in major scale, 73, 115, 140
    in melodic construction, 213–14

minor, 115
    in minor scale, 115, 140, 141
    names of tones, 71
    primary, 237
    progressions of, 237–40
    simple position of, 69
trill, 41
triple meter, 26, 160
triplets, 29, 183–84
tritone, 105–06
turn, 41
twelve-tone row, 46

U

unison, 59
upbeat. *See also* anacrusis.
    in conductor's beat, 159–60
    (defined), 28
    melodic patterns in, 204

W

waltz, 293
whole note, 26
whole step, 15
whole tone, 15
whole tone scale, 142

Index of CD #1: Chapters 1, 4-15

Track	Chapter	Section	Exercise #s	Time
1	1	A	1-10	1:05
2	1	B	1-10	1:29
3	1	C	1-10	1:26
None	2	A	1-10	2:01
None	2	B	1-10	2:13
None	2	C	1-10	2:10
None	3	A	1-10	2:15
None	3	B	1-10	2:09
4	4	A	1-10	2:35
5	4	B	1-6	1:42
6	4	C	1-5	1:07
7	5	A	1-4	0:59
8	6	A	1-10	2:08
9	7	A	1-10	4:52
10	7	B	1-6	3:17
11	7	C	1-10	2:56
12	7	D	1-6	0:58
13	7	E	1-6	1:23
14	8	A	1-10	1:21
15	8	B	1-10	2:07
16	8	C	1-10	2:12
17	8	D	1-10	1:52
18	9	A	1-6	1:48
19	9	B	1-6	1:30
20	9	C	1-5	1:17
21	9	D	1-6	1:12
22	10	A	1-8	2:07
23	10	B	1-8	1:53
24	10	C	1-8	1:42
25	10	D	1-5	1:01
26	11	A	1-6	1:33
27	11	B	1-6	1:36
28	11	C	1-6	1:21
29	11	D	1-8	2:10
30	12	A	1-7	1:48
31	12	B	1-10	2:26
32	12	C	1-6	1:06
33	13	A	1-6	1:36
34	13	B	1-6	2:05
35	14	A	1-10	1:59
36	14	B	1-6	1:06
37	14	C	1-12	5:01
38	15	A	1-6	2:28
TOTAL PLAY TIME				72:58

Index of CD #2: Chapters 16-30

Track	Chapter	Section	Exercise #s	Time
1	16	A	1-12	2:39
2	16	B	1-8	1:31
3	17	A	1-8	2:23
4	17	B	1-6	1:36
5	18	A	1-6	1:59
6	18	B	1-6	1:43
7	18	C	1-6	1:22
8	18	D	1-6	1:24
9	18	E	1-6	1:22
10	19	A	1-6	1:46
11	19	B	1-7	1:27
12	20	A	1-6	1:14
13	21	A	1-6	1:18
14	21	B	1-6	1:21
15	21	C	1-8	1:45
16	22	A	1-8	1:35
17	22	B	1-12	2:13
18	23	A	1-10	1:52
19	23	B	1-6	1:55
20	23	C	1-6	1:09
21	24	A	1-6	2:14
22	25	A	1-6	2:23
23	25	B	1-6	2:20
24	25	C	1-4	1:35
25	25	D	1-4	1:45
26	26	A	1-6	2:29
27	26	B	1-6	1:50
28	26	C	1-4	1:37
29	27	A	1-12	2:38
30	27	B	1-8	3:23
31	27	C	1-5	2:01
32	28	A	1-6	1:44
33	28	B	1-8	1:10
34	28	C	1-6	2:25
35	28	D	1-6	1:39
36	28	E	1-6	1:14
37	29	A	1-6	2:27
38	29	B	1-6	2:01
39	30	A	1-10	1:23
TOTAL PLAY TIME				**73:24**